Society &
Social Institutions

Society & Social Institutions

Nadeem Hasnain

STERLING PUBLISHERS (P) LTD.
Regd. Office: A1/256 Safdarjung Enclave, New Delhi-110029.
CIN: U22110DL1964PTC211907
Phone: +91 82877 98380/ +91 120-6251823
e-mail: mail@sterlingpublishers.in
www.sterlingpublishers.in

Society & Social Institutions
© 2023, Nadeem Hasnain
ISBN 978-93-93853-45-5
Edited by Sanjiv Sarin

All rights are reserved.
No part of this publication may be reproduced, stored in a retrieval system or transmitted, in any form or by any means, mechanical, photocopying, recording or otherwise, without prior written permission of the original publisher.

Printed and Published by

Sterling Publishers Pvt. Ltd.,
Plot No. 13, Ecotech-III, Greater Noida - 201306, Uttar Pradesh, India

Contents

Section One

1. **Social Institutions**   3

2. **Societies**   6
   Concept of society; Simple/primitive society; Complex society; Folk society; Peasant society; Urban society; Industrial society; Post industrial society.

3. **Some Important Prevalent Concepts**   17
   Globalization; Post modernism; Ethnicity; Diaspora; Civil Society; Multiculturalism; Rural-urban continuum; Social exclusion; Empowerment.

Section Two

4. **Marriage**   35
   Introduction, Concept and definitional issues, Functions of marriage, Rules of marriage, Incest rules, Exogamy and incest, Preferential marriage rules, Cross cousin marriage and parallel cousin marriage, Plural marriages, Polygyny and polyandry, Hypergamy, Fictive marriage, Choosing a mate, Group marriage, Marriage payments, BrideDowry, Divorce, Live-in-relationship and marriage, Indian scenario, 'Marital rape, patriarchy, and right of sexual autonomy in Indian society', Marriage selection in cyber space: technology mediated romance, Feminist critique of marriage.

5. **Family**   64
   Meaning and concept of family; Elemntry/nuclear/extended family; The household; Universality of family; Functions of family; Typological and processual approaches to the study of family; Joint family; The other types; Stability and change in family; Reimagining/Alternative family; Impact of industrialization and urbanization on family; Change in family over time; Indian scenario.

6. **Kinship: The Core of Social Organization**   84
    Introduction, Kins and kinship, A brief history of kinship studies, Types of kinship and category of kins, Functions of kinship, Principles of descent and descent groups, Kin groups, Kinship terminology, Kinship behaviour, Kinship diagrams, Feminist critique of kinship, Impact of industrialization and urbanization on kinship practices.

7. **Economic Organization**   105
    Introduction; Economic organization; Economic System, Primitive Economy and Primitive Economic System; Distribution and Exchange; Types of Exchange; Reciprocity; Redistribution; Reciprocity and Redistribution Compared; Market Exchange; Tribal Markets; Money, Trade,and Market; Market as Social Institution; Property; Peasant Economy; Technology; Division of Labour; Production Relations and Mode of Production; Work; Organization of Work; Work and Technology; Work, Technology, and Society; Formal and Informal Economy; Economy in Capitalism and Socialism.

8. **Political Organization**   132
    Meaning and concept of political organization; Concept of power and authority; Forms of social distribution of power: Marxist, Elitist, and Pluralist; Locus of authority; Systems of authority: Unicentric authority system, multicentric authority system; Kin based segmentary societies; nonkin based organizations; village councils; Centralised authority system; State and stateless societies; Primotive states; Chiefdoms and kingdoms; Leadership; Elements of democracy in primitive societies; The forms and functions of government; Primitive governments; Concept of law, law and justice in primitive societies; Sanctions of primitive law; Justice; legitimacy and the state; Civil society.

9. **Religion**   158
    Introduction; Notion and definition of religion; Question of origin of religion (psychological theories, EB Tylor, James Frazer, animatism/manaism, sociological theories); Functions of religion; dysfunctions of religion, modern sociological view: primitive religion; Functionaries of primitive religion; Totemism; Taboo; Divination; Rites of passage; Religion, majic and science; Religion and symbolism; Religion and economy;

Religion and politics; Monotheism and polytheism; Sects and cults; Classical theoretical perspective (Durkheim, Weber, Marx); Secularism and secularization; Religious revivalism and fundamentalism; Religious/communal conflict and violence.

10. **Caste and Caste System** 189

Introduction and definitions; Varna model and jati model of caste; Functions of caste system; Jajmani system, its decline and consequences; Untouchability; Perspectives on the study of caste system: Ghurye, Srinivas, Dumont, and Beitelle; Ritual aspect or binary opposition between pure/impure(pollution); Caste system as viewed by contemporary social anthropologist; Caste: cultural and structural view; Caste mobility and sanskritization; Changes in the ritual and economic aspects of caste; Caste system and its transformation; Caste and politics; Caste and non-Hindus (Muslims, Sikhs, and Christians); Dalit identity and consciousness; Future of caste system.

Bibliography 225

Preface

Study of social institutions is an integral part of the discipline of sociology and anthropology. At the same time, it is also important to the other social sciences as well. It is a part of every syllabus of sociology and anthropology at the undergraduate (UG) and postgraduate (PG) levels as well as in the civil services exams. I believe that a sound understanding of social institutions necessarily requires having a fair idea about the different types of societies. The students should also be familiar with the important basic concepts being used in social sciences. In view of this, the most used and abused concepts have been explained in this book.

I hope the book will be helpful to the students studying sociology or anthropology at the UG and PG levels. Using my experience of guiding civil services aspirants for more than three decades, I have tried to make this book equally valuable for the civil services aspirants opting sociology or anthropology.

As always, I welcome feedback from the readers to make the book more useful.

Lucknow

Nadeem Hasnain
(nadeemhasnain@gmail.com)

Acknowledgements

First of all, I would like to thank my friend and wife, Nishaat, for freeing me of the responsibilities of running the household as well as helping me with her sociological imagination. I also thank Sayead who, as earlier, has typed the manuscript diligently and accurately.

I extend my sincere thanks to my publishers for taking up the work urgently and the team which has been involved with the publication of this book.

Section One

1

Social Institutions

Chapter Outline: *Concept; Definitions; Characteristics*

Learning Objectives
- Why is the study of social institutions important to understand a society?
- Do social institutions of a society help in social control?
- Why are stability and endurance considered essential for social institutions?

'Institution' is a term widely used in social sciences. An institution is an enduring set of ideas about how to accomplish goals generally recognized as important in a society. The rules that govern them are usually ingrained in the basic cultural values of the society, as each institution consists of a complex cluster of social norms. When we refer to social institutions, we usually imply forms of standardized action or behaviour linked to a set of complex and interdependent norms and roles and applying to a large population of people within a society or territory. Family, Marriage, kinship, economy and caste are good examples of social institutions. Some of the important definitions of social institution are:

> *A social institution is a structure of society that is organized to meet the demands of people chiefly through well established procedures.*
> (Bogardus)

> *Social institutions are the social structures and machinery through which human society organizes, directs, and executes the multifarious activities required to sustain society human needs.*
> (Barnes)

While social groups are observable entities which can be classified and categorized, institutions refer to certain kinds of action procedures characterizing group activity. Sumner conceived of social institutions as consisting of a concept and a structure. Gillin and Gillin defined social institutions as the functional configuration of culture patterns including actions, ideas, and attitudes.

According to Maciver and Page, 'Institutions are the established forms of procedure, characteristic of a group activity'. According to Young, an institution is a set of folkways and mores integrated around a principal function of society. As such, in every society, certain recognized and established set of rules, traditions and usages are collectively called as institutions, that is, certain forms of procedure, recognized and accepted by the society, governing the relations between individuals and groups. Besides family, marriage, and so on, law, education system and systems of governance are some of the main institutions.

In view of this, the concept of institution characterises:
1. Means of controlling individuals
2. They involve group activities
3. Have standardized set of behaviour as norms
4. Have an aim, that is, the institution is directed to the fulfilment of certain primary needs of humans

Thus, institutions are not groups, but they involve group activities; the actors are provided by the groups associated with the institution, called as associations. For example, a family is the association which provides an individual marriage for the actuation of the institution of marriage; a government is an association providing actors for the institution of law; universities, colleges, and institutes are the bodies or associations feeding the personal requirements of individuals for education.

Social anthropologist Malinowski carried the concept of institution to a great theoretical elaboration and considered it as an important tool of cultural analysis. Malinowski developed what is called the functionalist model. He defined the institution as being characterized by a group of people united for a purpose called the 'charter' of the institution. They have the organization for carrying out the purpose and have culture, both material and ideal, to assist them. The charter also includes a set of ideas about the way things should be done. Personnel and norms are the other important ingredients of the institutional structure. Institutions fulfil the needs of human beings and of society.

S.F. Nadel pointed out the elements of repetition and recurrence as important characteristics of the concept of institution, which also induces an element of prediction in the concept. Some of the key characteristics of social institutions are:

- Stability and endurance
- Set purpose, providing better chances for human survival
- Roles that need to be filled
- Rules that govern social institutions are found ingrained in the basic cultural values of the society
- Capacity to govern the behaviour and expectations of the group
- Each institution performs some function

In earlier sociological usage, the term 'institution' referred to something which is established or constituted in society. Sumner (1960) in his work *Folkways* held that an institution consists of a concept (ideas, notions, doctrines, interest) and a structure. Tracing its development from the folkways and mores, he treated the institution as a super folkways. Maciver and Page (1949) and E. Chinoy (1962) emphasized that the term should be used to refer only to a pattern of approved or sanctioned behaviour or as established forms of procedure. However, Maciver and Page found it more useful to distinguish between the concept of an institution and an association.

All societies are organized into different types of groups. A group or an aggregate of few individuals become a social group when the members mutually interact with one another with some definite purpose of fulfilling certain aims. They also develop a consciousness or a sense of belongingness to the group. It involves a plurality of person's interaction in a specific context. Social groups differ in terms of their size, stability, aim, content, the nature of relationship between its members, and so on. As such they may be consanguineal (i.e., members are related by birth or blood). They may be a primary group (such as associations), formal or informal, and so on. The way these groups are inter-related and inter-dependent is called a social organization. Even two individuals may develop social relations and a group consciousness to form a dyadic group.

Critical Thinking Questions
- Why are social institutions regarded as established forms of procedure and characteristic of group activity in any human society?
- What may happen if a large number of members of a society defy the norms in a social institution?

****

2

Societies

Chapter Outline: *Concept of Society; Simple/Primitive Society; Complex Society; Folk Society; Peasant Society; Urban Society; Industrial Society; Post-Industrial Society*

Learning Objectives

- How do you distinguish between 'society' and 'a society'?
- Why is a simple society referred as 'simple'?
- How do you distinguish between simple and complex society?
- What are the criteria for distinguishing the industrial society from the post-industrial society?

Society, in the usual and most popular usage, refers to the totality of human relationships. Society may be referred to as any self-perpetuating, human grouping occupying a relatively bounded territory, possessing its own more-or-less distinctive culture and institutions.

Society, as a term, may have two distinct meanings, that of 'a society' and that of 'society' in general. In the general sense it is synonymous with social organization or social structure, while in its individual sense it is synonymous with social system. There are as many problems in defining a society as a discrete analytical unit, as there are in defining a culture. A society is generally conceived of as a human group which is relatively large, relatively independent or self-perpetuating in demographic terms, and which is relatively autonomous in its organizational or social relations. But it is the relativity of each society's autonomy, independence, and self-perpetuating nature, which is the crucial factor, and the distinction of one type of society from another is often arbitrary. In anthropology, it is important not to allow these arbitrary divisions to distort our vision of systems of local, regional, national, and international social 'relations' (Charlotte Seymour-Smith, 1993).

The predominant types of social relationships existing in a society forms the basis of classifying it into a particular type. There is no ideal classification. However, in loose and broad terms, societies may be categorized into two types: Simple and Complex. Apart from this broad classification, in this chapter we shall also discuss other forms of societies such as Folk, Peasant, Industrial, Post-industrial, and Urban.

Simple or Primitive Society

The term 'simple society' was often used interchangeably with 'primitive society'. A simple society may be described as the least internally differentiated and the earliest form of human society. The 'simple' nature of a simple society is not related to the simplicity of the lifestyle of its members. Here, it refers to the relatively simple technology which sustains its members. The most characteristic features of simple societies are:

1. Small scale or small sized populations.
2. A relatively simple technology.
3. A limited control over the environment which implies that they can neither manipulate their environment nor create an artificial one.
4. Lack of formal markets; markets, if any, are small scale.
5. Lack of specialization in the division of labour or lack of occupational specialization.
6. Relatively egalitarian social structure that lacks well-defined social ranking.

Most of the tribal societies, traditionally, come under the category of simple societies. The economies of simple societies are often characterized by production of material goods meant for subsistence. Thus, in most of the simple societies, the producer and consumer are one and the same persons. Further, profit making is not the prime motive in their economic transactions. A system of barter or exchange exists in which, often, the line of demarcation between economic and non-economic transactions gets blurred.

The social organization in simple societies includes elaborate systems of family, kinship, marriage, religion, and political systems. The simple societies, generally, act as corporate groups in performing a number of social, economic, political, and religious activities.

Most of the simple/primitive/tribal societies have existed in their geographical territories as self-sufficient economies based on the practise of simple technology. However, since the 18th century, because of emergence of European colonialism, the harmony of their life got disturbed. Since most of the areas inhabited by the tribal societies were rich in forest and mineral wealth, they were subjected to the worst types of exploitation. Most of the simple societies in Latin America, Africa, Asia, and Oceania were badly hit by colonialism. Unfortunately, their situation did not improve even in the post-colonial period. Their continued exploitation resulted in deprivation and pauperization. They lost control over their traditional resources. Their cultural and political autonomy was eroded beyond repair. Economic development proved counterproductive in most of the areas inhabited by them. In fact, they became 'victims of progress'.

Complex Society

The term 'complex society' is often used with its implied contrast, the 'simple society', to distinguish modern industrial societies from traditional or pre-industrial societies. Like any simple dichotomy, this classification raises many problems when its appropriateness or its application to the diversity and range of human societies is examined. The so-called simple societies may be extremely complex in certain aspects of their social and cultural structures. The criterion of simplicity or complexity is generally taken to be the nature of their social networks (predominantly large scale and 'open' in the complex society) and/or the level of technological development. It is immediately clear, however, that the term cannot be used with any precision nor can a definite border be drawn between the simple and the complex.

Complex societies have the following important features:
1. Larger territory and large-scale population.
2. Greater internal differentiation and occupational specializations.
3. Complex and advanced technology.
4. Quicker rate of change in values and institutions.
5. More emphasis on individualism and individual rights.
6. Profit making is the prime motive in economic transactions.

There is no clear difference between the rural and the urban community. Hence this rural–urban dichotomy is an important factor in the failure of any neat and clear demarcation between simple and complex societies. The term 'complex society', which was once very popular, is seldom used now.

Folk Society

'Folk society' is a term used in ethnology, anthropology, and sociology to refer loosely to traditional rural, peasant societies in which oral traditions predominate. The term was used by Robert Redfield to denote small, isolated groups characterized and controlled informally by sacred values. Kinship relations predominate, and culture is orally transmitted. The moral order is paramount, resulting in a relatively static society that develops indigenously.

The economy of the folk societies is self-sufficient and is different from the food-gathering hunting economy of the primitive societies. The folk societies maintain contacts with the centres of intellectual ideas and their evolution is known as civilization. Briefly speaking, a folk society is any small, unlettered society with homogenous cultural traditions, which is religious-oriented rather than secular in its outlook. Such a society is found exhibiting a high degree of unity and group solidarity.

In the 19th century the folk stratum was considered to be an inferior and backward residue existing within a modern nation and folk culture was therefore treated as a collection of survivals from earlier evolutionary stages of society. 'Because of the pejorative connotations of the term, many modern anthropologists and sociologists have avoided its use and that of such terms as "folklore" and "folkways". Many writers have therefore preferred the terms "oral tradition" and "oral literature" and more recently the prefix "ethno" to indicate the study of popular or pre-literate traditions' (Redfield 1947).

Redfield developed this as an abstract model of pre-industrial communities but this model is clearly based upon his classic studies of peasant society in Mexico in the 1930s. This concept was used by Redfield to designate one pole of a continuum between folk and urban societies.

Peasant Society

A peasant society is a small-scale social organization in which peasants predominate. Anthropologists have defined and explained peasant societies in different ways. A.L. Kroeber was the first anthropologist who tried to provide a formal definition of them. He described peasant societies as a 'part society', indicating its dependence in technological, economic, political, administrative, religious, and moral spheres on a larger society. George Foster, taking clue from Kroeber, described a peasant society as a 'half society'. He implied that a larger society, such as a nation, may consist of two parts – the first part consisting of a cultivating class living in villages, and the second part consisting of upper classes living in urban centres. The part of a larger society which is composed of cultivating classes is a 'peasant society' or 'half-society'. Robert Redfield followed Kroeber and also defined peasant society as a 'part society'.

Until the 1960s, the peasantry was largely ignored in sociology as having no significant role to play in history. This was despite the fact that peasants had existed for most of the recorded history of humankind in most parts of the world. From the 1960s, the publication of key works such as Erie Wolf (1966) and Barrington Moore (1967) began to change this perception, introducing perspectives developed in anthropology and political economy to sociology. The role of peasantry in the Vietnam War, and the growth of peasant political activity in Latin America and Asia raised questions about the assumed passivity of the peasants. Within Marxist work, partly under the influence of Maoism and events in China around the 1949 Revolution and subsequently, there emerged the question of whether the peasantry in the Third World represented the revolutionary force of socialism. Inter-disciplinary peasant studies is now a major area of study. The debate still continues over whether a distinctive category of peasantry can be identified both conceptually and empirically. Sahlins presents one of the strongest and most influential defences of the concept. Drawing his inferences from various peasant studies in the 21st century, he argues that there are four inter-related characteristics of the peasantry (Sahlins, 1982; (ed.)1988, 'Introduction').

1. The family farm is the major economic unit around which production, labour and consumption are organized.
2. Land husbandry is the main activity combined with minimal specialization and family training for tasks.
3. There is a particular 'peasant way of life' based on the local village community which covers most areas of social life and culture and which distinguished it from urban life and from those of other social groups.
4. Peasants are politically, economically, and socially subordinate to non-peasant groups against whom they have devised various methods of resistance, rebellion, or revolt.
5. A specific social dynamics involves a cyclical change over generations, which irons out inequalities over time via land division and the rise and fall of the availability of family labour through the domestic cycle.
6. Especially in the contemporary world, a common pattern of structural change, drawing peasants into market relationships, often through the influence of outside bodies such as agribusiness and incorporation into national politics. The precise outcome of these common changes is not predetermined (David Jary and Julia Jary, *The Dictionary of Sociology*).

Robert Redfield, in his landmark work *Peasant Society and Culture* (1956), places peasant society between folk and urban communities, and describes the following three as the most important features of a peasant culture:

1. Highly reverent attitude towards land.
2. Acceptance of agriculture as the noblest, best, and the ideal job.
3. A pronounced industrious attitude of the people, demonstrating a firm belief in the dignity of labour.

Among the important features of a peasant society are:

1. Family is the primary unit of the multilateral social organization.
2. The main source of livelihood is land and agriculture, which fulfil almost all the requirements of life.
3. The people maintain a distinctive, traditional culture in terms of day-to-day life and its schedule.
4. Usually, the people are dominated by outsiders.

For peasant societies, agriculture is not an enterprise but a way of life which cannot be given up in favour of any other activity promising more money or profit. If agriculture becomes an enterprise instead of way of life, a peasant becomes a farmer like the rich farmers of Punjab, Haryana, Maharashtra, or Karnataka. Thus, peasants are subsistence cultivators of agricultural land. They may be owner-occupiers or tenants, participants or non-participants in the market. Some writers (for example, Chayamov and Eric Wolf) have attempted to isolate a distinctive peasant economy; others (for example, Redfield) have stressed the notion of a peasant culture.

As this description indicates, all definitions of peasants agree on emphasizing the importance of the opposition or contrast between the peasant stratum and the urban elite. The peasantry and the urban centre are two opposing poles of a single socio-economic system, and this is reflected not only in their economic interdependence but also in the complex relationship which exists between peasant and urban culture. This may be seen in the concepts of Great/Little Tradition and folk–urban continuum. Among the anthropologists, Eric Wolf emphasises the economic aspect when defining peasantry. Wolf (1969) in his book Peasants defines the peasants as those whose surplus production is transferred to a dominant ruling group, which employs this surplus both to maintain itself and to redistribute it to other non-agricultural sectors of the population.

Peasants can be most clearly distinguished in agrarian societies. Significantly, cultivators are not the only segment of population constituting a peasant community. There are also people who are not defined as peasants but are still a part of the peasant community. They may be traders, labourers without land, and artisans with close social and economic links with the peasants. Further, people who are defined as 'peasants' will often engage in some of these non-cultivation activities for a part of their time.

Thus, while definitions of the peasantry sometimes rest on the functioning of a household, it is essential to see how a definition is firmly integrated into a wider social, political, and economic network. David Lehmann (1985) stated, 'It seems best to discard the term "Peasant" as a comprehensive descriptor of rural population of any sort and to use it instead as an adjective describing features of rural production systems without pretensions to exhaustive definition.'

Industrialization and Industrial Society

In loose terms, industrialization refers to sustained economic growth through the application of inanimate sources of electricity to mechanize production. In *The Social Science Encyclopaedia* (eds. Adam Kuper and Jessica Kuper, 1989) John Cornwell, taking a broader view, describes industrialization as the process which is 'meant to denote a phase in economic development in which capital and labour resources shift both relatively and absolutely from agricultural activities into industry, especially manufacturing'. The rise of the factory system, increasing urbanization, and movement from rural to urban areas are parts of the process. Agricultural employment undergoes an absolute decline as the rapid growth of productivity, coupled with the relatively slow growth in demand for agricultural output, generate surplus labour in the agricultural sector. The expanding industrial sector, in turn, pulls in the surplus agricultural employment as the output of industry takes on increasing importance.

In terms of mode and factors of production, industrialization may also be described as a process of transformation of a predominantly agricultural economy into one where the manufacture of goods increasingly contributes to overall output and exports. As a corollary, the percentage share of contribution to the economy by people employed in agriculture declines and that in the industry increases.

Industrialization initially took the form of factory production, later spreading to agriculture and services. Compared with pre-industrial organizations, this has involved division of labour; new social relations of production between the owners of capital, managers, and workers; urbanization and the geographical concentration of industry and population; and changes in occupational structure. Initially, a development within capitalist economies, industrialization now transcends every single economic system.

The process of industrialization is closely linked to the overall modernization of societies, especially the process of urbanization, the development of science and technology, and political modernization. Each of these changes can be viewed as either (a) a prerequisite of industrialization, or (b) a direct consequence or requirement of it, or (c) both of these. The process of industrialization is directly linked to the Industrial Revolution, usually dated 1760–1850, when the massive interrelated economic, technological, and social changes occurred and the United Kingdom became a manufacturing economy based on new technology which used machines and the factory system. As a result of these changes, UK became the first industrial society.

The term 'Industrial Society' was coined by Saint Simon to denote a society dominated by industrial production, and it is frequently used in this very general sense. Saint Simon chose this term to reflect the emerging central role of manufacturing industry in 18th century Europe, in contrast with the previous term the pre-industrial society and agrarian society. Nicholas Abercrombie et al. in *Dictionary of Sociology* (1988) wrote that the basic characteristics of an industrial society are:

1. The creation of cohesive nation-states organized around a common language and culture.
2. The commercialization of production and the disappearance of a subsistence economy.
3. The dominance of machine-based production and the organization of production in the factory.
4. The decline in the proportion of the working population engaged in agriculture.
5. The urbanization of the society.
6. The growth of mass literacy.
7. The enfranchisement of the population and the institutionalization of politics around mass parties.
8. The application of science to all spheres of life, especially industrial production.
9. The gradual rationalization of social life.

As the basic form of modern society, the term industrial society covers both capitalist societies and socialist societies and the underlying assumption is that all industrial societies share a number of basic, interrelated features.

Post-Industrial Society

The concept of a post-industrial society was first formulated in 1962 by Daniel Bell and subsequently elaborated in *The Coming of Post-Industrial Society* (1974) to describe the economic and social changes in the late 20th century.

The concept highlights the declining dependence of the societies on manufacturing industry, the rise of new service industries, and a new emphasis on the role of knowledge in production, consumption, and leisure. Daniel Bell is of the view that modern societies such as the US and many European societies are increasingly becoming information societies, that is, societies centred on knowledge and the production of new knowledge. An indication of this is the increased importance of higher education within these societies. According to Bell, knowledge is becoming the key source of innovation and the basis of social organization in these societies. This being so, new knowledge-based professional and occupational groups are also seen as increasingly achieving dominance within the class structures of these societies.

The post-industrial society is different from the classic industrial society as the latter was from pre-industrial agrarian society. The post-industrial society is a highly educated society and, indeed, knowledge is its central resource. Industrial society ran on practical knowledge, the knowledge that comes from doing rather than from pure research. The post-industrial society depends on theoretical knowledge, the knowledge that is developed in universities and research institutions. It not only looks to theoretical knowledge for many of its characteristic industries, such as the chemical and aeronautical industries, it increasingly puts a good part of its natural resources into developing such knowledge, in the form of support for higher education, and research and development activities. This shift of emphasis is reflected in the increased importance of the knowledge-class scientists and professionals and of 'knowledge institutions' such as the universities. These will eventually displace businessmen and business organizations as the ruling complex in society (Krishna Kumar in *Social Science Encyclopaedia*, 1985).

The term post-industrial society is also used sometimes as a synonym for 'post-capitalist' society, in which case it operates as a critique of the Marxist theory of the capitalist mode of production. Here the argument is that capitalism has transformed itself without proletarian revolution into a society in which the problems of affluence can be more easily resolved.

Several scholars have severely criticized the concept of post-industrial society for its exaggeration of the power and importance of new professional and technical occupations. Their contention is that there is still no conclusive evidence that these people constitute a distinct social class or that they effectively control business corporations, or that they exercise significant political power, while it is true that 'theoretical knowledge has become steadily more significant as a force of production throughout this century, this implies no change in the locus of power in the economy nor within society'.

Urbanization and the Urban Society

The term 'urbanization' appears in the literature of nearly every social science; within each it is used loosely when the theories of that particular social science are applied to the study of urban units, their populations, or individuals living in urban places. The concepts of urbanism and urbanization denote the predominance and growth of urban centres in society. Like other concepts, such as those of civilization, development, or industrialization, the concepts of urbanism and urbanization are beset by ethnocentric bias and theoretical and analytical confusions. The definition of city itself is a point of considerable controversy, with different authors focusing on such varied aspects as ecological, demographic, economic or political, depending on their theoretical orientation.

While not getting into the theoretical and methodological debates, some important features of urbanization that may be identified as:

1. Urbanization refers to a growth in the proportion of a country's population living in urban centres of a particular size.
2. It also refers to the social processes and relationships which are both the cause and consequence of the urban rather than rural way of life.
3. The rate of urbanization describes changes in the proportion of urban-to-rural dwellers over time (the reverse process is described as the rate of deurbanization).

Although in Europe, urbanization and industrialization occurred at around the same time, it would be a mistake to see these two processes as necessarily contingent upon each other. For example, urbanization preceded industrialization in England. The development of cities as centres of industrial activity came later. Likewise, today in many parts of Africa, Asia, and Latin America, there is a rapid urban growth via migration and natural increase without any significant development of an industrial economy. *The Social Science Encyclopaedia* (1985) says that the term 'urbanization' does have two interrelated, more specific, meanings:

1. Demographers, who use it to refer to the distribution of population between rural and urban areas, have given it its most specific meaning at

a conceptual level, but the demographic study of urbanization has failed to produce an internationally accepted set of criteria defining 'urban'.
2. In a number of other social sciences, most notably economics, geography and sociology/anthropology, urbanization refers to the changing morphological structure of urban agglomerations and their development.

When we talk of an urban society, we are constrained to comment that its beginning marks a turning point in the history of humans. Historically, the emergence of the urban society is linked to the rise of city-states and nation-states. The earliest urban centres may be traced back to 4000 BC. These urban centres associated with early city-states and nation-states were the seats of government or the locus of political power. They were islands of literacy and refinement surrounded by villages. The urban centres were economic parasites on the peasant population. They survived on the surpluses produced by the peasants. Following are some of the characteristics of the urban society:

1. Heterogeneity is a hallmark of the urban society because it offers varying economic and social opportunities to a variety of people.
2. It is a twin of the peasant society as both are born simultaneously.
3. It has a social system based on highly impersonal relations. The large numbers, the density, and the diversity of people are the main reason for the lack of personal relationships.
4. It has an economic system based on a complex division of labour and production for trade. The major occupations are industrial in nature and there is a lot of economic competition.
5. It is more receptive to change than the rural–agrarian society.

Another term which has often been used in the context of intermixing of rural and urban societies is 'rurban society'. As larger cities are not able to accommodate the whole population who work within the city limits, many people live in villages. In many cases the clear demarcation between 'country' and 'city' becomes difficult. Beyond the city limits there is a large area where farm and urban homes overlap to such an extent that it is no longer possible to speak of an urban or a rural area. These composite regions are called 'r-urban'. The term 'rurban' was first introduced by C.J. Galpin in 1918.

Critical Thinking Questions
- Why is society taken as the totality of human relationships?
- Why is the self-perpetuating nature of society accepted as a crucial factor?

****

3

Some Important Prevalent Concepts

Chapter Outline: *Globalization; Post-modernism; Ethnicity; Diaspora; Civil Society; Multiculturalism; Rural-Urban Continuum; Social Exclusion; Empowerment*

Learning Objectives
- What are all the important concepts for the understanding of the prevalent and emerging situations in the world?
- Why is the concept of ethnicity so important to understand the issues of identity?
- Where do you draw the line of demarcation between modern and post-modern society?
- In what way is the concept of pluralism different from multiculturalism? Do you consider Indian society to be a multicultural society?

Some important basic concepts being used to describe and analyse different social, cultural, economic, and political situations come from social science discourse and have also been used effectively in our day-to-day life. Most of these are used in the analysis of post-colonial situations in different parts of the world, including India, in different contexts and situations. These are suitable to be used in the Indian society, which is highly stratified and demonstrates glaring social inequalities.

Globalization

'Globalization' has emerged as one of the most important and talked-about phenomenon of the present age with its social, economic, and political dimensions. *The Blackwell Dictionary of Sociology* (1995) describes globalization as a 'process in which social life within societies is increasingly affected by international influences based on everything from political and trade ties to shared music, clothing styles and mass media'. Perhaps, the most powerful form of globalization is economic, in which planning and control expand from a relatively narrow focus – such as a single firm doing business on a regional or national basis – to a broad global focus in which the entire world serves as a source of labour, raw materials, and markets. When business is conducted at a local level, for example, activities of dealing with workers, obtaining raw materials and other goods, transportation, and selling the final product, all take place within the same social framework. In a globalized economy, however, transnational corporations operate in many different countries at once and exploit variations in local conditions for their own advantage. If workers in a more affluent industrial society such as Britain or the United States, for example, go on strike in order to improve pay or working conditions, a transnational corporation can simply shift work to another country where workers are more compliant and have lower expectations.

Analysing the necessity of international economic and socio-political management in the face of globalization, Samir Amin (1997), a renowned and strong voice on the issue of globalization and its implications for third world countries, says that the globalization of the capitalist system is certainly nothing new, but it has undeniably taken a qualitative step forward during the most recent period. Moreover, this deepening economic interdependence between nations occurs at a time when there is a crisis of accumulation, and the earlier boom has given way to stagnation. The advance of globalization has not been confined to trade; it also affects productive systems, technology, financial markets, and many other aspects of social life. The new globalization erodes the efficiency of economic management by nation-states though it does not abolish their existence.

Rise of ethnicity as a political response to economic globalization is yet another important dimension of globalization. Samir Amin (ibid) says that the 'present epoch is surely characterized by an awakening, or reawakening, marked by collective social identifications which are starkly different from those defined by membership of a nation-state or a social class. Regionalism, linguistic and cultural assertion, tribal or ethnic loyalties, devotion to a religious group, attachment to a local community, are some of the multiple forms this reawakening has taken.'

In Africa, the dissolution of national unity sometimes seems to have given way to ethnicity as a basis for the legitimate renewal of competing forces. In India, in Afghanistan, in Eastern Europe, in the former Soviet Union and the former Yugoslavia, even in Western Europe, in Spain, national unity has been put in question.

When we take a close look at the thesis put forward by the advanced and dominant countries and the system in support of globalization, we find that the management of the political and social systems by the single virtue of the market is a utopia. Concerned at the rise of ethnicity and religious fundamentalism in third world countries, Samir Amin (1997) puts forward an alternative agenda of action – the question of ethnicity should be replaced in the strategic framework by an action one can sum up thus: respect diversity, unite in spite of it. Respecting diversity means renouncing the empty discourse of power which pretends to act 'in the national interest' (which this power more often than not betrays) by pretending to internalize the ideology of the nation-state.

The passive acceptance of the inevitability of globalization in its present polarizing form, equating development with the expansion of the market should be resisted. Each society should be allowed to negotiate the terms of its interdependence with the rest of the global economy. National development can be pursued in a pluralistic world. The very goal of homogeneity may also be divisive, especially in the case of the pluralistic, third world countries.

Ethnic violence of the worst type is an alarming trend in the face of globalization. Arjun Appadurai (2001) in a UNESCO sponsored study on keys to the 21st century puts forward a thought-provoking agenda of action.

> There should be a concerted effort to delink ethnicity from citizenship: State policies should be developed to move away from monoethnic and majoritarian forms of citizenship to forms of citizenship that are dual, serial and multiple, so as to accommodate a world of growing hybridity and diversity in cultural identities. Secondly, nationalism should be consciously allied to multicultural projects (stressing the future-orientation, openness and non-exclusivity of social identities) rather than mono-cultural histories that tend to breed ideologies of purity and cleansing. Finally, States as well as non-governmental organizations of every type should encourage the use of mass media (both popular and official) to create a public sphere that stimulates, legitimizes and circulates images and narratives of hybridity and mixed identity. In this way, public spheres, both national and transnational, will grow habituated to indeterminacies and new mixtures in social life, and uncertainty about the 'other' will be less likely to produce terror and ethnocide.

Post-Modernism

Like globalization, post-modernism too has emerged as an omnipresent phenomenon in every discourse concerning human society today. There is hardly any field of intellectual activity which has not been touched by the spectre of post-modernism. From architecture to zoology, forestry, geography and from law to history, literature, arts, medicine, politics, philosophy, and sexuality, it has not left any field untouched. The term was probably first used by Arnold Toynbee, the great British historian, in 1939 in his monumental work, *A Study of History*. In this work he suggested that the modern period ends in the third quarter of the 19th century, that is, sometime between 1850 and 1875. This means that the period 'after modernism' or post-modernity is located not in the 20th century but in the 19th. By the time, he wrote the fifth volume of this work that was published in 1939, he used the term 'post-modern' for this period. At this point he had shifted the chronology a bit, suggesting that 'modern' now comes to an end during the First World War, that is, during 1914–1918, and the post-modern begins to form and shape itself in the years between the two Wars, that is, between 1918 and 1939. But the term 'post-modern', from its very inception, is characterized by an ambiguity.

Marvin Harris (1999), while elaborating post modernism, displays a high degree of clarity. According to him, post-modernism is an intellectual movement or orientation that promotes itself as the anti-thesis of modernism. The term itself was introduced by architects in the late 1940s, while the themes of post modernism actually originated long before anyone started to design post-modern buildings.' Extending the elaboration further, he identified the disparagement of Western science and technology as the most prominent intellectual strand. Other strands that follow from this central tenet include:

1. The representation of social life as a 'text'.
2. The elevation of text and language as the fundamental phenomenon of existence.
3. The application of literary analysis to all phenomenon.
4. The questioning of reality and of the adequacy of language to describe reality.
5. Disdain for, or rejection of, method.
6. Rejection of broad theories or meta narratives.
7. Advocacy of polyvocality.
8. Focus on power relations and cultural hegemony.
9. Rejection of Western institutions and achievements.
10. Extreme relativism and tendency toward nihilism.

The concept of post-modernity belongs to social thought because it alerts us to some tremendously important social as well as cultural shifts taking place at the end of the 20th century. In order to understand the main currents of post-modern thought, it helps to step back and review the thinkers who anticipated post-modernity. Undoubtedly, the most significant figure is Friedrich Nietzsche. He announced that 'nihilism stands at the door'. Nietzsche achieved notoriety for proclaiming 'the death of God'. His slogan, 'the death of God', means that we can no longer be sure of anything. Morality is a lie, truth is fiction. While these lies may seem abstract, a generation before Nietzsche, Karl Marx viewed the same process in a much more mundane light. What Nietzsche saw as a predicament for science, rationality and metaphysics, Marx attributed to the 'banal everyday workings of the bourgeois economic order'. In other words, under capitalism, people allow the market to organize life, including their inner lives. By equating everything with its market value – commodifying - we end up seeking answers to questions about what is worthwhile, honourable, and even what is real, in the market place. Nihilism can also be understood in this practical, everyday sense.

David Lyon (2002), taking a refreshing look at post-modernity, says that big questions remain unanswered. 'The post-modern may refer to the exhaustion of modernity but does this invite obituaries or merely a call to make a room for a fresh appraisal of modernity? Is logo centrism dead or dormant? Would we fall into the trap of modern linear logic if we imagined that the path from Providence to Progress and from thence to Nihilism is a one-way street with no return?'

Ethnicity

The intellectual history of the term 'ethnicity' is relatively short. Prior to the 1970s, there was little mention of it in social science literature and text books contained no definition of the term. Since the mid-1970s, the concept has acquired strategic significance in anthropological theory, partly as a response to the changing post-colonial geo-politics and the rise of ethnic minorities' activism in many industrial States. This has resulted in a proliferation of theories of ethnicity, explaining such diverse phenomena as social and political change, identity formation, social conflict, race relations, nation-building, assimilation, and so on.

Among a variety of definitions, the most generalized one may be the one given in the *Blackwell Dictionary of Sociology* (1995) which describes ethnicity as a concept referring to a shared culture and way of life, especially as reflected in language, folkways, religious and other institutional forms, material culture such as clothing and food, and cultural products such as music, literature, and art. The collection of people who share an ethnicity is often called an ethnic group, although technically the use of 'group' is inappropriate in sociological usage because a group is a social system with some degree of regular interaction among its members. Ethnicity, however, typically includes far too many people for regular interaction. Etymologically speaking, the term 'ethnic', derived from the Greek word 'ethnikos', refers to: (a) nations or peoples not converted to Christianity; (b) races or large groups of people having common traits and customs; or (c) groups in an exotic primitive culture. But in sociological-anthropological parlance, an ethnic group can be defined as a historically-formed aggregate of people having a real or imaginary association with a specific territory, a shared cluster of beliefs and values connoting its distinctiveness in relation to similar groups, and recognized as such by others. The definition thus has five components:

1. A subjective belief in real or assumed historical antecedents.
2. A symbolic or real geographical centre.
3. Shared cultural emblems, such as race, language, religion dress, and diet, or a combination of some of them which though variegated and flexible, provide the overt basis of ethnic identity.
4. Self-ascribed awareness of distinctiveness and belonging to the group. and
5. Recognition by others of the group differentiation. It is thus a self-defined and 'other-recognised' status.

Barth (1969) says that an ethnic group refers to that population which (a) is largely biologically self-perpetuating; (b) shares fundamental cultural values realised in overt unity in cultural forms; (c) makes up a field of communication and interaction; and (d) has a membership which identifies itself and is identified by others as constituting a category distinguishable from other categories of the same order. While race is a biological concept, culture is purely social in nature.

By concentrating on what is socially effective, ethnic groups are seen as a form of social organization. There are three competing approaches to the understanding of ethnicity. They can be roughly categorised as:

1. Primordialist
2. Instrumentalist
3. Constructivist

Sergey Sokolovski and Valery Tishkov (1996), commenting on these three approaches, say that roughly speaking, primordialist theories assert that ethnic identification is based on deep, 'primordial' attachment to a group or culture; instrumentalist approaches treat ethnicity as a political instrument exploited by leaders and others in pragmatic pursuit of their own interests; and constructivist approaches emphasize the contingency and fluidity of ethnic identity, treating it as something which is made in specific social and historical contexts, rather than (as in primordialist arguments) treating it as a 'given'.

If we have a close look at these three approaches, we find that primordialist view asserts that ultimately there is some real, tangible foundation to ethnic identification. It accepts that ethnicity should be viewed as a predominantly biological phenomenon, closely related to culture and history. Pierre L. van den Berghe (1981), an exponent of this approach, has explored the contribution of socio-biology to the explanation of ethnic phenomena and suggests that these are rooted in a genetic predisposition for kin selection, or 'nepotism' which in the long run leads to primordial loyalties. Clifford Geertz is also a known exponent of this view and he conceives of ethnicity as an inchoate but powerful characteristic of human life. To him, the congruities of blood, speech, custom, and so on are have an ineffable, and at times, overpowering coerciveness in themselves.

Unlike the primordialists, the instrumentalists define ethnicity 'as an instrument for the pursuit of material interests by competing cultural groups within complex societies' according to Jean Popeau (1998). The extreme stand, taken by some instrumentalists, conceives of ethnicity objectives in the contemporary world, and therefore needing no historical or cultural explanations. Sergey Sokolovski and Valery Tishkov (ibid), expanding on this point, further say that for instrumentalists, claims to ethnicity are a product of political myths, created and manipulated by cultural elites in their pursuit of advantage and power. The cultural forms, values, and practices of ethnic groups become resources for elites in competition for political power and economic advantage. They become symbols and referents for the identification of members of a group, which are called up in order to facilitate the creation of a political identity. Thus, ethnicity is created in the dynamics of elite competition within the boundaries determined by political and economic realities.

The constructivist approach found the first voice in a seminal contribution of Fredrik Barth and his colleagues titled as *Ethnic Groups and Boundaries* (1969). They treated ethnicity as a continuing ascription which classifies persons in terms of their general and inclusive identity, presumptively determined by origin and background, as well as a form of social organization maintained by inter-group boundary mechanisms.

Besides the three approaches we have described, sociologists refer to some more approaches such as Marxist and Neo-Marxist approach and Weberian approach. For the former, ethnic conflict emerges at two levels: (a) at a general level in which ethnicity is viewed as a device detracting from the consciousness of class interests, and (b) in a situation where there has been a 'cultural division of labour', when members of an ethnic group are placed in a subordinate position within a given State (internal colonialism) or in the global context (international division of labour). For Marxists and Neo-Marxists, ethnic relations are antithetical to the development of class solidarity. Mobilization on an ethnic basis evokes false consciousness. It weakens class solidarity. In the Weberian approach, ethnicity does not constitute a group; it only facilitates group formation of any kind, particularly in the political sphere.

As Sergey Sokolovski and Valery Tishkov (ibid) rightly point out, all the approaches to understanding ethnicity are not necessarily mutually exclusive, so one possible avenue of research is the integration of the soundest aspects of existing approaches into a coherent theory of ethnicity. There are reasons to believe that a constructivist conceptualization could serve as the nucleus of such a synthesis. Another direction for ethnicity research is the assimilation of relevant knowledge from other social sciences.

Diaspora

Diaspora is another new field of study in sociology and social-cultural anthropology. Derived from a Greek word, it means dispersion or scattering. In sociological-anthropological literature, it refers to the dispersion or scattering of a population to far off places. This term was initially used in the context of exile of the Jews to different parts of the world, explaining the protracted exile of the Jewish people and cultural contacts with different regions and populations, cultures, philosophies, and ways of life. Richard Marienstras (1989) says that this interpretation is somewhat metaphorical. The idea of diaspora implies or may be held to imply the idea of 'centre' and 'periphery'; the idea of a relationship or lack of relationship to the soil and the territory; the ideas of 'majority' and 'minority'. But it is only recently that this term has come to describe minority groups whose awareness of their identity is defined by a relationship, territorially discontinuous, with a group settled 'elsewhere' (for example, the Chinese diaspora, the Indian diaspora, etc.).

The diasporic community may be occupying an ambiguous status of being both an ambassador and a refugee. 'Further, categories emerge, through the use of such words as immigrant, exile, and refugee. Their use attempts to give some indication of the ideologies, choices, reasons, and compulsions which may have governed the act of migration,' according to Jasbir Jain (1998).

Right from its very inception, there has been a search for a theoretical framework to integrate this area of study. Ravindra K. Jain did pioneering work on the Indian diaspora and in his seminal volume Indian *Communities Abroad* (1993), provides an important discussion on several frameworks to deal with cultural persistence. This is the retentionist view of Indian culture overseas and the studies falling under this category have recorded the ability of the Indians to retain, reconstitute, and revitalize many aspects of their culture in an overseas setting. One of the best examples of this perspective is Morton Mass's study of East Indians in Trinidad, published in 1961.

Studies of cultural persistence fall under the general rubric of acculturation processes. The second perspective is purely and simply an adaptationist one. Studies falling under this category are chiefly concerned with the question of the adaptation of the social group or an immigrant society of the social environment of the host society. R.K. Jain's (1970) work on south Indian migrants in a typical Malaysian setting is a study of the process of adaptation of people of Indian origin to conditions of life and work in a particular Malayan environment, namely rubber plantation.

The third perspective is that of the plural society, first advocated by Furnivall (1948) in the context of the colonial society of South East Asia. According to him, this kind of society possessed three characteristics – cultural, economic, and political. Culturally, a plural society consists of incongruous and incompatible cultural sections between which communication is hampered. Economically, the relationships between the cultural sections are those of a market place. Politically, this kind of plural society is held together only by the fact of being dominated by an external colonial power. R.K. Jain (1986) has argued that the concept of a plural society in the sense used by Furnivall is applicable only to 'settlement societies' and not to civilizations.

With the globalization of ethnicity as the post-modernist phenomenon of our times the diaspora studies have assumed further importance. From India's viewpoint, such studies are of immense importance in assessing not only the implantation of Indian society and culture in all parts of the world but also the economic and symbolic capital which the non-resident Indians may contribute to the development of India. From a purely academic view, the Indian diaspora is one of the most varied, representing several religions, regions, and castes.

Multiculturalism

'Multicultural' and 'Multiculturalism' are words frequently used to describe the ethnic diversity that exists everywhere in the world today. However, there is some confusion about what precisely they signify. Do they simply describe diversity or are they advocating a particular response to that diversity?

We must be very clear as to why multiculturalism has overtaken pluralism as the dominant concept. Cultural pluralism is not a modern phenomenon. History provides many examples of different communities and cultures existing side-by-side, within the same society, co-existing peacefully, and many times amicably. Cultural plurality, thus, has been a hallmark of many societies, including the Indian society, for a long time.

This is a very useful concept to understand and analyse the social situation in countries which have diversity. It has been fashionable to describe Indian society in terms of pluralism – social, cultural, linguistic, religious, environmental, and racial/ethnic.

Thus, pluralism is merely an acknowledgement of diversity. Multiculturalism is a step forward. It denotes not only the acknowledgement of diversity but also recognition of the contribution of various groups to different spheres of life and it also demands their special protection under the law. Several such minority groups, even in modern democracies, suffer discrimination, oppression exclusion, and marginalization in different ways and in varying degrees. Multiculturalism calls for not only protection of the interests of such minority groups but also a reasonable share in power structure. Their contributions should be recognized and should not be disregarded. Their identities should also be respected and not mocked since they are different from the dominant population. Many minority groups face these problems.

Multiculturalism does not support cultural assimilation into the dominant majority but encourages a respectful integration so that the minority groups feel they are an integral part of the larger society. Thus intentional homogenization is not considered desirable. Multiculturalism looks at the society with diversity, not as a 'melting pot' but as a 'salad bowl' or a 'cultural mosaic'.

Some of the theorists are firmly of the view that minority cultural groups should not only enjoy equal rights but also special group rights. This requires the majority dominant population to be educated and trained to not only accept this but also advocate for it whenever they come across any deviation or departure from the desired goal. This leads to an ideology where the values of no specific or particular community, including the dominant group, are treated as 'central'.

Although the Indian Constitution goes near the ideals of multiculturalism, the Indian society, in practice, cannot be described as multicultural. At most, it may be said that it is a plural society trying to be multicultural.

Multiculturalism, as a coherent theory, with its distinct conception of democracy and citizenship, has emerged only in the recent past. As Gurpreet Mahajan (2002) points out, 'The simultaneous presence of many cultures and communities within the same social space points to a plural social fabric, but it does not betoken the presence of multiculturalism. The latter entails something more than the mere presence of different communities, or the attitude of tolerance in society. Multiculturalism is concerned with the issue of equality: it asks whether the different communities, living peacefully together, co-exist as equals in the public arena.'

It is this emphasis on equality that distinguishes multiculturalism from pluralism. Within the framework of plurality, the major concern is peaceful coexistence and amity. Pluralism, in other words, indicates the presence of differences and marks a departure from policies aimed at annihilating the other, but that is all. It remains silent about the public status of these communities.

The multicultural condition like the condition of post-modernity cannot be reductively defined. Rather, it can be described phenomenologically. David Theo Goldberg, in his seminal work Multiculturalism: A Critical Reader, writes that 'Multiculturalism stands for a wide range of social articulations – ideas, and practices that the "-ism" reduces to a formal singularity, fixing it into a cemented condition, the ideology of "political correctness".' Multiculturalism has a history. One needs to understand clearly about mono-cultural commitments due to which multiculturalism arose, in response. The term 'multiculturalism' has come to be used primarily in connection with demands on behalf of black and other minority groups for equal representation in USA.

Unlike multiculturalism, 'Pluralism and tolerance are often most visible when the dominance of one community is unambiguously acceded. The dominant community asserts its supremacy by stamping its presence in public places and challenges to these symbols are taken as a sign of rebellion, to be strongly resisted. In India, from the 6th century AD onwards, rulers established their dominance by removing the idols of the local deity and replacing them with their own gods' (Mahajan, ibid).

On the other hand, multiculturalism makes a value statement. It asserts that the many cultural communities that are present in the society must live as equals in the public domain. Multiculturalism, thus, speaks of issues that are central to democracy and egalitarianism. Any discussion on multiculturalism should take place along with an assessment of its core agenda. In the case of India, the society has always been characterized by pluralism or cultural mosaic, but the post-independent Indian polity based on the Constitution is trying to reach the ideal of multiculturalism.

Anthropologists have been 'reluctant' students of multiculturalism. As Terene Turner rightly points out, 'There are a number of ways that anthropologists could contribute constructively and critically to multiculturalist thinking and practice, and a number of ways also that they might expand their own theoretical and practical horizons by doing so.'

Rural-Urban Continuum

Discussing the distinctiveness and difference between a village and a city or rural and urban has been an old pastime of a number of scholars of human and settlement geography, anthropology, and sociology. The concept of 'continuum' in the present context was first developed by the cultural anthropologist Robert Redfield in the wake of his study of the Mexican rural society, *Folk Culture of Yucatan* (1941).

Let us first look at the literal meaning of the term 'continuum'. It is anything that goes through a gradual transition from one condition to a different condition without any abrupt changes. This may also be a continuous sequence in which adjacent elements are not perceptibly different from each other although the extremes are quite different. The underlying idea, obviously, is about continuity. Thus, in this context, the process of continuity between the rural and the urban societies is being sought to be understood. A civilization consists of both rural and urban societies. A village of today gets transformed into a town and city tomorrow. Thus it is not a total break in culture and traditions even though we may find a strong distinction between the rural and the urban in terms of occupation, environmental factors, size of the community, density of population, pace of social mobility or change, migration pattern, social stratification, level of literacy or education, and systems of interaction between people (including levels of anonymity). When Robert Redfield was studying Yucatan, he encountered the problem of differentiating between the folk culture and the urban culture. He noticed that beyond a point, the folk culture (beliefs, social practices, values, etc.) and the urban culture were merging with each other and thus he found it impossible to tell where the folk culture came to an end and the urban culture began. He concluded that they should not be considered as two totally disjointed, independent and separate entities. Rather, it would be prudent and logical to treat both in terms of a continuum.

Thus, we find that it is almost impossible to draw a clean and sharp line of demarcation between rural and urban culture. There is always some overlapping and commonality between them. Every rural society possesses some elements of an urban society and every urban society carries some elements of a rural society.

Urban people usually maintain an attitude of superiority by describing the rural as 'rustic', superstitious, crude, and unsophisticated and lacking refinement. The superiority in terms of technology may be true, but in terms of beliefs, faith, and rituals, the urban population exhibits the similar amount of superstition and sometime even more.

In the process of urbanization and expansion of the city limits, we may come across villages in the city and city in the villages. Thus, the phenomenon of 'urban peasants' is not rare. Moreover, the concept of 'rurban' may also be applied in any situations.

In every civilization, there is a process of cultural continuity that is largely responsible for the justification of the concepts such as the rural–urban continuum. The advent of mobile phones (now smartphones) is providing more connectivity, automobiles such as bikes more mobility, and cheaper and accessible college education (even of indifferent quality) more social equality and caste anonymity. In their own ways, they are further enlarging the rural–urban continuum in the Indian society.

Social Exclusion

In a broad sense, social exclusion is the denial of equal opportunities to some people or groups which leads to their inability to participate in the basic social, economic, and political functioning of the society. As a result, individuals or entire groups or communities are systematically blocked from various rights, opportunities, and resources which are normally available to others. When certain groups are systematically disadvantaged because they are discriminated against on the basis of their race, ethnicity, religion, caste, descent, or sexual orientation, their social integration with the larger society also suffers. Social exclusion is a multidimensional discrimination that occurs in public institutions such as education and health services, and in employment as well as in day-to-day social life. It takes forms such as denial of housing, shop, office in private spaces. It encompasses social, cultural, economic, and political dimensions.

Social Science Encyclopedia (2009) says social exclusion is a flexible and somewhat an amorphous term to use, but its core features which separate it from marginalization and poverty are:
1. It is multidimensional.
2. It is conceived as a social, not an individual problem.
3. It is regarded not as a particular local problem, but as a development that has global roots.
4. It suggests the imperative of inclusion.

Social inclusion is the opposite of social exclusion. It is affirmative action to change the circumstances that lead to social exclusion. In the Indian context, the scheduled castes and the scheduled tribes and to a lesser extent the other backward classes and religious minorities, especially Muslims, may be included in the segment of population suffering from social exclusion in varying degrees. The LGBTQ community is another such category of people. Sometimes the exclusion becomes doubly sharper, for instance, in the case of Dalit women who have to suffer on both counts—being Dalit as well as women. Thus, the Dalit women's deprivation and exclusion is further compounded by caste as well as gender.

Empowerment

The concept of empowerment and other related concepts and ideas such as social empowerment, disadvantaged groups, vulnerable groups, and weaker sections have never been more in vogue in the analysis of society including the Indian society than the post-Independence period. Empowerment, in general terms, is the process designed to increase the degree of autonomy and self-determination in the lives of the people in order to enable them to represent

Some Important Prevalent Concepts 31

and protect their interests, to overcome their sense of powerlessness to use their resources and opportunities.

Empowerment has emerged as a key concept for all the weaker sections of the society. Obviously, the disempowered or those lacking power in comparison with others need empowerment. In the Indian context empowerment is the key requirement for the Dalits, Adivasi (tribal) communities, women, minorities, and others lacking power and facing discrimination in a variety of ways. Women's empowerment is now a central concern of the women's movement. Empowerment also includes acquiring knowledge of the structures that oppress the people, and to seek to alter the power imbalance in the society.

Social empowerment is largely understood as a process of accessing opportunities and resources in order to make personal choices such as what to eat, wear, where and how to live, and so on.

Being disadvantaged and vulnerable are the other key ideas. Disadvantage means an unfavourable circumstance or condition that reduces the chances of success or effectiveness. Thus, a disadvantaged group may be defined by a denial or lack of accessibility to resources and barriers it faces. Overcoming disadvantage, then, means overcoming or removing barriers to self-sufficiency. A disadvantaged group becomes vulnerable or susceptible to exploitation because of disempowerment and unfavourable conditions. For instance, all the weaker sections mentioned earlier may also be described as vulnerable groups and also recognized as such by the Government of India. Thus vulnerability – social, economic, or political, leads to social exclusion and exploitation.

Critical Thinking Questions

- Is social exclusion an individual or a collective problem of a group?
- How do all the concepts discussed in the chapter help in the analysis of the contemporary Indian society?

****

Section Two

4

Marriage

Chapter Outline: *Introduction, Concept and definitions, Functions of marriage, Rules of marriage, Incest rules, Exogamy and incest, Endogamy, Preferential marriage rules, Cross cousin marriage, parallel cousin marriage, Levirate and Sororate, Plural marriages, Polygyny and polyandry, Hypergamy, Fictive marriage, Residence after marriage, Choosing a mate, Group marriage, Marriage payments, Bride wealth or bride price, Dowry, Divorce, Live-in relationship and marriage, Indian scenario, 'Marital rape, patriarchy, and right of sexual autonomy in Indian society', Marriage selection in cyber space: technology mediated romance, Feminist critique of marriage*

Learning Objectives

- Define marriage sociologically–anthropologically.
- Explain the near universality of marriage.
- State the Important functions of marriage.
- Make and assessment of the universality of taboo of incest.
- Why is live-in-relationship replacing marriage in some societies?
- How does technologically-mediated romance intervene in the institution of marriage?
- How is the traditional Indian society coping with romance in cyberspace and live-in-relationships?
- On what grounds do the feminists critique the institution of marriage?

Introduction

Human beings, like all mammals, mate, copulate, and have children. Like all animals, they rear a family. But humans, unlike other animals, marry.

In almost all societies of the world, marriage is a central structure in the formation of families and the linkages between wider relations. Thus, marriage and family are key structures in most societies. Marriage, the creation of families, and kinship systems offer solutions to several problems faced by human societies. Sociologists and anthropologists have always been keenly interested in both, as well as in the relationship between these two social institutions. They consider marriage as a 'cultural universal' as it exists in some form in all societies.

Concept and Definitions

The term 'marriage' refers to the various customs and rules concerning special a relationship between two persons of the opposite sex (though same-sex marriage is also now a reality) which also creates a set of obligations and roles for them as well as for their kin groups. It also refers to the sanction which the society provides to such a relationship. Sociologically, it means certain procedures of action and the rules concerning such relations having social approval. In this sense, marriage is a social institution.

Defined in the context of a relationship between an adult male and a female, it includes sexual relations between the two and the children born out of such a relationship.

There could be many ways to define marriage. Since the concept involves reference to a set of rules, customs, and practices, and the social approval or legitimization which differs greatly from culture to culture, there cannot be a universally applicable definition of marriage which has no exceptions. Hence, instead of learning about it through definitions propounded by the anthropologists and sociologists, it is better to learn about it by analysing its nature and content. The social characteristics of marriage include:

- In most societies marriage is considered a permanent social and legal contract.
- It is based on mutual rights and obligations between the spouses.
- A marriage is based on a romantic relationship in the Western society and arranged by the family in other societies.
- It signals a sexual relationship between two or more people.
- It is codified as a social institution.
- Because a marriage is recognized by the law and religion and also involves economic ties between the spouses, a dissolution of marriage (divorce) also involves a dissolution of relationship in all these spheres.

Although the earlier evolutionary scholars of the 19th century, like Morgan, talked about a situation in human society called promiscuity, a condition nearer to animality regarding sex between adult males and females, the evolutionist Westermarck, in his book *The History of Human Marriages* (1891) wrote that he accepted the presence of marriage as a social institution even at the earliest stage of human existence. Malinowski goes to the extent of regarding marriage as demarcating the state between humanity and animality. In line with these 19th century discussions about the origin and evolution of marriage, ethnographers have not found any society where marriage in some form or the other does not exist. Its near universality and relative stability compels us to think about its functions, which leads us to a better understanding of the concept.

Functions of Marriage

The importance of the institution of marriage may be gauged by the fact that it has several social functions within societies and cultures:

- Marriage determines the roles that the spouses play in each other's lives, in the family, and in society at large. Sociologist Talcott Parson outlined a theory of roles within marriage and household. The social status of the spouses is determined on the basis of their assigned roles and a hierarchy of power is created between the spouses.
- It regulates sexual access between males and females.
- It finds ways to organize labour, assign responsibility for childcare and is guided by certain cultural rules.
- It also determines family names and lines of familial descent.
- It socially legitimizes sexual union between individuals.

Sexual mating is a biological process of reproduction by which species are maintained and generations extended. But the presence of the psychological dimension in humans as compared to animals brings about the question of individual likes and dislikes and selection as well as the sense of exclusiveness of such a relation. It does not simply remain a question of satisfaction of a biological drive. It also brings to light the thought of male and female individuality and ability.

All these considerations complicate the situation and call for a role of society and culture. Also, the fact that the human child is born in a most helpless condition, and the mother is also physically handicapped for some time after the child's birth, and the prolonged infancy and dependence of the human child are the biological compulsions which require social and cultural intervention.

As a result, there are three basic problems in every society for which it must find some cultural solution. Firstly, the regulation of sexual access between males and females. Secondly, devising some kind of division of labour between males and females and thirdly, the need to assign responsibility for childcare.

Sexual competition can prove to be a source of serious conflict if not regulated. Because the birth of children involves responsibility and there is a question of inheritance of property, the relationship must be relatively permanent and socially approved or legitimized. Basically, it is these social concerns which are of great importance, rather than merely the biological question of satisfaction of sexual needs, and acquire larger significance in the concept of marriage.

Marriage involves the establishment of a relatively permanent union or relationship between an adult male and female who belong to two kin groups. The establishment of this relationship does not limit itself to the levels of the two individuals but is extended to the two families. Kin groups also become related variously in different societies, also involving economic exchanges.

The culturally controlled and socially sanctioned marital relations result in the formation of a group called 'family'. Marriage and family are so intertwined that it is difficult to talk about one without making a reference to the other. Though rooted in the biological satisfaction of sex and biological compulsions of the prolonged dependence of the human child on adults, the concepts are social–cultural. Since family comes into existence by marriage, family, marriage and human culture are coeval with one another and constitute the foundation of society.

Anthropologists take the view that the most useful way to approach the study of marriage and family is not by establishing definitions that apply to every known group but to look at the different ways in which the basic needs of sexual regulation and infant care, and the establishment of rights and obligations are legitimized in different societies.

It is because of this view that a debate about the possibility of a universally acceptable definition of marriage has also emerged. Taking the *Notes and Quarries on Anthropology* definition of marriage, Edmund Leach pointed out several shortcomings and limited character of this definition. Later, after the publication of the book *The Nuer: A Description of the Modes of Livelihood and Political Institutions of a Nilotic People* by E. Evans Pritchard, the prevalence of 'ghost marriage' and the marriage between two women in that society became exceptions which were not covered by any definition current at that time. Hence, Leach and his followers concluded that a universally applicable definition of marriage was not possible. The instance of the Nayar society also became a point of contention. In that society, *Tali–Kettu–Kalyanam* was the real marriage which was never consummated; the temporary *sambandham* alliances were without the status of a husband, but were functional in sex regulation; and none of the two had any economic obligations for the care and upkeep of the children born to the women. Indeed, the situation was interpreted by some anthropologists as a case of no-marriage. This also added strength to the view that no universal definition of marriage was possible.

Since the word 'legitimacy' formed a part of all the definitions of marriage and legitimization being a highly culturally-variable aspect, Leach asserted that legitimacy cannot be a basis for any universal definition. However, Kathleen Gough, who also studied the Nayar society and recognized the presence of marriage there, modified the *Notes and Queries* definition to evolve a definition which could resolve all the limitations pointed out by Leach and could be accepted as a nearly universal definition. Thus, according to Gough (1954):

> Marriage is a relationship established between a woman and one or more other persons which provides that a child born to the woman under circumstances not prohibited by the rules of the relationship, is accorded full birthright status common to normal members of the society.

This definition, largely functional, meets most of the objections pointed out by Leach. But Leach is also critical of functional definition, as according to him, Marriage performs different functions in patriarchal and matriarchal societies. In patriarchal societies, it establishes the legal father of a woman's child while in matriarchal societies it establishes socially significant relationship of affinity between a husband and his wife's brothers.

Broadly speaking, marriage may be defined as 'a socially sanctioned sex relationship involving two or more persons of opposite sex whose relationship is expected to endure beyond the time required for gestation and birth of children.'

According to Paul Bohannan, marriage is a complex phenomenon. 'It is the final stage of successful courtship and the initial stage of family formation'. The husband-wife relationship can be given many different sorts of cultural contents. This means that the roles of husband and wife must be factored into several different aspects before any cross-cultural comparison becomes meaningful.

Socially, marriage is associated with parentage; the element of social approval makes it a legal contract. It is always a public affair. At times, religious blessings are also associated. In no culture is it entirely a free choice. People related in certain ways may be debarred from or expected to marry. An almost universal rule prohibits marriage between siblings and parents. The universality of marriage does not mean that everyone in every society gets married. It simply means that most of the people get married at least once in their lifetime.

It is critical to point out that instead of using 'male-female' or 'husband-wife', using the term 'partners' would be more realistic. Though same sex relationship was accepted in Western societies, same sex couples could not legally marry anywhere in the world. It was only in 2001 that Netherlands became as the first country to legalize same sex marriage. It was followed by some other countries of Europe such as Belgium, Spain, Norway, and Sweden as well as Canada. Later, South Africa also legalized it. Meanwhile, some states and cities of USA followed, such as Connecticut, Iowa, Maine, Maryland, Massachusetts, New Hampshire, New York, Vermont, and Washington DC. It took almost two decades for India to 'decriminalize' Section 377 of the Indian Penal Code, allowing same sex relationship but no marriage.

Rules of Marriage

Marriage in every society is subject to certain rules, which may be prohibitive, prescriptive, or preferential. These rules answer the question – who can marry whom? In all societies, there are some prohibitions on marrying persons in certain relationships or from certain groups.

Incest Rule

Just as some form of marriage exists in essentially in all cultures, all cultures also have some form of incest taboo or rules that forbid sexual relations between certain close relatives. Beyond the immediate family, incest taboos vary from culture to culture, the most universal being that of mating between kins such as mother and son, father and daughter, brothers and sisters.

Such prohibition or taboo also extends beyond the immediate family group. This rule is called as the rule of 'incest'. The violation of this rule in primitive societies is invariably associated with a sense of horror as a result of expected divine punishment. In modern societies, however, ethical notions may be associated with this rule as such matings are also considered as 'uncivilized'. These matings are considered as disastrous for the society. But explanation confuses incest taboo and exogamy, because having incestuous sex relations does not mean a dislike for others.

The rule of incest widens the network of social relations. It also prevents confusions which cross-generational matings are likely to create. It stops conflicts within a family and prevents inbreeding. Since sexual access is one of the most important rights conferred by marriage, incest taboos effectively prohibit mating as well as marriage among certain kins, the notable exception being the royal families of ancient Egypt and Hawaiian society.

Exogamy and Incest

The word 'exogamy' means 'marrying out'. The term specifies that an individual must marry outside particular groups. Because of the association of sex with marriage, prohibition of incest produces an almost universal rule of exogamy within the family group of parents, children, and brothers and sisters. Very often, the descent groups based on blood relations such as lineages and clans are also exogamous. Members of the same totemic group also generally avoid marrying between themselves.

Apart from reducing conflicts over sex in co-operating groups such as hunting and fishing units, practise of exogamy leading to alliances between larger groups are of great adaptive significance for humans. Such alliances may have economic, political, or religious components. Wandering early-hunting and food-gathering bands exchanged women to make peace and ensure social ties of co-operation. These alliances are important among people who must move around in search of food. Exchange of women ensures inter-group sociability. In peasant societies in North India, the rule of exogamy applies to the entire village.

Endogamy

The term 'endogamy' refers to marriage within one's own group. The group may be defined in order to keep the privileges and the wealth of group intact. Practice of endogamy further consolidates the group by establishing group identity in terms of 'we' and 'they' as in-marrying groups. Tribal endogamy is a universal phenomenon. Endogamy forms the backbone of the structure of caste system in India. In America, racial groups and social classes tend to be endogamous. Classes, opportunities, cultural norms, and similarities of lifestyle, all contribute to maintaining endogamy though, theoretically speaking, social classes are identified as open groups.

Preferential Marriage Rules

Beyond explicit incest taboos, all cultures have norms about who is a legitimate or preferred marriage partner. There are certain rules, called 'preferential marriage rules', which specify the groups or categories of relations from which marriage partners are drawn as a matter of preference. While the categories of prohibitive and prescriptive rules entail some form of social punishment in case of their violation or non-observance, preferential rules are only indicative of the desire or preference of the society in the selection of mates and their violation does not amount to any serious breach of norms. Yet, in all societies where they are operative, these rules are followed by a large majority.

Cross-Cousin Marriage

The most common among the preferential marriage rules is of cross-cousin marriage. In some societies, cross-cousin marriages are accorded social preference. There are two types of cross cousins – one's mother's brothers' children are matriarchal cross cousins. Similarly, one's father's sister's children are patriarchal cross cousins. In a particular society, the rule of preference for cross-cousin marriage may be for either of the two types of cross cousins or for both the types. In the former case it is known as asymmetrical cross-cousin marriage and in the latter case it is known as symmetrical cross-cousin marriage.

Cross-cousin marriage is related to the organization of kinship units larger than the nuclear family. In a society organized in unilineal kin groups, cross cousins belong to unilineal groups and their marriage is considered as lineage exogamy. Cross-cousin marriage reinforces ties between kin groups established in the preceding generations. The reason for preference for cross-cousin marriage is similar to exogamy, that is, establishment of alliances between groups. But whereas exogamy establishes alliances between different groups, preferential marriage rules like cross-cousin marriage intensify the bonds of relationship between a limited number of groups generation after generation. In some of the middle Indian tribal groups such as Gonds, Baigas, Pradhans, and so on, a prevalent term for cross-cousin marriage in their tribal languages is *doodh lautawa* (the return of the milk). This is indicative of the advantage of return of the bride wealth (earlier called 'bride price') to family 'M' which was paid by family 'A' to 'B' generations before. This economic advantage associated with cross-cousin marriage cannot be brushed aside lightly, particularly in the context of simple or tribal societies.

Parallel-Cousin Marriage

The children of two brothers or of two sisters are parallel cousins. With only a few exceptions, parallel-cousin marriage is prohibited in all societies the world over. But a few societies allow parallel-cousin marriage. It is not only just practised customarily but is a preferred form of marriage in them.

Among these societies, nuclear family exogamy is associated with male-descent group endogamy. It is widely practised by pastoral nomadic Muslim Arabs. They are fighting-predating pastorals, with a low level of political organization. There are two main functions of this type of marriage among them – it consolidates their male-power, significant in the context of nomadism and fighting tradition. Marrying in a descent group consolidates their property, which is mainly in the form of their livestock. It also reinforces patrilineal authority. The system finds favour with the Qoranic acceptance of marriage between parallel cousins or even between half siblings.

Frederik Barth, in one of his studies among the Kurds, has observed that among the village-settled farmers of the Middle-East, lineage endogamy is replaced by village endogamy. Another instance is provided by the royal families of ancient Egypt who preferred brother–sister marriage to avoid fragmentation of the royal wealth. A sense of high-ranked status consciousness also got satisfaction with this practice.

Levirate and Sororate

Preferential marriages are often used as a device to promote inter-familial cordiality. The practice of a woman being an actual or potential mate for her husband's brothers is called 'levirate'. Often, it is obligatory in these societies on the part of the brothers of the deceased husband to marry the widow. In case she marries the younger brother of her husband, it is called junior levirate. If she marries the elder brother of the deceased husband, it is called senior levirate.

Similarly, the husband of a barren woman or a deceased wife can marry her sister; this is called 'sororate'. In the former case, at least some of the children born out of the union may be considered as the children of the first wife. A man having more than one wife, who are sisters, is known as 'sororal polygyny'.

Both, levirate and sororate attest the importance of marriage as an alliance between two groups; death does not dissolve the marriage contract. They emphasize the inter-familial obligations and the recognition of marriage as a bond between the two families and not just between two individuals.

All forms of preferential or prescribed forms of mating limit the number of possible marital linkages. According to Levi-Strauss, the main purpose served by these preferred or prescribed forms of marriage is to strengthen the solidarity within a tribe. However, others have doubted the primitive people's ability to understand what is good for them. Probably psychological-emotional concerns, as well as other features of their tribal society, might have led these rules.

Plural Marriages

The number of spouses one may have is another basis for some other types of marriages prevalent in some societies. One person having one spouse seems to be very logical rule and in most societies people have only a single spouse. This is called as monogamy. But monogamy is not a universal feature. As the ethnographic evidence reveal, plurality of spouses, known as 'polygamy', is a widespread phenomenon. It has two forms – a man having more than one wife is called 'polygyny' and a woman having more than one husband is called as 'polyandry'.

Polygyny

In modern industrialized societies where divorce laws have become easier, a man or a woman will not necessarily remain married to the same person for the whole life. Because of religious prescription and ethical notions, plurality of spouses is resented, and they continue to remarry and live with a single wife or husband – a situation called as 'serial monogamy'. But several societies permit or prefer plural marriages and, very often, polygyny.

Polygyny, as a cultural option, may be related to different factors in different societies. Africa is a prime example of polygyny. A lower proportion of males may give rise to the custom of polygyny in a society. Usually there are other social and economic factors as well that influence this practice. In most of the societies practising polygyny, it is a means of improving one's social status and increasing social dominance. Having more than one wife is a reflection of one's economic capacity to sustain bigger families. It also implies one's economic capability of paying bride wealth again and again, while adding to the number of wives. In many societies, apart from social prestige, it is also indicative of heroism. Look at the Nagas of India, where the number of wives is not added by payment of bride wealth but by capturing them in raids on the villages of their traditional enemies, a practice now hardly in vogue. In societies having a military tradition, the male population gets reduced due to the wars, adding to the number of widows, and polygyny may be the most adaptive (though not necessarily always) cultural option. At times, certain customs such as the practice of hypergamy generates problems for which polygyny becomes the most practical solution. Sometimes there may be a preferred means of taking another wife by taking the wife's sister, called as sororal polygyny.

In primitive societies and medieval feudal societies, kings and feudal lords kept and maintained several wives as a mark of prestige and a status symbol. Despite male dominance, the status of women in these societies was not always low. Rather, in some societies, women welcomed the addition of a co-wife as it eased their workload. The system permitted a high degree of sexual freedom to women.

Three types of new relationships appear in a polygynous households– the co-wives, half-siblings, and step-mother – because of which family management requires specific measures such as isolation of co-wives and socialization of children in accordance with the multiplicity of relations.

The system has some advantages, too. Particularly among farmers in regions with high rates of infant mortality, hands are always needed to manage the cultivation. Hence several wives and more children become an economic asset. Apart from farmers, in Africa and Middle-East among herding people and primitive farmers with backward technology, hard physical labour and frequent threats of violence are a way of life and polygyny serves to protect their interests. But among the hunters-and-gatherers, where children are a liability, only a widow may be accepted as another's wife and polygyny can never be a preferred form of marriage. In modern 'civilized' and industrialized societies with greater mobility, polygyny has no advantage to provide.

Concubinage is an institution whereby a man may have extra-marital relations with a number of women who do not have the status of a wife, but their children are taken care of by the man. In societies where these types of relations are permitted, there are cultural means to legalize the children born of such relationships and provision for their financial welfare. The women, or concubines as they are called, have no rights and are entirely at the pleasure and mercy of their masters. In medieval China, where monogamy was the strict rule, the kings and feudal lords kept a number of such women for sex, who were financially provided and their children were treated at par with the children of their wife, but these women did not enjoy the rights and privileges available to the married women. As such, concubinage is no polygyny.

Polyandry

Polyandry, that is, the plurality of husbands, occurs primarily in the Himalayan range – from Jaunsar-Bawar to Ladakh, Tibet, Nepal, and some isolated pockets. It is also reported among the Eskimos of Siberia. It is an adaptation to a shortage of females as among Todas and Pahari Hindus of Himalayan foothills. Among the Todas, the traditional custom of female infanticide led to the shortage of females. Among the Tibetans where this institution has the oldest roots it is the shortage of land which led to the fraternal polyandry where several brothers have a common wife. Khasas/Jounsaris practise fraternal polyandry, while among Nayars it used to be of non-fraternal type, whereby the husbands of a woman used to be unrelated to each other and their co-wife used to live with each one of them intermittently. Occasionally, non-fraternal polyandry is also reported among the Todas. However, due to the restricted female infanticide and the impact of Christian missionaries deploring infanticide as well as polyandry, Toda people today are largely monogamous.

In a polyandrous society, since the question of the biological father always remains enigmatic, there are cultural ways to establish social fatherhood. Among the Khasas and in Tibet, the privilege of social fatherhood is given to the elder brother who actually marries the women and his other brothers become husbands of the common wife by custom. Among the Todas, there is some amount of liberalism in this respect where social fatherhood was acquired, in turn, by performing a simple bow ceremony at the time of the pregnancy of the woman.

Polyandry restricts the number of children that are born and also the fragmentation of meagre cultivable land as the brothers, as common husbands, own it jointly. This has played an important adaptive role among the Khasas and Tibetans. However, among the Khasas, the developmental activity in the region by the state government providing irrigation facilities, has changed the economic prospects because many people taking to cash crops. As a consequence, among the Khasas, to a great extent, polyandry has been replaced by monogamy. In the interiors of the vast area where the impact of development has not reached, one may find a family or two still being polyandrous. With a number of outsiders from the neighbouring urban areas settling down in this region, who ridicule this type of marriage, the Khasas may be hiding this custom from outsiders.

Hypergamy

Hypergamy is a system of marriage promoted by a rigid stratification of the society, with selective openness. This type of a system existed as the varna system in ancient India. The four varnas in which the traditional Hindu society used to be divided were unequal in their social status and arranged in their order of superiority. A girl born in the topmost varna had no choice but to marry a boy from her own varna of birth. But a boy had access to the girls of his own varna as well as to the girls from any other varna below his own in the hierarchy. This type of marriage is known as 'hypergamy'. The opposite of it, which was not permitted, is called 'hypogamy'; if performed, the persons were subject to dire consequences.

Fictive Marriage

This refers to a type of marriage between the members of the same sex. This is done for the sole purpose of passing property. There is no sexual dimension in the marriage. Among the Nuers of Africa, in a marriage between two women, one is acknowledged as the husband-woman, and the other as the wife-woman. The husband-woman's brother or cousin indulges in sex relations with the wife-woman. However, the incidence of such marriages is very rare. Yet, their presence in one or two societies endorses the important point that marriage is deeply enmeshed in any culture.

Residence after Marriage

Some anthropologists tend to accept residence as a criterion for marriage. But since the question of residence, 'who lives where after the marriage' is a post-marital phenomenon and affects the character of family set-up, it should not form a basis for the typology of marriage.

Choosing a Mate

In every society, there are different methods of choosing a mate. In most societies, the system of arranged marriage prevails where parents of the bride and bridegroom and their families have greater say. In certain other societies such as in North America and the Europe, decision of the individuals is given more importance and it is here that the institution of courtship got developed.

In India, the popular way of distinguishing between the traditional and 'modern' way of marriage is to describe them in terms of 'arranged marriage' and 'love marriage'. In case of arranged marriages, it is the parents and families of the persons concerned who ultimately negotiate and put the stamp of approval on the decision. This has given rise to the institution of a go-between who has information about a wide network of the families. In the event of the prevailing rule of preferential or prescribed marriages, the go-between or the middleman loses his/her importance. Matrimonial advertisements in newspapers and caste/community magazines, collective caste marriages and registering on matrimonial websites are also forms of arranged marriage. In simple societies, choosing a mate or a life partner is the individual's affair, yet the ways and means adopted by the individuals and the approval of the parents and families and of the society accorded to them, are much different from the courtship concept of the modern Western societies.

Hoebel (1949) undertook a classification of marriages on the basis of mode of courtship. He listed eight important ways, all of which are represented in Indian tribes. They are probationary marriage, marriage by capture, marriage by trial, marriage by purchase, marriage by suitor service, marriage by exchange, marriage by mutual consent and elopement, and marriage by intrusion. A ninth mode, which is prevalent among the Nagas of India, is marriage by widow inheritance. Most of these modes are adopted to avoid the payment of bride wealth, a widely prevalent custom in primitive tribes the world over. In all this, the involvement of the parents and the families of the two individuals is obvious. However, since finding and choosing a mate or a life partner is largely a premarital exercise or a mode of courtship, it is doubtful if these modes of acquiring mates in different tribal societies constitute a typology of marriage.

Group Marriage

What should the word 'group marriage' mean has always remained a bone of contention among scholars. In essence, the term refers to a situation which may be called as 'sexual communism', that is, no individual has exclusive sexual rights on any other individual. This is a state of free sex, almost similar to the situation that exists in animals.

Morgan used the term 'promiscuity' for such a state of free sex in the earliest stage of human society and culture – a stage having no taboo or rule of incest. Morgan conceived of 'group marriage' at this stage. He did not elaborate on the idea as to what the 'group marriage' of his conjecture actually meant in practice.

What one concludes about the usage of this term is that a group of males and females indulging in sex or mating among themselves. Morgan based this conclusion about the condition of promiscuity and group marriage on two observations. He referred to the use of certain kinship terms which could best be explained by visualizing a group marriage. He also referred to the lax sex morality in some primitive societies due to which premarital or extra-marital sex relations are permitted in them. Morgan explained that this situation was probably an improved situation of promiscuity and group marriage and as a consequence of evolution of marriage. But at present, the condition of group marriage and promiscuity does not exist, no one practising it.

Marriage Payments

Marriage as a social institution is a public affair as it involves social sanction and also transfer of certain rights and obligations among the participating parties. The foremost are the rights of sexual access between husband and wife and the obligations of both of the care of children born as a consequence. The families and the kins of the bride and bridegroom also get certain rights in each other's goods and services.

In all human societies everywhere, the transfer of these rights and privileges are invariably associated with some exchange of goods and services. Quite often, this exchange may be simply an expression of goodwill and nursing the relationships created. But in other cases, the exchange of goods and services is considered essential for the transfer of marital rights without which it is not considered to take effect – it becomes an essential condition to complete the process of marriage. Three kinds of such exchanges or payments are prevalent in different societies and cultures. They are the bride wealth or bride price, dowry, and bride-service or suitor service.

Bride Wealth or Bride Price

Bride wealth or bride price, as it was commonly recognized in the earlier sociological and anthropological literature, refers to goods presented to the bride's family by the family of the bridegroom. Dowry, not prevalent in primitive societies, but very common in India and less common in Europe, refers to the payments made by the bride's side to the bridegroom's side. In small, pre-literate societies, payment of bride wealth is a must. Initially, missionaries, traders, and administrators coming across this practice among the tribal people, interpreted it as a sort of a sale–purchase transaction and named it as 'bride-price'. But later on, as more and more ethnographic evidences came to light, better understanding of this practice has developed.

At present, the earlier term 'bride price' has been totally abandoned as it fails to express the intended connotation. The term 'bride wealth' is considered more appropriate.

A major function of bride wealth is legitimation of marriage. In many African societies, the infertility of a woman is enough condition for the refund of the bride wealth to the family and the kins of the woman. Bride wealth also remains as an assurance for the proper conduct and the behaviour of the bride. Any proper termination (subject to specified conditions) of marriage also requires refund of the bride wealth.

Another function of bride wealth emphasized by scholars is that it entitles the husband to domestic and sexual rights over his wife. Also, the condition of refundability of bride wealth in the event of divorce serves as a deterrent to the misuse of the provision of divorce. Thus, it stabilizes marriage. It is also considered by some as a symbolic compensation to the bride's family as marriage involves social and economic loss to her family members since she moves away to her husband's family after marriage. Some scholars have also associated the payment of bride wealth with the question of status of women. But cross-cultural studies do not corroborate this view.

Dowry

This refers to the payment made by the bride's side to the bridegroom's family. It is commonly practised among the 'civilized' societies. Unlike bride wealth, there is no provision for the refund of the payment made as dowry. While some anthropologists consider it as a compensatory payment by the bride's family in consideration of the denial of property rights to the married girls in their parent's families, others view it as a payment to ensure the economic rights on the husband's earnings and her rights in the property of her husband's family. The main consideration which supports this practice is that the woman is treated as an economic liability.

Divorce

Barring Hindus, marriage everywhere is a social contract with the provision of dissolution of marriage by seeking divorce. Adultery, barrenness, and incompatibility of temperament are some common grounds for seeking divorce. In certain cases, the party desiring the dissolution of marriage must pay compensation to the other party. Once the divorce is effected between the two individuals, they cannot remarry. Divorce is always a public affair. In every society there are rules which decide the fate of children after the divorce.

However, the provision of divorce has not disturbed the life in primitive societies. But in modern Western societies, particularly in America, the rising rate of divorce has created an alarming situation. In these societies, the law concerning divorce has been liberalized to accommodate the rise of individualism. This has led to the multiplication in the number of broken families and a widely prevalent sense of economic insecurity.

Live-in Relationship and Marriage

In the past few decades, relationship dynamics has undergone a paradigm shift. Couples living together without going through the process of marriage is no more a rare practice in the West. This has generated a 'marriage versus live-in relationship' debate. Marriage is more a legal and socio-religious form of relationship between couples.

Earlier, in most of the societies, the idea of virginity, especially of women, played an important role within the institution of marriage. Thus for the traditional societies, physical relationship outside the wedlock was been unacceptable. However, non-marital cohabitation or live-in-relationship is rapidly emerging as an alternative to the traditional institutions of marriage and kinship.

In broad terms, a live-in-relationship may be described as an arrangement for cohabitation in which a couple live together in relationship without undergoing marriage and are therefore free of marital obligations. This arrangement may be heterosexual or homosexual and may last for a short or a long period. Compared with marriage, which is based on stability, a live-in relationship may or may not be strong or stable.

In Western societies, especially in North America, live-in-relationship is as commonplace as getting married. In most of the societies, marriage may be seen as an alliance, in varying degrees, between families whereas a live-in-relationship is essentially between two individuals or partners. They may or may not have children. In many cases, it is seen that after spending quite some time in relation, when the couple wants children, they get married. In several other instances, the couple enter into wedlock after having a child or children.

In any case, commitment is a key difference between marriage and live-in-relationship. There is no formal agreement in a live-in-relationship and cohabitation may be ended informally. Further, division of assets and parenting are the grey areas in this relationship. Despite all these problems, live-in- relationship has emerged as a serious challenge to the institution of marriage and it is becoming more prevalent in the Indian society as well.

Indian Scenario

In Indian society there is a wide variety and types of marriages. Wedding traditions vary across religion, region, caste, ethnicity, and so on. A vast majority of Indians still go for 'arranged marriage' in traditional ways, practising endogamy in terms of caste or jati and religious affiliation. Most Indians are opposed to inter-faith (inter-religious marriages) but its frequency has been increasing, though on a very slow pace and largely confined to the big urban centres and metros. Such marriages have got mired in allegations of 'love jihad' which spread hatred between religious communities.

Though monogamy (marriage between one male and one female) is followed by an overwhelming proportion of the population, other types of marriages are also prevalent in small numbers such as polygyny (one husband and two or more wives), polyandry (one wife and two or more husbands), bigamy (one husband and two wives), and so on. Among several tribal communities, multiple ways of acquiring mates through different modus operandi are followed, such as marriage by probation, marriage by ceremonial capture, marriage by elopement, and several others.

The status of pre-marital and extra-marital sex relations also varies from group to group and so do the ways of dissolution of marriage. Caste endogamy (marriage within the same caste group) is still a strong norm among the Hindus, Muslims, and Sikhs. Though in cities a few inter-caste marriages take place, but in most of the cases these are arranged by the couple with or without the consent of the parents. Child marriages still happen, but in very small numbers.

Kinship groups in the Indian society demand a strong social loyalty and hence marriage, to a large number of people, is an affair deeply impacting the entire family and kins. Thus, traditionally speaking, marriage is not merely an alliance between two individuals but between two families. In the so-called arranged marriage, criteria of caste, horoscope, physical appearance, and family background are very important.

But the criterion of dowry is equally and, for some, most important. With the growing materialism, consumerism, and consumer culture, the craving and the amount of dowry has been rising phenomenally. The arranged marriages are settled through matchmakers such as the family pundit, the family barber, relatives, or other middlemen. Biodata and pictures are exchanged. After the scrutiny of various criteria and negotiation for dowry, the marriage is fixed. Notwithstanding the legal ban on seeking dowry, the practice continues and there is only a small minority of people who forego or refuse to accept any dowry in either cash or kind. The evil of dowry among the Muslims was earlier confined only to the lower castes/classes, but now it has engulfed almost the entire population.

Among the educated classes, earlier there was also a practice of giving matrimonial advertisements in newspapers and also in the magazines of particular caste associations, but with the advent of internet, several matrimonial websites have emerged and millions of marriages are fixed through them. These websites are popular among all castes and communities.

With the increase in education, social mobility, and freedom, and the resultant empowerment of women, the number of inter-caste marriages have increased manifold, but these are mostly self-arranged and are popularly called 'love marriages'. Such marriages are mostly confined to cities and towns. In many instances these are solemnized in an Arya Samaj temple in a simple and austere ceremony. Despite the promulgation of Special Marriage Act, 1955, facilitating interfaith and inter-religious marriages, the society at large is still very hostile and prejudiced to such alliances. In villages and towns, in most of the cases, it may create even law-and-order problem but in cities, especially in metros, it does not attract much attention. As several couples entering into wedlock under this provision narrate, the State is secular but not many of those who have been assigned the responsibility of implementing the rules and they put unnecessary hurdles. The marriage is supervised and registered by a designated Special Marriage Officer in each district, who is usually a magistrate. Under special circumstances, the Special Marriage Officer is authorized to perform the formalities even outside the premises of his or her office.

The traditional system of marriage faced the first big challenge from interfaith marriages, but now has to reconcile with live-in relationships which may or may not result in a formal, legalized marriage. The live-in couples cohabit rather than marry for a variety of reasons. In many cases it is just to assess mutual compatibility, gay–lesbian couples do it for financial reasons. Some people claim that such cohabitation was permissible even during the Vedic times. Many of our tribal communities have been liberal enough to allow live-in in the form of 'marriage by probation'. Though the Indian society is opening up in some ways, for the overwhelming majority, live-in is socially unacceptable, even in metros where it is just tolerated but not accepted.

Economic boom in big cities coupled with women's empowerment has facilitated in the incidence of certain practices. Substantial population in metros consists of non-locals who may not be concerned or interested in the affairs of others. Urban anonymity gives courage to a number of young couples to adopt a live-in relationship without the knowledge of their close relatives. In smaller cities and in towns and villages, one cannot live in anonymity and may get punished or socially ostracized because of such relationships. In metros, people do enjoy much more freedom to indulge in practices which the traditional orthodox society terms as 'deviant' and 'corrupt'.

In May 2013, in a landmark judgment, the Supreme Court observed that if a man and a woman in love decide to live as a couple, it will be within their 'right to life' and by no means can be deemed as a criminal offence. This provided the much-needed legal protection to such couples. Obviously, it has not gone down well with the traditional and conservative people.

Even before the Supreme Court verdict, the Government had taken several measures to protect the interests of the live-in partners. In one such move, the Government extended economic rights to women in live-in relationships under the Protection of Women from Domestic Violence Act, 2005. Similarly, in 2008, the Maharashtra State Government granted approval to a proposal stating that a woman involved in cohabitation for a 'reasonable period' should be given the status of a wife.

In the same year, the Ministry of Women and Child Development was urged by the National Commission of Women to include female live-in partners in the definition of wife as described in the Section 125 of Cr.P.C. The objective of this recommendation was to harmonize the various other sections of law with the Protection of Women from Domestic Violence Act, 2005. Justice Malimath Committee of the Supreme Court recommended that this be turned into law by all the states. The committee had observed, 'If a man and woman are living together as husband and wife for a reasonably long period, the man shall be deemed to have married the woman.' The Malimath Committee also recommended that the word 'wife' under Cr.P.C. be amended to include any 'woman living with a man like his wife'. In spite of all these judicial verdicts, the fact remains that the larger society is not prepared to accept live-in relationships. But in the future, the society has to accept them as a part of an individual's rights, which have to be respected.

Divorce

In Indian society, marriage carries religious–social sanctity and hence there has always been a great impact of religion and culture on the practice of divorce. Marriage is a religious sacrament among the Hindus but only a civil contract among the Muslims.

Since marriage carries religious sanctity among the Hindus, solemnized with Agni as witness and with the blessings of gods and goddesses, its dissolution was never considered desirable. This continued for centuries. Dharma forced people to remain married even if the marriage did not work. Being divorced carried a strong stigma and individuals had to bear the cross of an unhappy marriage in order to protect their image as an 'ideal Indian family'. It was only with the promulgation of the Hindu Marriage Act, 1955, that dissolution of marriage became permissible under the law. But it continued to be considered undesirable socially.

Community disapproval is stronger for divorced women than it is for divorced men. That is why remarriage for men is much easier than for the women. This is not the case with the Dalit (both Hindu and Muslim) and tribal communities who take divorce in the normal course because women in these societies enjoy much more cultural autonomy. Unlike the higher castes, the strongly patriarchal value of *pati parmeshwar* (husband is the highest god) and gender discrimination are not so strong in Dalits and women do not have to face sexual harassment and character assassination the way they face in the higher castes.

All major religious communities in India have laws governing divorce. Hindu, Sikhs, Jains, and Buddhists are governed by the Hindu Marriage Act, 1955; Christians by the Indian Divorce Act, 1869; Parsis by the Parsi Marriage and Divorce Act, 1936; and Muslims by the Dissolution of Muslim Marriage Act, 1939. Unlike the Western societies, there are only a few grounds for seeking divorce, the most important of which are adultery, desertion, cruelty, impotence, mental derangement, conversion to another religion, and chronic diseases. Through an amendment in the Hindu Marriage Act, non-compatibility in temperament was also allowed as a valid ground for divorce. Among the Hindus, divorce is a difficult process while among a substantial section of Muslims, it is relatively easier. However, among the Shia Muslims and many Sunni Muslims the instant triple talaaq (pronouncing divorce three times in one go by the husband) is not permissible. It is to be pronounced in three sittings with a substantial time interval, in the presence of witnesses, so as to give the couple sufficient time to reflect and introspect and make a possible reconciliation. But among all Muslims, it is much more difficult for a woman to seek divorce, though it is permissible. The obnoxious practice of triple talaaq has already ruined the life of millions of Muslim women and the progressive sections of the Muslims have been demanding a total ban on this practice the way some Muslim countries have already done. The practice of instant triple talaaq has now been banned by law and is considered a criminal offence.

However, it has another aspect. The cases of bride burning/killing and dowry related atrocities and female foeticide/infanticide are much lower among the Muslims. One reason could be that they can divorce the wife much more easily and go for another marriage, unlike the Hindus where it is not easy to get divorce. Hence the unhappy and greedy husband finds it easier to eliminate the wife and go for another marriage. Thus, the plight of women is almost the same in both religions.

Marital Rape, Patriarchy and Right of Sexual Autonomy in Indian Society

For the overwhelming majority in Indian society, the very mention of 'marital rape' is shocking. How can a husband rape his wife? First, let us look at the definition of rape. The popular and common-sense meaning of rape is understood as unlawful sexual activity, most often sexual intercourse, against the will of the victim through force or the threat of force or with an individual who is incapable of giving legal consent because of minor status, mental illness, mental deficiency, intoxication, or deception. But the legal definition of rape has changed substantially since the late 20th century. The definition of rape as codified in Section 375 of the Indian Penal Code includes all forms of sexual assault involving non-consensual intercourse with a woman.

Under normal circumstances, rape or sexual harassment would be considered heinous. However, there is one kind of rape in the Indian society that is not considered illegal or heinous and the culprit is not criminal in the eyes of law or the society. That is 'marital rape' or rape of the wife. In this case, consent of the woman is not required as it is presumed that she has given her consent, for all times to come and in all situations, to her husband by virtue of entering into marital alliance with the man. It is an implied consent, and the husband has every right to get access to his wife for sex anytime he wishes. It becomes illegal only if the wife is minor. It is to be noted that India is now one of the only thirty-six countries that still have not criminalized marital rape.

Sexual relations with an unwilling wife in the Indian society has never been considered a bad thing in the value system of the strongly patriarchal society. If we look at the section 375 of the Indian Penal Code (IPC), we should remember that it was drafted in 1860s by the British when the wife was considered as a personal property or chattel of her husband. She was not considered an independent legal entity.

Manu Smriti says that 'Women do not deserve independence'. Other religions too consider it a wife's duty to comply with the wish of the husband in consonance with the religious and cultural expectations of subordination of the wife. Such values and ideas were challenged in the Western societies in 1960s and this consciousness began spreading to all parts of the world. Post the 1960s, the movement for self-determination for women intensified and their rights over their bodies and sexuality became a topic of debate.

Resistance to Criminalization of Marital Rape

The reluctance of the society and judiciary to criminalize and consequently prosecute marital rape is largely attributed to the traditional views on marriage and glorification of the status of husband. Husband has been described as *pati parmeshwar* (husband is the highest god) in the traditional Hindu system. Submission to the wishes and authority of the husband is considered the desired goal of a wife in popular Islamic values. The Indian society has a deep-rooted belief that allowing women sexual autonomy and rights over her body shall threaten the very foundation of family and marriage. The popular view in the society is that defiance by a woman and assertion for her rights shall corrupt the society. Without saying so, it is assumed that after a woman gets married, her body becomes her husband's property and she ceases to have any autonomy over it. The patriarchy expects the woman to meekly accept her role as a means for the perpetuation of *vansh* and *kul* (lineage) through her reproductive capacity and at the same time to fully satisfy her husband's sexual desires so that he does not go to any other woman. Not making marital rape a criminal offence is a message, loud and clear, to women that their consent to any sexual activity ceases to matter. A pertinent issue that may be pointed out is that the society accepts an unmarried woman's right over her body and its violation (if not consensual) invites punishment, but the same woman loses all her rights over her body after her marriage. The society not only discriminates between a married woman and an unmarried one, but also decides that the consent of a married woman below the age of 18 is valuable but not the consent of a married woman above this age.

Rape should be accepted as rape and the age, gender and marital status of the victim should not matter. It must be accepted that a no is no whether it comes from the wife, girlfriend, or any other person, even from a sex worker.

Prevalent Views against Criminalization of Marital Rape

Not only the orthodox sections of the Indian society, but also large sections of judiciary have been, directly or indirectly, showing their dislike and disagreement against the demand for making marital rape as criminal offence. Following are some of the most important points of discussion pertaining to the issue of marital rape:

- Situating rape within the institution of marriage is not in consonance or conformity with India's culture. Those holding this view also claim that it will create absolute anarchy in families and the larger society. They also maintain that a husband can never rape his wife because a good wife will obediently and dutifully submit to her husband.
- Consent is not sought every day. It is implicit that at the time of marriage, the wife gives a permanent and perpetual consent. The desire for submission of a woman before her husband is so deep-rooted in the patriarchal Indian society that any departure is taken as deviant behaviour and antisocial, worthy of condemnation.
- Among different sections of the society, there is a strong apprehension that any law against marital rape would be misused by women and this will be a perpetual source of harassment of men and spoil their image. It will lead to 'distortions' in the institutions of family and marriage as sanctified in the Indian society. The same arguments were floated when such legislative measures as Protection of Women from Domestic Violence Act was passed.

Another argument against a law against martial rape is that a remedy is already available through section 498A which says that the 'husband or relative of the husband of a woman subjecting her to cruelty . . . shall be punished with imprisonment.' But in this section, 'cruelty' has been described in such a manner that marital rape can hardly be included under its preview.

Restitution of Conjugal Rights and Sexual Autonomy of Women

This topic pertains to Section 9 of the Hindu Marriage Act, 1955. This Act is a powerful tool in the hands of men (husbands). The liberal elements of Indian society describe it as an 'archaic remedy'. The Act says:

> When either the husband or the wife has, without reasonable excuse, withdraws from the society of the other, the aggrieved

party may apply, by petition to the district court, for restitution of conjugal rights and the court on being satisfied of the truth of statements made in such petition and that there is no legal ground why the application should not be granted, may decree restitution of conjugal rights accordingly.

A similar remedy is also available under the Special Marriage Act and provisions of Muslim, Parsi, and Christian personal laws. Divya Srinivasan (2018), a lawyer and women's rights activist, says that the concept of restitution of conjugal rights was brought to India by British Raj, imported from British ecclesiastical law at a time when the wife was considered chattel or property of her husband. This matrimonial remedy has long since been abolished in the United Kingdom and numerous other common law countries. But inexplicably, it continues to be held and implemented by Indian courts.

On the face of it, the idea that a court could legally require an unwilling spouse to live in the same house as his/her partner seems absurd, not to mention a violation of the fundamental rights of privacy, freedom of movement, dignity, and equality guaranteed under the Indian Constitution. However, the provision has been upheld by the Supreme Court in Saroj Rani vs Sudarshan Kumar Chaddha (1984) case as constitutionally valid on the ground that it performs an important social purpose of preserving a marriage. This outmoded notion which prioritizes the so-called sanctity of marriage over individual rights and freedoms, particularly those of the wife, is in keeping with the Indian societal and jurisprudential tradition, which has long been loath to concede that fundamental rights apply within the home. Do constitutional rights not apply to marriage?

The existing social structures enforce the position of a woman as an unequal participant in a marriage. The court's recent willingness to strike down discriminatory religious practices as seen in the triple talaaq and Sabarimala case raises the hope that the Indian constitutional regime no longer considers the introduction of constitutional law in the home as akin to introducing a bull in a china shop. The time has come to delegitimize the patriarchal structures within the home and the family.

Marriage Selection in Cyber Space: Technology Mediated Romance

Ian Kwok and AB Wescott (2020) aptly describe marriage selection in cyber space as cyber intimacy through technology-mediated romance in the digital age. With a swipe or click, people now seek and sustain romance in unprecedented ways. Emerging research shows that cyber intimacy, or the phenomenon of technology-mediated communication between partners and potential romantic interests, significantly impacts the way we form, maintain, and even extinguish romantic relationships. These new digital courtship rituals mean that emerging opportunities for cyber intimacy are also accompanied by unanticipated challenges. As Kwok and Wescott (ibid) say, an emerging phenomenon, besides some others, is cyber-sex, defined as 'online sex oriented conversations and exchanges', which have the potential to disrupt romantic relationships and can even lead to separation or divorce.

Internet-based social media and cellular phones (now smartphones) are playing an increasing role in our personal and social lives. There are serious discussions among scholars regarding their positive or degrading role in romantic relationships. In an important study titled *Marriage, Choice, and Couplehood in the Age of the Internet*, Michael Rosenfield (2017) raises the question whether the new technologies improve or degrade the commitment and longevity of our primary relationships. Examining the data from a nationally representative study of American couples followed for six years, he studied the efficacy of couples meeting online with reference to the rate of breakups. He says that heterosexual couples dating online transition to marriage more quickly than other heterosexual couples.

There are hundreds of online dating platforms and a majority of them follow almost similar processes of registering the interested individuals. After exchange of messages online between interested individuals (online dating), offline meetings may follow, resulting in a one-night stand or a live-in-relationship or a marriage, or simply parting of ways for another relationship.

Online dating is relatively new phenomenon in Indian society. It is an increasingly popular method among the younger generation, especially those in urban areas and metros, for meeting romantic partners. It is gradually displacing the traditional ways of looking for the mates.

In the past, matrimonial advertisements in newspapers and magazines used to be the most popular method of selecting a bride or bridegroom. Then came matrimonial websites such as jeevansathi.com, shadi.com, and so on, where either parents or the potential bride/bridegroom uploaded their photos and personal details. Interested parties then established contact, followed by an offline meeting. This does not mean that the traditional means of establishing matrimonial alliance of taking the services of intermediaries or pundits/purohits are gone. These are still there, but now largely confined to villages and towns.

Feminist Critique of Marriage

Despite its universal presence, the institution of marriage has always been debated and criticized on different counts by a number of scholars, especially feminist and Marxist scholars. They are of the view that girls, from a young age itself, are indoctrinated about the virtues of marriage, which contributes to maintaining and perpetuating traditional gender roles. Neel Burton (2020), extending the arguments further, says, 'Beyond a certain age, a man who remains unmarried is thought of as independent or intelligent, whereas a woman who remains unmarried is assumed to be desperate, at once a figure of pity and scorn. A woman who is strong minded enough to forgo marriage and live out her own life is constantly made to doubt her resolve.'

Feminist scholars and activists have critiqued the very institution of marriage on the ground of its historical, legal, and social inequalities. A number of feminists strongly believe that women cannot achieve freedom without the abolition of marriage. Their ideas may be summarized as follows:

- The institution of marriage is the chief vehicle for the perpetuation of oppression of women.
- The roles prescribed for a wife are largely responsible for the subjugation of women.
- Marriage may also be seen as legalized prostitution.
- Marriage is not an inclusive institution of the society.
- Marriage reinforces the idea that women exist to serve men.
- In marriage, women live in subordination to men in exchange for subsistence.

Feminists maintain that because of socialization and indoctrination in early childhood, people are not able to form an objective opinion and assessment of marriage. For the feminists, marriage is nothing but society-sponsored discrimination. 'Marriage benefits the economy by producing new workers and consumers, largely through the unpaid work of women, and by making it difficult for workers with families to support to withdraw their labour. A wedding alone generates spending of, on average, £31,974 (about $38,000), and probably that again on the gift list and the travel and other expenses of the wedding guests. And even that pales into insignificance compared to the £230,000+ required to raise a child, let alone two or three' (Burton, ibid).

Some critics, looking at the history of marriage, are of the view that the institution of marriage should not be accepted in the 21st century as it would be ignoring the abuse of women over centuries and millennia. Marriage will always symbolize the subordination of women. Elizabeth Brake (2016), attacking the common view of marital life as 'private' and outside the purview of public intervention, says that it only allows violence and exclusion against women to flourish. Marital rape is another serious issue. Is sexual intercourse without wife's consent not rape? In most societies men have sexual authority over their wives, in law and in practice. Often wives have no power to stop unwanted sex and the resultant pregnancy.

Among the Marxists, Fredrick Engels in his celebrated work *The Origin of Family, Private Property and the State* (1884) expressed the view that the origin of marriage was not for the purpose of love but, instead, of private property rights.

In Indian society the custom of *kanyadaan* is an integral part of Hindu marriage rituals. Literally meaning 'giving away one's daughter' to the groom, this practice is severely criticized by women's rights activists and feminists as demeaning for women, reducing them into a commodity or private property.

In any discourse on feminist critique of marriage, the early 'second wave' feminist literature, the following works especially shall always serve as a beacon:

Sexual Politics (1969) by Kate Millet

The Female Eunuch (1970) by Germaine Greer

The Women's Room (1977) by Marilyn French

The Future of Marriage (1972) by Jessie Bernard

The Dialectic of Sex (1970) by Shulamith Firestone

Beside these works, another work of critical importance is Second Sex by Simone de Beauvoir, published in 1949, who argues that marriage is an alienating institution.

Critical Thinking Questions

- Do you find the institution of marriage still as relevant as it was in the past? Does the traditional marriage system require any changes?
- What are the changes taking place in marriage practices?
- Where do you situate live-in-relationship within or around the institution of marriage?
- To what extent do you agree with the feminist critique of marriage?

****

5

Family

Chapter Outline: *Meaning and concept of family; Elementary/nuclear/extended family; The household; Universality of family; Functions of family; Typological and processual approaches to the study of family; Joint family; The other types; Stability and change in family; Reimagining/Alternative family; Impact of industrialization and urbanization on family; Change in family over time; Indian scenario.*

Learning Objectives

- In what way is family a universal social institution?
- What are the variations in forms of family?
- What are the factors that affect stability and changes in the institution of family?
- What is the impact of industrialization and urbanization on family?
- What are the emerging alternatives to family?

Family occupies a central position in the study of human society. It has been studied for more than hundred years by a variety of scholars. Yet, we are not very sure about the imperatives under which it developed. One of the most enduring views on the origin of family come from Fredrick Engel's *The Origin of the Family, Private Property, and the State* published in 1884. The importance of this classic work may be understood by the fact that even today, the question of the origin of family is not discussed without bringing in the economic argument.

Meaning and Concept

'Family' is one of the words most commonly used in sociological and anthropological writings and everyday life and yet its meaning is neither always clear, nor a matter of consensus. Generally speaking, a family is a social and economic unit consisting minimally of one or more parents (or parent substitutes) and their children. 'Marriage lays the legal foundation for the family but the family can coexist without marriage. A family is a domestic group in which parents and children live together' (Lucy Mair, 1965).

Thus the term 'family', as used in everyday life, refers to a group entity where children are born, taken care of, and socialized. The membership, size, and the structure of the group differ in different societies. Family also refers to culturally and historically specific social practices.

The form of family varies from society to society and even within societies, but all societies have families. 'Members of a family have certain reciprocal rights and obligations, particularly economic ones. Family members usually live in one household but common residence is not a defining feature of families' (Ember and Ember, 2019). In simple societies, the family and the household tend to be indistinguishable but in complex societies some members may be living elsewhere.

While some social scientists have seen family as a universal social institution, others have tended to use the term to refer to a distinctive characteristic of social life of particular cultures. While functionalist scholars have tended to regard family as universal and omnipresent in human societies, the others, particularly historically-oriented scholars and even Marxists scholars, speak of the emergence of family over a period of time. Morgan talked about the earliest stage in the human society when there was no family, characterized by promiscuity and group marriage. A few of the scholars even envisage the eventual disappearance of the family. All these views assume that 'family' refers to an entity. Whether the entity is held to be universal or limited to particular localities depends upon the way one chooses to define it.

The functionalists, in tune with their theoretical stand, have tended to define family in terms of what it does, what it is meant for in terms of certain activities, and the effects on social structure of the society of which it is a part. This mode of definition makes it a near universal feature of every human society, defining family as a residential group composed of parents and young, dependent children called the 'nuclear-family'. The functionalists also say that the nuclear family is very often a part of some larger residential group.

Anthropologists and sociologists have also used the term 'family' as a concept having universal application instead of using it to refer to an empirical type. Family has been conceptualized by them as a process of procreation involving a male and a female, entailing the biological relations of mating, filiation, and siblings. These relations form the basis of group formations. The term 'family' also carries the implications of group membership. Such groups may be distinguished as groups composed of parents and young, dependent children as well as groups composed of the parents and mature, dependent children. The groups having dependent children are called nuclear families. Groups with this composition constitute the smallest possible kin groups. The nuclear and post-nuclear families are elementary or immediate families at different stages of their development cycle. Post-nuclear family is a system of collective parenting where a number of children are raised in a single household.

This shows that the study of family involves concerns which are universally applicable since mating and procreation are universal activities. But these universal activities do not constitute main principles of organization of kin groups in every society. In general, the term 'family' refers to a particular set of questions and to a particular form of social organization.

Anthropologists have identified two basic types of families – elementary or nuclear families and extended families. The activities of mating and procreation do not necessarily require but normally tend to result in co-residence of the persons involved. Nuclear families are normally residential groups as mating, procreation, and the associated activities of child rearing require residence in same dwelling (or in close proximity) and the co-operation of the members in provision of domestic services. Families may also be the owners of property and engaged in economic production.

In quite a large number of societies, nuclear family exists as an embedded unit in larger kinship units consisting of co-residence groups called 'extended family'. An extended family is not just a collection of nuclear families. It is a different family system in which it is the kinship ties and not the conjugal ties (as in nuclear families) that are important and involved in organization of the family group. The ties of lineality between the generations are more important than the bonds of marriage. When the group includes vertical extension in the same line, it is called a vertically extended family and when it is the extension of generations of siblings, it is called a horizontally extended family.

The independent or isolated nuclear family is the ideal either in hunting and food gathering societies or in industrialized Western societies – both characterized by the excessive mobility of their populations. Extended family is the ideal in almost half of the world's societies.

Extended families they may be organized around males or females. The former are called patrilineal extended families and the latter called matrilineal extended families. Matrilineal extended families, organized around a woman and her daughters, are found among the Nayars of South India or Khasis of Meghalaya. Patrilineal extended families, organized around a male and his male descendants, were also the ideal in traditional Chinese society. The elder members are lost through death and the new members are added through birth. Dissolution of the marital ties between some of the members does not affect the continuity of the group. Most extended family systems give some recognition to the nuclear family with the only exception of the Nayars of South India among whom conjugal ties are completely absent.

Extended family systems are the opposite of nuclear family systems. It is more precisely to transform conjugal to filial system. That is, to contrast groups composed of spouses and dependent children with groups composed of parents and adult children, their spouses and offsprings.

The extended family is clearly adaptive under certain economic and social conditions. The main advantages of this type of family are economic, particularly in predominantly cultivating societies. Due to its larger size, it can provide a larger number of workers compared to a nuclear family. Primitive conditions being labour intensive, an extended family is useful both for food production and for producing and marketing handicrafts. The settled cultivators own land which should not be divided into smaller pieces, which renders it unproductive, through inheritance. The extended family is a way of keeping land intact. It also inculcates companionship and a sense of participation as most of the everyday activities are carried out jointly. Apart from economic advantages, it also provides social security to the elders, along with a sense of dignity.

In the last few decades, research on the history of family has successfully demolished previous myths about family behaviour. Sociologists had earlier assumed that modern family and population behaviour were innovations resulting from industrialization and that the predominant household form in the pre-industrial society had been the extended family. It was argued that industrialization destroyed the three-generation co-resident family structure and led to the emergence of the isolated nuclear family – a structure more compatible with the demands of the modern industrial system. Some of the scholars like Peter Laslet and his Cambridge group have firmly established the predominance of a nuclear household structure in the industrial Western Europe and its persistence over at least the past three centuries. A critical distinction was made between family and household structure, often including non-kins in the latter, in addition to the members of family.

The most important conclusion emerging from the first wave of historical research was that industrialization did not break down the traditional extended family and lead to the emergence of isolated nuclear family. In many respects, the household continued to function as an economic unit even after it had been stripped of its major functions in production. As a flexible unit, the household expanded and contracted in response to the family's needs.

Prior to the emergence of the welfare State, the kinship network of the household formed the base of social security. As a subsequent development, researchers have documented the continuity of kinship ties in the process of migration and the important role of kins in adapting to new environments. The overall tendency was to include non-kins in the households rather than kins outside the nuclear family.

It is generally held that although the extended family has advantages among cultivators or economically marginalized populations, these advantages become liabilities with urbanization and industrialization. But Milton Singer (1971), in his study of industrial leaders in the city of Madras (now Chennai) in India, has found that the existing set-up of the joint family and extended kins has been successfully transferred to the management of modern corporations.

The Household

Though family is frequently defined as a social group consisting of parents and children, this only refers to a nuclear family. But in actual experience and empirical evidence we find that this form of family set-up is by no means universal. There are many societies where people live in groups in which one or more of the three elements constituting a nuclear family are missing. Or they may be living in groups with members either related otherwise or not related at all but fulfilling all the functions of a family. Hence anthropologists have conceived of the idea of 'domestic groups' or 'households', a concept which emphasises on common living.

A domestic group or a household is not the same as a family. Although domestic groups most often contain related members, non-kins may also be part of them.

Members of a family may be spread over several domestic groups of households. The composition of domestic groups is affected by the rules a society has regarding residence after marriage. Neolocal residence exists when it is the norm for a married couple to establish an independent domestic unit. This is related to the high degree of mobility required in an industrial system and to a value system that makes emotional bond between husband and wife, privacy, and independence as primary concerns.

Most societies have a rule of 'patrilocal residence' in which a woman, after marriage, lives with her husband's kins. In societies with a rule of 'matrilocal residence', the husband lives with the wife's kins after marriage. But if the couple has the choice to live with either the husband's or the wife's family, the rule is called 'bilocal residence'; this is also called 'cambilocal residence'. A very rare pattern of residence is the 'avunculocal residence' where the married couple is expected to live with the husband's mother's brother. The patrilocal residence is also known as 'virilocal residence'. For matrilocal residence, the term 'uxorilocal residence' is also used. Another very rare rule of residence, where the couple is expected to live with the husband's father's sister's family, is termed 'amitolocal residence'.

Anthropologists have generally emphasized economic factors to explain the reasons for choosing a particular pattern of residence after marriage. While matrilocality is associated with horticulture where women have important role in economy, patrilocality is generally associated with the dependence on big game hunting and intensive agriculture where men must co-operate and take part collectively in these economic activities. But cross-cultural data does not approve of this kind of association. Where societies have a fighting tradition between lineages or villages – male co-operation in warfare is very important – the rule of patrilocal residence prevails. Very often, residence rules are only ideal or preferred norms and many specific or individual situations make the couples to decide differently. Who should live where after marriage and who actually lives where are both important in the social organization of a society.

Universality of Family

In a study titled 'Social Structure', Murdock examined the institution of family in a wide range of societies. After studying 250 societies ranging from small hunting and gathering bands to largescale industrial societies, he concluded that some form of family existed in every society and that the family was universal. He defined family as a social group characterized by common residence, economic co-operation, and reproduction. A family included adults of both sexes, at least two of whom maintain a socially approved sexual relationship and one or more children (own or adopted) of the sexually cohabiting adults.

Many other social scientists also maintain that the nuclear family, even when embedded in other kinship structures, is universal and that this universality is based on its necessity of carrying out the basic and necessary sexual, economic, procreative, and educational functions required by every society. The functionalist theorists emphasize on the biological human compulsions of the helpless condition of the human child and the mother and the prolonged infancy of human child, which make a family necessary.

The question of whether the nuclear family structure is universal or necessary is becoming increasingly relevant today with divorce having acquired greater incidence in Western industrialized societies and many families headed by a single parent. In Israel, kibbutz (communities) were created, without any nuclear family.

But both before and after Murdock's study, exceptions have been cited, specifically the Nayars of Malabar, but Murdock's judgment has met with general approval. An examination of the kibbutz led Spiro (1954) to conclude that from a functional and psychological viewpoint, it is possible to see the kibbutz as a large extended family. The kibbutz may have eliminated the nuclear family (by deliberate effort of antifamilism), it did so only by converting the entire community into a single gemeinschaft.

In another study, Levy (1955) investigated whether the nuclear family was institutionalized in all societies. He pointed out that even though the father, mother, spouses, sister, and brother may be present, they may not function as a nuclear family unit. According to Adams (1960), social organization is flexible enough to permit different forms of family to co-exist; in many cases, some parts of a nuclear family may not function at all as a family unit. These exceptions are present in every society. They may function differently as there are more elemental forms of family, besides nuclear family such, as:

Maternal dyad: A residential unit composed of the mother and one or more children.

Adult dyad or sexual dyad: Composed of a man and a woman (not necessarily husband-and-wife), based simply on the sexual act which may be subsequently sanctioned by marriage.

Paternal dyad: Composed of father and one or more children (found very rarely in societies).

The identification of maternal dyad as distinct from the nuclear family is made on the basis that there is no husband–father as a regular resident. There may be households with a male head or a female head. In Brazil, the presence of maternal dyad is not a matter of limited or local significance. In Central America, the 1950 census data of four countries about maternal dyad families revealed that the percentage of mother dyad families present was as follows:

Guatemala 16.8%, El-Salvador 25.5%,

Nicaragua 26% and Costa Rica 17.2%.

Similarly, T. Smith (1956), who studied negro towns in British Guiana reported a significant percentage of mother dyad families there. These cases provide ample evidence that in contemporary populations with bilateral descent systems, woman-headed households are quite common. These female-headed households (mother dyad families) have also been called 'mother centred' or 'matrifocal families'.

In USA, in 1971, 29 per cent of all Black families were matrifocal families. The percentage is often higher in other new world societies. Nancie Gonzalez, in her study of Livingston Honduras in 1956, found that 45 per cent of Black Caribbean families had female heads. Poverty and a background of slavery in the past are stated to be the most potent factors for matrifocalism in these societies. In some of the Black communities in large American cities such as Washington, matrifocalism has become a part of the cultural traditions. In certain cases, matrifocal families have become an expected and accepted alternate to the standard nuclear family.

These facts raise certain pertinent questions regarding the universality issue. Firstly, should matrifocal family be regarded as an exception to Murdock's claim that the family is universal? Or, if it is accepted as a family, an exception to his claim that a nuclear family is a universal social group. Supporting Murdock's argument, we find that, statistically, the female-headed family is not the norm either in Black communities or in societies where they exist. Also, a matrifocal family is often a nuclear family that has been broken by permanent desertion of the husband or due to divorce. Even the Blacks with matrilocal family regard a nuclear family as the ideal. Many scholars tend to view matrifocal families as a product of social disorganization and not as a viable alternative to the nuclear family.

Certain other arguments support the view that matrifocal families should be recognized as an alternative to the nuclear family. Firstly, it cannot be ignored simply on the ground that it is a statistical minority in any society. In low income Black communities, they have come to stay as accepted forms of a family. Matrifocal family can be viewed as a positive adaptation to circumstances of poverty. A matrifocal family can be regarded as the basic minimum family unit – as a primary building block.

Functionalist anthropologists emphasize that the family is a group where children are born, brought up, and socialized. They define family as a fundamental universal social group – this fundamentality does not refer to any specific type of group but simply to some sort of social group to take care of broader universal human concerns. No human survival is possible without some such group. The matrifocal family consisting of the mother and her dependent children, though not a widely common form, yet it is nearly universal and structurally more elementary than a nuclear family. Two or more matrifocal units linked together resemble a consanguineous group such as Nayar Tharwads.

In trying to define a fundamental structure of the human society, at best we can agree that in human society there is usually some pattern of regular mating such that the children born tend to have a recognized father as well as an obvious mother. But to proclaim the husband–wife–children unit to be the nucleus of human society is to force categories onto facts. In an empirical situation we must examine the operative arrangements and not prejudge the issue.

Functions of a Family

The roles that a family as an entity or a social group, plays in the life of an individual have many dimensions and the individual remains under its impact all through his or her life. Anthropologists have tried to discuss some of the basic or primary functions of a family in the context of an individual as well as the society.

The family owes its universal character to the biological needs of the mother and child at the time of the child birth and the prolonged infancy of the human child. It also has important provisionary functions in terms of organized economic activities and a judicious division of labour among its members. Being bound by strong sentiments, the bio-psychological needs of the members get fulfilled. These sentiments are expressed in patent ties of conjugal relations and filiation. Also fulfilled are the important needs of regular satisfaction of sex and the socialization of the children who must grow up to be responsible members of the society as adults.

In most of the societies there are other non-familial institutions such as controlled prostitution, extra-marital sex relations, concubinage, homosexuality, and so on as a means of regulating sex. According to Talcott

Family

Parsons, a stable attachment of a man to a woman with inclusion of sexual relationship taken for granted, almost automatically results in a family.

George Peter Murdock talked about at least four major functions of family:

1. Sexual function: Regulation of sex, fulfilling bio-psychological need of motherhood, and sexual gratification.
2. Reproductive function: Procreation and child rearing.
3. Economic or provisonary function: Production of goods/services and division of labour within the family.
4. Education: Socialization, that is, enculturation and transmission of culture.

The family does not perform these functions exclusively, but it has immense utility in making major contributions on all them.

Talcott Parsons reduced the family to two major functions:

1. A primary socialization of the child involving humanization–internalization of one's own culture, which is important in the structuring of the basic personality.
2. Secondary socialization, that is, personality moulding–stabilization in later years when the other agencies also get involved.

Thus, the functionalists assertion that family is the most fundamental and universal social group, is broadly directed to all these important roles that it performs in the context of individual as well as the society.

Typological and Processual Approaches to the Study of Family

Sociologically, a family can be defined and discussed from two different angles. Often, we look at the family as an entity or a group or an association, but it can also be viewed as a process. The process called 'family' can be divided into three or four well-defined stages on the basis of the changing needs of an individual at different stages of life. In the formative stage, as a growing child the individual is prepared for his or her adult roles as a responsible member of the society. This follows the pre-nuptial and nuptial stages when, after getting married, an individual concentrates on his or her family for 'procreation', though not entirely delinking themselves from their family 'orientation' (using Warner's terminology) in which they were born and brought up. In modern Western societies, the tradition of neo-local residence after marriage weakens, if not totally disrupts, the relation between the families to which an individual belongs. In most of the tribal societies, in the pre-nuptial stage the youths prepares themselves psychologically for the adult married life and procreation of children. In Western societies the institution of courtship constitutes the pre-nuptial stage. But in societies where there is the tradition of child marriage and parents-arranged marriages, such a pre-nuptial stage does not exist. In the post-nuptial stage of the process, the family is very significant from the point-of-view of the broader interests of the society, where one generation passes on the traditions to the new generation which has come of age. This is the family cycle where individuals are born and die, but the process continues.

The typological approach basically emphasizes the study of the family as an association of certain persons related by proximate kinship bonds and the group is directed to serve important cultural roles. The various typologically different forms that this group might acquire in different societies and cultures depend on demographic, economic, and political factors. These typological forms have always remained in a state of flux in accordance with the changing cultural needs of the society.

Apart from nuclear and extended families, many other types have also been recognized. Family being a group concerned with the training, education, and discipline of the child, some authority must prevail in decision making about the affairs of the family and the children. In matrilineal or matriarchal societies often associate with matrilocal residence, women who inherit the property have greater say in the affairs of the family. The term 'matriprotestal family' has been used for them. In patrilineal or patriarchal societies associated with patrilocal residence, it is the authority of the male spouse that prevails; such families are called 'patriprotestal families'.

Linton has found it useful to distinguish between a consanguineal family predominantly exhibiting the role of kins in their co-residence with the nuclear family and the conjugal family where the two spouses predominantly have important roles in the affairs of the family. A nuclear family being an ideal form of such a role, is also called as conjugal family. The emphasis in this distinction is on the assertiveness and decision making rather than on the number of persons involved in the group.

Joint Family

A family based on blood relations extending over three or more generations, known as 'extended family', acquires a slightly different form when its structural construct is subject to certain cultural norms converting it into a corporate group. A joint family has vertical as well as horizontal extensions and has a bigger size as compared to a family which is only vertically extended. A joint family may sometimes also include distant kins.

The main characteristic feature of the joint family is the indivisibility and common sharing of property. The property belongs to the family. The family members have an obligation to maintain it and share the benefits with everyone. Since this requires proper management and someone to be responsible for it, traditionally the eldest male member has the right to manage the property and the responsibility to see that no one is deprived of its benefits. As the manager or the 'karta' of the joint family, he also wields authority and enjoys the respect and confidence of other family members. A characteristic pattern of Hindus in India, this system has developed as a philosophy of life where individual preferences have to be suppressed in favour of the family interest.

Not all members in a joint family will have similar capacity and skill to work. At times this leads to bickering among the more active and therefore the more productive members. It is here that the judicious role of the manager becomes important. The rule of distribution of work according to capacity and skill and disbursement of benefits according to the needs makes the joint family as the source of social insurance and is especially beneficial for members who are physically disabled, mentally abnormal, or the victims of protracted illness. Their spouses and children do not have to suffer because of the disability of the bread winner.

The joint family is also characterized by a common kitchen and a common code of conduct for all the members. This family system is compatible with the agrarian background of the Indian economy. Though the system has predominantly male preference for many privileges, women enjoy a little status or freedom too.

With the advent of British rule in India, there were many changes which had a long-term influence on this institution. The first and the foremost was the Western education which brought about a value system in which individualism acquired the prime motive for all the behaviour and which also opened up opportunities for women in education, gave them right in property, and so on. This was a severe blow to the prevailing philosophy of life which had sustained the institution of joint family for a long time. Britishers also gradually started establishing industries which suited their economic interest. A number of urban centres were created around these industrial hubs. There was mass scale exodus of people from rural joint families to grab the employment opportunities. Thus, industrialization and urbanization made erosions in the structure of the joint family so that the system came to the verge of collapse, if not totally broken and set apart.

Other Types of Families

Since a family comes into existence as a consequence of marriage, therefore the incidence of plural marriage in a society gives rise to the types known as polygynous and polyandrous family types characterized by plurality of wives and husbands respectively. Evans Pritchard conceived of a couple producing children without getting married as a 'natural family' and using the terms 'simple legal family' (for nuclear or monogamous families) and 'compound legal family' (for polygamous and polyandrous families).

Although the concept of family is not tied up with the conditionality of common residence or essentially being a domestic group, yet in practice it is found to be so. That is why the mode of residence after marriage also becomes a basis for the typology of family as patrilocal, matrilocal, or avunculocal families. The mode of inheritance of the family name and property, of reckoning descent and succession to rank and office, may lead to a two-fold division as patrilineal or matrilineal families.

Morgan, an evolutionist, denied the presence of family at the earliest level of human society and conjectured that a state of promiscuity and group marriage prevailed at that time. According to Morgan, the only form of group that existed then was mother–siblings. Free and unrestricted sex relations and ignorance of the role of males in begetting a child rendered the concept of father and husband as redundant. Later on, with changes in economic conditions, emergence of the notion of property and attitude towards sex, the idea of marriage, regulated sex behaviour, and the rules for inheritance of property led to the gradual evolution of a family. This evolution, according to Morgan, took place in five stages. These were:

1. *Consanguineous family*, consisting of a group formed on the basis of intermarriages – between brothers, sisters, and cousins.
2. *Puncduan family*, where various sisters inter-married each others' husbands. The joint husbands were not necessarily related to each other. Sometimes several brothers inter-married several wives who were not necessarily sisters.
3. *Syndyasmain family*, that is, marriage between single pairs without any exclusive right of cohabitation. Such marriages always lacked stability.
4. *Patriarchal family*, which was based on the marriage of a man with more than one female.
5. *Monogamian family*, which was based on the marriage between one male and one female, with both having exclusive cohabitation rights over the other.

However, this unilinear scheme of evolution of the family and the condition of no marriage and no family at the earliest level of human existence was objected and disagreed even by some of the contemporaries of Morgan.

Family and Social Stability

A unique feature of family is that the concept embodies stability as well as change, depending upon how we understand it. The functionalist approach stresses upon certain universal human needs, important for the survival of the individual as well as the society, to be the basis of the organization of the family. These constitute the basic bio-psychological factors of human nature in which the family is rooted. Thus analysed as a permanent universal social institution, it represents the elements of stability.

But one cannot resist the temptation of studying the family as a group in which children are born, brought up, and educated. This group may be differently organized in different societies, but the common basis of their organization in every society are the strong bonds of filiality and kinship. Thus studied as a social group, the historical perspective brings about the patterns of change exhibited by this group over time.

Family stability is an essential component of social stability and social protection. In many developing and third world countries, family is the only source of social security and hence any instability or disintegration in the family gives rise to a crisis situation. There could be several reasons threatening the stability. Some of them are:

- Urbanization and industrialization
- Economic independence of women craving for emancipation from subordination from the male authority
- Education and empowerment of women
- New sexual morality and infidelity
- Childlessness
- Incompatibility between husband and wife
- Persistent interference of in-laws (husband's parents) in joint families
- Emergence of multiple new occupations promoting high mobility

Alternative Family or Reimagining Family

The very idea of 'alternative family' is based on the diversity within the institution of the family. The traditional concept of a family, when confronted by the new alternatives that emerged in the 20th century, was threatened by a number of alternatives. Alternative family could be seen in a variety of types such as:

- Fostering and adoption
- Surrogacy
- Co-parenting
- Single parent by choice
- LGBT (Lesbian, gay, bisexual, and transgender) parenting
- Live-in relationship

To nurture a child through fostering care has been a traditional and time-tested way of the childcare which may or may not lead to adoption, which is a formal way of commitment to take care of a child. Adoption is a legal process giving the child a legal status. Creating a family through surrogacy is a relatively new idea. It involves renting a womb. The term 'surrogate family' refers to a family formed with the help of a third party who rents her womb for the gestation of the child. It functions as a traditional family with the only difference that here maternity is a bit complicated. Surrogacy provides an opportunity to individuals who cannot conceive and also if both the parents are of same sex. Co-parenting refers to a situation where the parents are not married. This may include an absence of cohabitation as well as a romantic relationship. In this type of parenting, there are no pre-ordained roles of parents and everything is negotiated. Single-parent-by-choice is a growing trend in many societies. Since more and more women are becoming career conscious in the Western as well as the Indian society and no stigma may be attached, several women are preferring to be single parent by choice. Many women who are busy with their careers, get their eggs frozen, to be used later.

Until a few decades ago, same sex families were inconceivable even in America. In 1990 came the book *Brave New Families*, published by Judith Stacey, in the backdrop of contemporary post-industrial family life due to changes in economic realities, changing gender roles and concepts of kinship. In a landmark study *Family We Choose* (1991), Kath Weston argued that gay and lesbian families are based on love rather than biological connections. LGBT parenting is also a growing trend, though more prevalent among the Western societies. An LGBT person has many options of becoming a parent, including IVF (in-vitro fertilization) as well as IUI (intrauterine insemination). Lesbian couples who are parenting together often divide household and family responsibilities evenly. Beliefs that gay and lesbian adults are not fit parents have no empirical foundation.

Thus, in a fast-changing world, different types of alternative families will continue to grow. However, a nuclear family of a mother and father with children born through intercourse is expected to continue as the dominant mode of family.

Impact of Industrialization and Urbanization on Family

Industrial revolution in the West not only impacted Western societies but also the developing and underdeveloped countries. The process of industrialization induced changes in the structure of family and also in the different aspects of family and family life. Some of the most important effects on the family organization were:

- Transformation of the family from the principal unit of production to a unit of consumption. This was largely due to the transformation from an agrarian society to an industrial society.

- With the emergence of alternative occupations because of machine-oriented production systems, dependence of young adults on their parents ceased. This economic independence contributed to a weakening of familial authority.

- Universal, compulsory education to children freed them from the requirement of contributing to the family income. In this process, their dependence on the family increased. They ceased to be economic assets until the time when they would be, after completion of education, be able to contribute to the family income.

There are innumerable published accounts showing that the structure of the family has undergone changes due to the impact of industrialization and urbanization. Different aspects of family life were affected. Following is a summary of the important changes:

- In Western societies, especially United States, we see a seismic change in the last five decades or so. There was a shift from the traditional nuclear family and a number of family forms could be seen – single parent families, step families, grandparents raising grandchildren, gay and lesbian families, parents living apart and so on.

- Nuclearization of the family is the most obvious change in the structure of the family. With the progress of industrialization and urbanization the tendency towards nuclear family increased. The extended or joint family could not bear the onslaught of these twin factors of change.

- In the traditional societies, women never enjoyed cultural autonomy and had to live under the subordination of males in the patriarchal society. They did not have a right to choose their spouse and marriages were arranged by the parents and elders of the family. All this underwent a drastic change.
- In the agrarian societies, care for the elderly and the aged used to be an integral part of the value system. Widowhood was not a big problem as the joint families would take care of them. Under the new dispensation, things changed. Most of the Western countries witnessed a shift from high mortality–high fertility societies to low mortality–low fertility societies. The life expectancy has also increased, giving rise to a number of aged people.
- Female-headed households was yet another new trend. Young widows and divorcees emerged as the new heads of the family.
- Large scale migration from rural to urban areas and industrial towns altered the old norms of division of labour in the family, especially when both the husband and wife worked outside the home.

The traditional Indian society is steadily moving towards modernization. Both industrialization and urbanization have made a significant contribution towards this change. Due to the exposure to the forces of modernization, the structure of the family is also undergoing a variety of changes.

Changes in Family Over Time

Viewed as an association (as a social group), the family has always seen a transitional structure due to different socio-cultural factors existing in different societies at different times.

The evolutionist scholars of the 19th century like Morgan Lubbock, Frazer, and Briffault conceived of an earliest stage (sex, no marriage, and no family) of the human society. They presumed that in the later stages, realizations of economic advantages of having a man by the mother's side resulted in more permanent sex relations. The common prevalence of levirate, sororate and the practice of wife hospitality among the tribal people the world over, prevalence of classificatory terminology, and the reported ignorance of the role of the male in procreation, lead the scholars to form the functionalist view. The modern anthropological view, by and large, sticks to the functional view, holding that the origin of the family cannot be explained by any historical fact or situation.

E.B. Tylor thought of two stages in which the evolution of the family took place – the earlier as a matriarchal family and later as a patriarchal family and, in between, having a prolonged period of transition characterized by mixed features. The patriarchal family represented the medieval age in civilized societies. In Rome, the 'patriarch' or the 'pater' of the families used to be the sole owner of the family property. Among the Hebrews, Greeks, Romans, and Aryans, women were subject to the will of men. In Athens, wives and daughters were secluded in a separate apartment, not permitted to move out without the permission of the patriarch. In the earlier recorded history, this patriarchal system, derived from ancient civilizations, prevailed in Europe till feudal times. The demands of feudalistic socio-cultural environment (authoritarian mores) supported patriarchy and the suppression of women.

The age of Renaissance saw reformation and rational thinking, the influence of science and the induction of democracy. All these ideological factors brought about the downfall of patriarchy. The industrial revolution which involved substituting power machines for manual tools, supported the change. As a result, functions of the family were limited and replaced by secondary associations and State agencies. The involvement of women in factories, business establishments, and other jobs; modern education and inculcation of democratic values; and the development of an individualistic outlook, together undermined the authoritarian feudalistic practices. The status, rights, and privileges of women changed.

The modern family in the industrialized Western societies is characterized by a laxity in sex relations and economic independence asserted by women. With no religious control, smaller filocentric families (nuclear families) have become the most adaptive groups under the economic situations created by industrialization, urbanization, and excessive commercialization. Under the new economic set-up, the modern family has changed from a unit of production to a unit of consumption. Divested of the strong hold of kins, the isolated nuclear family has become more portable. It has become small, streamlined, and compact.

Some modern sociologists interested in the study of primary groups have studied the overall impact of this process of nuclearization of the family in modern industrialized societies. They have pointed out certain serious situations which speak of the nuclear family becoming dysfunctional.

Individualism and the egoistic behaviour of parents in modern American families leave many conflicts unresolved – sending wrong signals to their young children.

'The isolation of the nuclear family in modern industrialized societies,' according to Edmund Leach, 'has made it an overloaded electrical circuit the parents fight and the children rebel.'

Says David Cooper, 'Family operates as an ideological conditioning device where child is taught not how to survive in society but how to submit to it. The privatized, isolated family breeds suspicion and fear from the outside world.'

In modern American societies, the prevailing trend of 'moral relativism' among the youth is making marriage an undesirable burden and sex without marriage as a popular choice. The unmarried mothers demand legal status for their children. Probably, matrilocalism may become the preference in the future in the highly industrialized societies of the West.

Indian Scenario

A number of sociologists such as M.S. Gore, I.P. Desai, K.M. Kapadia, A.M. Shah and several others have analysed the emerging trends of family organization in India. On the basis of their studies and analysis, some of the important changes may be summarized as follows:

- Family as a social institution has been undergoing change both in its structure and function. Fission has been taking place in the structure of family. In increasing numbers, children prefer to live separately from their parents, thus creating nuclear families at the cost of extended or joint families. Yet, in many cases they continue to take care of their parents and the dependent unmarried brothers and sisters, thus fulfilling most of their traditional obligations.

- Family size has been reducing due to adopting the small family norm. Many people realize that they will not be able to maintain or improve their standard of living if they have a larger number of children.

- Emergence of female-headed families is also becoming more common. This is mainly because of two reasons. The first reason is the increasing frequency of divorce and dissolution of marriage and the husband leaving the children with the wife. In these cases, he may or may not provide support for the children. The second reason is the early death of the husband.

- The increase in the number of women in the work force has also induced changes in the family. These women contribute to the family income and the amounts are always a welcome addition. This has strengthened the

Family

position of these women in the affairs and management of their family. This is also altering the traditional gender-based division of labour.

- Migration within India as well as abroad has brought about any changes. In many cases, the entire family may not migrate and only the male head of the family goes away for a higher-paying job. In such cases, especially if the children are still young, the grandparents are called to live with the family, or the family moves to live with them, thus marking a reversal of the movement to the nuclear from the extended family.
- Empowerment of women because of education and employment is inducing significant changes in the status of women in the family. This has happened in the cities and also in the villages through institutions like anganwadi workers, Asha volunteers and self-help groups.
- The ideologies of equality and democracy in family relations coupled with the demand for gender equality have released new forces of change, impacting the nature of relationship between the husband and wife and between grown-up children and their parents.

As M.N. Srinivas, in his book *On living in a Revolution*, comments, Indian society has been undergoing a silent revolution in its values and institutions. Market economy and globalization have brought about a churning in the society and no social institution remains unaffected.

Critical Thinking Questions

- Do you think there may be a revival of the extended family?
- What are the social consequences of female-headed families?
- Technology is a factor of change in every sphere of life. How are technological changes reshaping the institution of family?

****

6

Kinship: The Core of Social Organization

Chapter Outline: *Introduction; Kins and kinship; A brief history of kinship studies; Types of kinship and category of kins; Functions of kinship; Principles of descent and descent groups; Kin groups, Kinship terminology; Kinship behaviour; Kinship diagrams; Feminist critique of kinship; Impact of industrialization and urbanization on kinship practices*

Learning Objectives

- Why have anthropologists and sociologists, especially socio-cultural anthropologists, spent so much time studying kinship?
- What are the functions of kinship?
- What are the various ways in which different societies categorise kins?
- Understand the structure of kinship and distinguish between various types of affiliation.
- Understand the terminology used in different systems of kinship.
- What is the importance of kinship behaviour?
- Why have feminist scholars criticized kinship practices?
- How is kinship changing in the modern world under the impact of industrialization and urbanization?

Introduction

Humans live in groups. As a species, they rarely live alone or in isolation. As Kenneth Guest (2018) very rightly says, 'Kinship is perhaps the most effective strategy humans have developed to form stable, reliable, separate, and deeply connected groups that can last over time and through generations.' Though also studied by sociologists, the study of kinship has always been a core topic in anthropology. Serena Nanda and Richard Warms (2017), acknowledging the significance of the study of kinship, say that such studies are anthropology's unique innovations for thinking about how culture works. Perhaps the most important comment on kinship comes from Robin Fox (1984) when he states that 'The study of kinship is the study of what man does with these basic facts of life – mating, gestation, parenthood, socialization, siblingship etc.'

Society being a network of social relationships, there are many ways in which these social relationships are organized in different societies and different types of groups get formed. In all human societies, the biological facts of marriage, birth, and death become the basis of cultural expression in the form of organizing persons into different categories and groups. For instance, in every society, with respect to any one person, there is a wide category of persons whom he or she may recognize kins and others may be related as non-kins.

Kinship determines the formation of social groups like families, forms the basis of classification of people in relation to one another, determines individual rights and obligations, and helps in regulating behaviour. Because all the elements of social life are interwoven, kinship is also referred as a 'system'.

Kins and Kinship

Reproduction is based on a basic human instinct and the most universal bond, called kinship, is based on it. Kinship is defined as the relationship through bonds of marriage and birth. The two persons of the opposite sex involved in the process of reproduction, giving birth to children, are termed as 'mother' and 'father' or 'parents'. Both parents, along with their children, form a small group called 'family' which is recognised as a kin group. A child who is born to a woman (called 'mother') indicates the biological bond between the woman and her child; the same may not be true for the man who is the procreator of the child for he acquires the status of 'father' only through the social bond of marriage. For getting recognition as the father of a woman's child, the person must be her husband too – a status provided by the social bond of marriage between the two. Thus, 'kinship' is defined as the fact of being related through the bonds of marriage and birth, marriage being the social recognition of the biological relation of sex and providing the basis for the social status of 'husband' and 'father'. Hence, kinship is the social recognition of the biological ties of marriage and birth and all those who are related to one another through these bonds are recognized as kins, as distinguished from 'non-kins' who may be related to one another in hundreds of ways, other than these two.

The three concepts of marriage, family, and kinship telescope with one another and have a common meeting point in the concept of the family, which is the fountainhead of kinship. The eight types of dyadic relations generated within the family become the building blocks of the kinship system in any society. These are the relationships or ties between husband and wife, mother and son, mother and daughter, father and son, father and daughter, between brothers, between sisters, and between the brothers and sisters. All these social relations are characterized by mutuality of obligations, rights and privileges, and co-operation. The understanding of these and their use for structuring different types of social groups constitutes kinship studies.

Two kins who stand in a particular relationship with each other are expected to behave in a particular manner. The study of such expected patterns of behaviour of kins in a particular society is called the study of kinship behaviour. Two kins, in recognition of their kinship ties, call or refer to each other by certain culturally coined and socially accepted terms. The study of the use of these terms and their social implications in a society is called the study of kinship terminology. While studying kinship in different societies and cultures, anthropologists try to learn about the categories of kins recognized, how these categories are organized in the social groups, the nature of expected behaviours between these kins, and the terms of calling or reference used by the people. All these studies of a particular society or culture constitute the study of kinship system of that society.

A Brief History of Kinship Studies

The history of kinship studies may be traced to the work of L.H. Morgan whose pioneering study was *Systems of Consanguinity and Affinity of Human Family* (1871). Morgan and Radcliff-Brown, considered kinship as an important social institution. They wrote about kinship terms, types of kins, classification of kinship and typology of kinship groups. The later scholars described this approach as a 'classical approach' and related it with interests in comparative legal institutions and philology. Because of their intense interest in kinship, cross-cultural comparison of kinship systems became the favourite topic of anthropology. Contributions to the study of kinship largely built the reputation of scholars such as Malinowski, Radcliff-Brown, Kroeber, Murdock, Meyer Fortes, Evans-Prichard, Levi-Strauss and many other anthropologists.

Until the last decade of the 20th century, kinship was regarded as the core of British social anthropology. The importance of kinship has been such that no thorough ethnographic study could afford to ignore the central importance of kinship, especially in stateless, non-industrial, simple or traditional societies of Asia and Africa.

By the 1950s, the study of kinship tended to become abstract and removed from the practise of actual lived relations. Anthropological and sociological studies of that period were characterized by highly technical or even mathematical models of how societies worked. In the 1960s, 1970s, and even later, the earlier kinship studies were challenged by the feminist and Marxist scholars.

Even before this, scholars such as Edmund Leach had expressed the opinion that kinship was not a thing in itself as it dealt with phenomena which had independent existence such as marriage, inheritance, property disputes, economy, politics, and so on. After considering all these aspects, kinship became a framework or guideline to regulate various aspects of human behaviour. But this approach further enhanced the importance of kinship. Contemporary kinship studies are more historically grounded. They emphasize on everyday experiences. Unlike the earlier studies, they tend to focus on representations of gender and power.

Robin Fox (1967) thinks that anthropologists have been too shy about making generalizations. This has resulted in the accumulation of a wealth of isolated data and case studies without building theories around them. Fox maintains that different family structures are based on four universal, or nearly universal, principles:

- The women have the children
- The men impregnate the women
- The men usually (i.e., for all societies until now) exercise control over property
- Primary kin do not mate with each other, meaning incest is tabooed

The Types of Kinship and the Categories of Kins

Since kins are defined as those related through the bonds of marriage and the bonds of birth, there are two types of kins. Those related to each other through the bond of marriage are called 'affinal kins' or simply 'affines'. They are not related to each other through the bond of blood. Those who are related to each other through the bond of birth are called 'consanguineous kins' and the relationship based on blood ties is known as 'consanguinity'. An individual's world of kins of both the types is referred to as kindred.

As real consanguinity is difficult to determine and our own scientific notions of genetic relationship are not shared by all peoples and cultures, the notion of consanguinity or blood ties varies considerably. A person may be having any number of blood kins whom he or she may not recognize. A child is equally a consanguineous to both the parents and their kins. But this is not the universal notion; our experience of different kinship systems in different societies shows that the idea of real consanguinity is somewhat useless in kinship studies. A consanguine is one who is recognized as such by the society, the blood relationship in the genetic sense may have nothing to do with it.

There are three types of consanguineal kins:

1. The direct descendants of a pair of common ancestors or the descendants of the same parents in a vertical line called as 'lineal kins'.
2. The brothers and sisters, that is, the children born of the same parents called as 'siblings'.
3. Those who are the descendants of the siblings of one's parents called as 'collaterals'.

Thus, consanguineal kins may be lineal, siblings, or collaterals.

A family is a social group consisting of persons related by the bonds of blood as well as of marriage, that is, it consists of consanguineal as well as affinal. The eight types of kins represented in a nuclear family – that is, mother, father, daughter, son, brother, sister, husband, and wife – are called 'primary kins'. The primary kins of one's primary kins are known as 'secondary kins', such as father's brother or mother's sister or sister's husband and so on. Similarly, the primary kins of one's secondary kins are known as 'tertiary kins'. This is how the network of kinship may extend to any degree. This is called the 'range of kinship'. In primitive societies, it is very common for the people to recognize kins up to the range of fifth or sixth degrees or even beyond. But in modern societies, this range seldom goes beyond the third degree kins. That is why primitive societies are categorized as broad-ranged kinship systems while modern societies are characterized as narrow-ranged kinship systems.

A cousin is a third-degree kin but at least four types of kins are covered by this word of English language. For example, a person's father's brother's child, father's sister's son or daughter, mother's sister's son or daughter and

Kinship: The Core of Social Organization

mother's brother's son or daughter – are all his or her cousins. But in practice, in different societies all these kins are categorized as either cross-cousins or parallel cousins. The sons and daughters of a brother and a sister are known as parallel cousins. In most of the societies, barring a few exceptions, parallel cousins do not marry while in a large number of societies, cross cousins are expected to marry.

When groups, already related by bonds of marriage, choose to restrict their lifemates among the same groups in the subsequent generation and thus renew and re-strengthen their relations, the practice is called 'alliance'. In a large number of simple societies, two groups (class) keep on exchanging their daughters and sons generation after generation, thereby strengthening their bonds of mutual cooperation in everyday life, particularly in economic activities.

Kins may also be categorized on the basis of generation, relative age, and sex. They may also be categorized as the kins on father's side, that is, 'patrilineal kins' or as kins on other's side, that is, 'matrilineal kins'. The kinship rules are applicable for many purposes and occasions, such as participation in rituals and ceremonies and also in passing on the family name from one generation to other. The rules of inheritance of property in every society are also restricted to the father's or the mother's side kins. The rule of recognition of kins (for different purposes) of either side only is known as 'unilateral' and the rule and practice of recognizing kins of both the sides is known as 'bilateral'.

As mentioned earlier, kinship though rooted in biological facts of birth, marriage, and death, is more a question of social recognition. In every society there is a category of quasi kins or putative or active kins. The disciples of the same teacher or the followers of the same godfather may behave as if they are consanguineal kins.

A universal example of social recognition is the practice of adoption. A ceremonial recognition of a child as equivalent to one's own biologically produced offspring speaks of overriding nature of social recognition. Among the polyandrous Todas of India, the ceremonial presentation of a miniature bow-and-arrow by a brother to the common wife confers the status of fatherhood. In all polyandrous societies, paternity is a difficult question. They need to have some social mechanism to solve the question of fatherhood. Among the polyandrous Khasa (Jaunsari) people, the elder brother enjoys the status and privileges of fatherhood by virtue of tradition and social recognition.

Functions of Kinship

There are three basic functions of culturally defined kinship ties and socially recognized kinship categories in all human societies. Firstly, they provide continuity between generations. Socialization of a child and initial childcare in all societies except the kibbutz (in Israel), is done in a kinship unit. Also, orderly transmission of property and social positions from one generation to the other takes place in kin groups.

Secondly, kinship defines a group of persons on whom to depend in the normal course. The smallest group is a domestic group. The other kin groups larger than this are significant in many societies having adaptiveness to different situations. In tribal societies, particularly in stateless societies lacking political mechanisms to maintain order and initiate other activities, the web of kinship provides the main structure for social action.

Thirdly, kinship regulates marriage by defining (among related persons) who can marry whom or who should not marry among themselves and extends the area of kinship to unrelated persons through the bonds of marriage.

In small sized, simple societies, kinship is the most important social bond. Most of the social groups are organized on the basis of kinship. Relationship between individuals is mainly governed by the kinship norms. People's world of kins extends to the entire society. Their world of non-kins is very limited.

In modern, industrialized Western societies, other principles of social organization such as work, citizenship, common economic and political interest, and other varied common interests operate as basis of organization of groups. But nuclear family continues to be the most significant kin group. A few larger groups of kins may also exist but their significance remains limited to ceremonial occasions only. Yet, a person claiming a relationship as a kin is treated with a different regard than one who is unrelated and is a non-kin.

Kinship systems serve a number of functions ensuring the continuation of the society. The most important ones are:

- They provide continuity between generations
- Their rules provide for the orderly transmission of property (deciding inheritance) and social position (succession) between generations

The importance of kinship stems from the fact that in most of the societies kinship is the single-most important social institution. There is a close interrelationship between the kinship system and other aspects of the social organization. 'Kinship is the system of meaning and power created to determine who is related to whom and to define their mutual expectations, rights and responsibilities' (Guest, ibid). In small-scale, non-industrial societies, kinship is the most important social bond and serves as the basis of group formation.

Principles of Descent and Descent Groups

Like birth and marriage, the biological fact of death also provides a socially significant encouragement to the people who are alive. There are many reasons for which people in a present generation may recognize, identify, and remember their ancestors who are no more.

Apart from the supernatural motives, there are many other practical social motives for which people may associate themselves with their ancestors. The way people in a society relate themselves to their common ancestors is known as 'descent'. In anthropological terminology, 'descent' refers to the culturally established affiliation with one or both parents. Those who establish their ties with a common ancestor or a couple of common ancestors utilize this sentiment for useful social purposes. In many societies, descent is an important basis of social group formation – often the groups are of consanguineal kins, who are lineal descendants of a common ancestor or a pair of common ancestors, extending beyond two generations. In societies where descent groups are formed, they have important functions to perform in the organization of domestic life; socialization of children; transfer and inheritance of property, political, and ritual offices; and so on.

Sexual and descent are two kinds of biological relationships. Each kind of biological relationship may be expressed in direct and shared form. Mates have a direct sexual union, but the co-spouses (in polygyny or polyandry) share a mate. Parent and child is a direct descent union, but the siblings and other collaterals share descent. Biologically, a child is equally related to both the parents by virtue of birth. However, differences are found in delineating descent in different societies through virtual neglect of either of the two parents or ancestors or by giving equal preference to both the common ancestors.

It is in this sense that 'descent' is a cultural rule – the way a society prefers to choose from the three options (male, female, or both) in the matter of reckoning descent. In a society where both the common ancestors (in the male line as well as in the female line) are recognized in considering descent, this rule or principle is known as the 'bilateral principle' of descent. If the rule or the cultural practice is to give recognition to either the male ancestor in the male line or to a female ancestor in the female line, the rule is known as the 'unilineal principle' of descent.

Under the principle of unilineality, if the female ancestor in the female line is recognized, the rule is known as 'matrilineality'. If a male ancestor is recognized in the male line, the rule is known as 'patrilineality'.

Using the principle of bilateral descent, all those who share a common ancestor are known as 'cognates'. That is why this rule of bilateral descent is also known as 'cognatic descent'. But in case the mode of recognizing descent is the unilineal principle (matrilineal or patrilineal) the co-sharers of the common descent in the male line only are called as 'agnates' while the descendants of a common female ancestor are called as 'uterine' kins. It is these cognates or agnates or uterines who, demonstrating their bond of common descendancy, group themselves variously in different societies.

But there are certain exceptions too. The principles of matrilineality and patrilineality may sometimes be operative simultaneously in peculiarly mixed or combined forms to give rise to certain other rules of descent which are not very common but do exist in some societies. These are known as 'double descent', 'parallel descent', and 'ambilineal descent' rules.

Double Descent: The adoption of a rule of descent by a society is based on the need to meet some real-life situations and different types of kinship groups are organized by them accordingly.

The problem with unilineal descent groups is that they are subject to demographic vagaries over population levels which affect the process of forming sub-lineages called 'segmentation'. A decrease in population results in diminishing numbers and sizes of groups.

A double descent system is a system in which both matrilineality and patrilineality are operative, but for different purposes and objectives. For example, among the Yako of Nigeria, the immovable property and assets are inherited patrilineally (in the male line) while moveable assets are inherited matrilineally (in the female line). In most of the double descent systems, the residential group is the patrilineage.

Historically, the double descent system often arises from matrilineal descent through a changeover to patrilocal residence. Thus, although most of the societies have only one rule of descent, sometimes both the principles of matrilineality and patrilineality are used to affiliate individuals with different sets of kins for different purposes, in which case both the rules of unilineal descent are operative simultaneously. Although theoretically it is a feasible option, yet practically it is a rare situation.

The group Yako of Nigeria is the best documented example of a double descent society. They live in one large town called Umer. The population of Umer is divided into wards known as 'Kepan' which are inhabited by a patrician. Umer is also divided into matriclans and the matriclans are divided into lineages of shallow depth. Matriclans are also important as ritual groups.

Parallel Descent: Like double descent, there is another situation of a rare descent rule. Margaret Mead, who studied the Mundugamer of New Guinea, found the operative descent system in them was a mix of agnatic and uterine systems. In them, land was inherited patrilineally. All other property and assets were inherited matrilineally from father to daughter and/or mother to son. Among the Apinaye of Brazil, there are matrilineal groups of females and patrilineal groups of males. The consanguines are excluded not on the basis of the son or the daughter of the parent alone but on the basis of same sex or opposite sex links between the parents and the child. All other goods (excluding land) including the sacred flutes are passed on from father to daughter and mother to son. These lines of inheritance are called 'ropes' by the natives. Sister exchange is a common form of marriage among the parallel descent societies. According to Mead, a sentiment of same sex hostility prevails in these societies – father hates son, mother hates daughter.

Ambilineal Descent: This term is used for the system prevailing among some people where there are no culturally prescribed norms for the adoption of matrilineal or patrilineal rules of descent. It is this ambiguity which is illustrated by this term. Some people in these societies affiliate through mother to daughter and others through father to son. Thus, both male and female descent groups are organized in the society.

Kin Groups

A kin group simply means a social group in which kinship is the basis for the recruitment of its members. A family or a domestic group is the most common type of kin groups in human societies. In most of the societies the mode of descent or the rules prevailing in them for reckoning descent from common ancestors becomes the basis for the organization of kin groups known as descent groups.

As mentioned earlier, there are two broad categories of descent groups called as bilateral descent groups and unilineal descent groups.

Bilateral Descent Groups

Bilateralism is a system of recognizing descent in which the ancestors are not differentiated on the basis of sex and an individual affiliates himself or herself with male as well as female lines of descent. The individual, along with the kins related from the mother's side and the father's side, forms an operative group which is known as a 'kindred group'. Since such groups are identified by individuals or an ego, they are called ego-centred groups. Since these groups include kins from both sides, therefore in order to be functional, they are smaller in size as larger groups become non-functional. An individual may simultaneously belong to many such groups.

All such kindred groups or cognatic descent groups cannot serve the same kind of function. They are never residential groups. But these groups have certain advantages in societies where they are organized. The moment a group becomes larger, it tends to become non-functional and it breaks up into smaller ego-centred groups by a process of fission. That is why they are also called as amorphous groups.

At least three kinds of bilateral descent groups can be identified. The first are 'unrestricted' kindred groups in which all the descendants of founding ancestors are included. They function with greater effectiveness than the other bilateral kin groups. The second type of groups are called as 'restricted' kindred groups in which all the descendants of the founding ancestors have a right to their membership but they can only exercise this right if they choose to live in the founder's territory. The third kind of kindred groups are 'pragmatically restricted' kindred groups in which all the descendants remain members of the group but in practice very few of them belong to these groups as they are territorial groups. They have to choose which are to affiliate with.

Among Sagada Iqrats of Philippines, the common grazing and land user people, these (pragmatically restricted) groups are simply ceremonial groups. Among the Lappes of Northern Europe, the reindeer grazing people, such groups are organized. The Ginsbert Island people (Pacific) and the Iban of Borneo are some of the societies with bilateral descendancy where these groups are organized.

It is the small size and individual or ego-centred character of these groups which makes them very effective in emergency situations like birth, marriage, and death. Their amorphous character always keeps on reorganizing them into more effective smaller universes of kindreds who can effectively co-operate with one another. The groups are of temporary nature, that is why they cannot be entrusted with responsibilities of long-term nature. Also, since an individual is simultaneously a member of many such groups, the membership pattern always remains ambiguous.

Unilineal Descent Groups

The term 'unilineal' signifies the practice of tracing descent either through a male line or a female line. In some societies like Iraquois of North America and the Khasis and Garos of Meghalaya in India, have the tradition of tracing their descent from a common female ancestor. In many other societies, descent is traced from father to son through a common male ancestor. All those tracing descent in only the male line are called 'agnates' while the descendants of a common female ancestor are called 'uterine' kins.

The application of the unilineal rule of descent provides groups with clear-cut and unambiguous kin members. The groups continue to operate as corporate units, affiliating members by virtue of being born in the group. Death of individual members does not change the tenor of these groups. This non-overlapping character of the unilineal kin groups is important as they can be entrusted with the responsibilities of a long-term character, including political administration at the local level.

There are different types of unilineal kin groups organized in different societies. A particular society may have only a few of them All the types are usually not represented in any one society.

The rule of descent becomes the basis for the recruitment of new members of these group. Although both sons and daughters born in a unilineal kin group became the members of the group, it is only the sons in the patrilineal descent groups who transmit the affiliation in that group through their children.

There are two advantages of such groups:

Firstly, they are self-perpetuating groups even as their members keep on changing like modern corporations. Effectively, they are permanent groups and may own property.

Secondly, they are ancestor based, facilitating unambiguous group formation. The group membership is easily and clearly defined. This membership ensures rights of ownership, social and moral obligations, and social roles.

Lineages and clans are two types of unilineal descent groups organized in different societies.

A group of consanguineal kins who can actually demonstrate their relatedness to a common male or female ancestor constitute a 'lineage' group. Depending upon the rule of unilineal descent being in male or female line, these lineage groups may be patrilineal or matrilineal. In different societies where they are organized, they vary in size.

In some societies, such as the Nuers of Sudan in Africa, there may be different levels of lineage groups. A large lineage group is called a 'maximal' lineage group which may be segmented into smaller, medium-sized lineage groups which themselves are segmented into still smaller lineage groups called 'minimal' lineage groups.

All of these groups perform different functions. In societies, where lineage groups hold land collectively and members are held responsible for one another's behaviour, they are considered as corporate groups. But in other societies they may not operate in that manner.

Lineages are generally local groups and are residential or domestic groups whose members cooperate each other in day-to-day life. They also regulate marriage as they are exogamous groups.

Clans are defined as unilineal kin groups whose members claim a common ancestry from a common male or female ancestor. The common ancestor may be a mythological figure or some aspect of nature from whom they cannot trace their relationship genealogically.

Clans are comparatively larger groups and have a large number of lineages. They are not residential groups; their members spread out in many villages and locations. Often, they perform political or religious functions. Being exogamous, they also regulate marriage. Clan exogamy extends the network of peaceful social relations within a society by incorporating different clans through bonds of marriage.

In stateless societies, in the absence of any centralized system of political control, kinship-based alliances are important mechanisms for peace-keeping as kins should not fight with one another. Because of the clan and lineage exogamy, kinship relations extend widely over the tribe. Residence after marriage and other concomitant factors distinguish matrilineal and patrilineal social systems. In patrilineal systems with patrilocal residence, the status of woman is more suppressed due to male predominance, and they tend to be more stable. In matrilineal systems with matrilocal residence, women enjoy better social status, the importance of their brothers is enhanced, and the loyalties of the males get divided between their own children and their sister's children.

Kinship Terminology

How various kins are classified in a society relates to their roles. A kinship term is simply a term or a word used for designating or referring a kin. Based on his observations of the North American Indian societies, Morgan, as early as the late 19th century, talked about two systems and called them as classificatory and descriptive systems of terminology.

Morgan observed that in some of the societies, people used the same term for calling more than one type of kin. He called this system as the 'classificatory' system of terminology. Here more than one type of kins are classified by one single term. Similarity of age, group, sex, and same generation are usually the basis for such a categorization. In societies where most of the terms of calling are separate terms to designate one single kin, the system is called the 'descriptive' system of terminology.

Under the classificatory system, several lineal kins as well as collaterals and even affinal kins are all referred by the same term of designation, whereas a descriptive term of designation describes the person's exact relation with whom he or she is interacting. Thus 'uncle' is a classificatory term while 'father' is a descriptive term.

Morgan, being an evolutionist, saw the same kind of evolutionary pattern in this type of categorization in societies. He thought that the classificatory system was characteristic of primitive societies while the descriptive system was characteristic of modern societies.

However, this dichotomy of terminological systems is by no means absolute. No system is purely classificatory or descriptive. Even in modern Western societies, some of the classificatory terms such as uncle, brother-in-law, and aunt, are used.

W.H.R. Rivers gave another justification for the significance of the study of kinship terms. He maintained that the kinship terms refer to social usages, certain marriage customs, and practices which are antecedent to their use. At times certain kinship terms prevail but the related customs and practices which brought them in use may not exist and may have vanished. Thus, their continued usage alert us to correlate them with some of the past practices.

Through them we can peep into the past, which is of great significance in the context of primitive societies lacking any recorded evidence of their past history.

Kroeber held the view that these kinship terms are no more than mechanisms of identification and distinction of various kins by just providing a word to name them and that it is futile to read anything more in them. According to Kroeber, the question of using terms is related to the type of language which may have an elaborate or limited stock of words.

British social anthropologists, under the influence of Radcliff-Brown, have devoted serious attention to the study of kinship terminology. Brown was rather overawed by his study of the kinship system of Australian aborigines which is highly complicated and more complex system than any other society. From this study at first and later from the study of African kinship systems – a collection of African kinship studies which he edited – he developed several new insights about the importance of the study of kinship terminology which he regarded a key to unlock or comprehend any social structure. Rejecting any preconceived evolutionary bias or conjecturing about the origin, he stressed upon the need to study kinship systems functionally from a synchronic point of view, that is, studying them as a systematic arrangement of living an orderly social life. He felt that in studying the kinship system of a people, study of kinship terminology should be the first step. Radcliff-Brown also made certain generalizations and called them as principles of kinship structure, such as:

1. Principle of inequality of proximate generations
2. Principle of the unity of sibling groups maintained by exogamy

Earlier anthropologists, based on the ethnographic data with them, spoke of at least six terminological systems based on cousin terminology. They are Hawaiian system, Iroquios system, Eskimo system, Sudanese system, the Crow system and the Omahu system.

Kinship Behaviour

A kinship relationship is characterized by the role-expectations which form the basis for mutual co-action and behaviour between different kins. There are some behaviours concerning certain categories of kins which show an element of regularity of occurrence across societies and more-or-less permanent behaviour with an element of universality. Anthropologists call them 'kinship usages'.

Avoidance, joking relations, avunculate, amitate, teknonymy, and couvade are some usages which have found their way in anthropological literature.

Avoidance

In most of the societies, father-in-law–daughter-in-law avoidance is found where the two kins tend to avoid each other. In different societies, other kinds of avoidances may also be found, for instance, the mother-in-law–son-in-law avoidance, among the Trobriand Islanders or brother–sister avoidance among the Veddas of Sri Lanka. In different societies, the practice of avoidance may be expressed in various forms ranging from limited familiarity to covering faces. While Tylor explained mother-in-law–son-in-law avoidance among the Trobriand Islanders as a result of an element of strangeness and matrilocal residence, Frazer explained brother–sister avoidance as a part of precautionary measure to avoid the breach of the rule of incest. So is the case with father-in-law– daughter-in-law avoidance where, along with the element of strangeness, it helps prevention of social strain by avoiding the development of any intimacy being between the two. Radcliff-Brown explained this as an arrangement to prevent any possibility of conflict between the kins.

Joking Relations

If avoidance means a restricted social interaction between two kins, 'joking' represents a tendency to increase proximity by allowing liberal social interaction between the two kins, for example, a woman's interactions with her husband's younger brothers or a man's interactions with his wife's younger sisters. All these kins belong to the category of relations who can even have sexual relations in their effort to be intimate with one another without the breach of any norm (other than adultery) of the society. The word 'joking' simply represents a situation of extreme familiarity. Modern functional anthropologists tend to explain this kinship usage as a safety-valve or a release mechanism for the tensions generated due to the imposition of restrictions.

Other Usages

The other kinship usages are relatively rare and limited to certain specific kinship relations. For example, the term 'avunculate' stands for certain special rights and obligation permitted and expected culturally from the maternal uncle. Similarly, the term 'amitate' stands for the culturally expected behaviour between an individual and his or her father's sister. The privileges in both the cases are associated with specific modes of residence after marriage.

'Couvade' is a term which refers to a unique though rare practice in which a husband imitates the behaviour of his wife at the time of childbirth such as using special and restricted diet and a self-imposed period of confinement. The practice has been reported as being followed by the Todas of South India and some of the Australian aborigines. Anthropologists have explained this as a show of sympathy for the wife as well as a cultural mechanism by which a genuine and equal concern for the child in a matriarchal complex where the biological role of the males in begetting the child and the role of father as well as the concept of fatherhood always remain eclipsed.

Kinship Diagrams

Kinship diagrams depict the different kin status more conveniently than describing and explaining them verbally. Diagrammatically, it is also possible to represent facts back to any number of generations. Certain conventions must be followed in preparing these diagrams.

Since tracing and establishing relationships involves a starting point or an individual from whom the relational structure spreads out, we call this initial individual as an 'Ego'. Normally, certain symbols are used to show gender difference. For example, a female is depicted by a small circle (o) and a male by a small triangle (Δ). When an individual is to be depicted without sex difference a small square (□) is the symbol used. For showing a person to be dead, the figure of the symbol is crossed like ∅ =.

For a marriage tie between to individuals the sign = is used, that is, two parallel small horizontal bars.

Single horizontal line (-) is used for a consanguineal tie and a single vertical (|) line indicates generation difference.

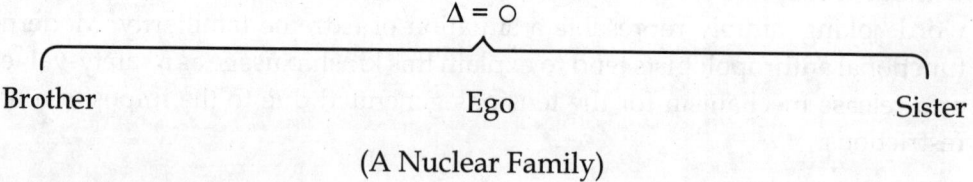

(A Nuclear Family)

There is yet another convention, though not so common, that is, a bracket opening upwards to indicate marital bond. But the same bracket in an inverted form depicts consanguinity. In such a depiction, two generations are differentiated by a single vertical line (|).

Indian Scenario

Both consanguineal as well as affinal kinship bonds are very important. Consanguineal kins are related by blood ties while the affinal kins come into existence as a result of marital bonds. The kinship bonds between the parents and children, and beyond that with all the kins related by blood, whether primary, secondary or tertiary, come under the category of consanguineal kins. The kins who come into existence as a result of the establishment of marital alliance such as husband–wife and their kins are the affinal kins.

Kinship system is not the same throughout India. For instance, the kinship system in the North and Central India are different from the rest. Even within this region there are variations. By-and-large, the people in this region marry outside the village as they consider members of their caste living in the same village as brothers and sisters. It is also a strongly patriarchal system. But in terms of the range of kinship (inclusion/exclusion of different degrees of kins – primary or direct, secondary or the primary of the primary kin and tertiary or secondary of ones' primary kin) local and regional variations are observed.

Among the majority of Hindus of different regions, the range of kinship along with the kinship expectations are very broad while most of the Muslim communities in India exhibit narrow kinship range. This may be seen when the list of invitees or participants are drawn and gifts given during family celebrations like marriage, along with kinship expectations.

Feminist Critique of Kinship

Like in several other areas of social life and enquiry, interpretation of the institution of kinship was also challenged by the feminist and Marxist scholarship in the 1960s and 1970s. Eleanor Leacock, an American Marxist-feminist scholar and some others pointed out that the earlier ethnographic accounts were concerned with only with men, and in the process a large body of information on the lives of women was left out. This was largely because of the dominance of anthropological–sociological scholarship by males. This was not an acceptable situation. Thus, women's experiences emerged as a legitimate subject of scholarship.

Feminist scholars gradually shifted from documenting the world of women to analysing the symbolization of gender itself. These studies of the 1970s and 1980s challenged the intellectual edifice on which the theory of kinship had been built earlier. It gave rise to a debate over the mutual definition of kinship and gender.

Thus, the very understanding of the phenomenon of kinship demanded some alteration with the advent of new technology, especially the new reproductive technologies (including in vitro fertilization) and family forms (such as same-sex marriage). These new developments gave a new lease of life to kinship studies in the late 20th and the early 21st centuries.

If we take a closer view, we find that the feminist challenge to kinship theory is based also on the critique of certain assumptions that were accepted without questioning them. Among such assumptions, the crucial one was the very base of kinship theory, that is, separation between the domestic domain and the public/politico-jural domain. It was assumed that the domestic domain was largely marked by the mother-child bond and the basic constitution of this domain was 'natural' as compared to the public domain which was consisted of politico-jural facts. It was further assumed that the domestic domain largely involves fulfilling sexual and child-bearing roles and responsibilities and the public domain was related to the authority, power, legal rules, and so on. Based on this assumption, it was accepted that the domestic domain was primarily associated with women and the public domain with men. This obviously tilted the power structure openly in favour of men which led to the curtailment of cultural autonomy of women, ultimately leading to their subordination.

Another point of critical importance in the criticism of the kinship theory by the feminists was the assumption about gender – that gender lies at the core of kinship studies. It was assumed in kinship theories that the creation of human offspring was a result of a heterosexual intercourse resulting in pregnancy and childbirth. The critics argued that beside these, there were several other activities which were involved in reproduction. Collier and Yanagisako (1987), giving voice to the feminist critique, ask, 'Given the wide range of human activities and relationships (other than parenthood and marriage) that can be viewed as contributing to the production of human beings, why do we focus on only a few of them as the universal basis of kinship?' Thus, we find that the feminist critique of kinship has contributed to getting a new insight to the scholarship on kinship studies.

Impact of Industrialization and Urbanization on Kinship Practices

Though social change in itself is a slow process, in a traditional society like India, the pace of change is still slower. Social institutions in any society are so deep-rooted that any alteration in the is a time-consuming process.

Among factors causing change, technological innovations and rural to urban migration are the most decisive factors. Introduction of a new technology impacts the value system of a society in a variety of ways. Population and environment are other factors contributing to social change.

Each change in one social institution leads to changes in all social institutions. Some of the notable changes in kinship and family as a result of industrialization and urbanization may be described as follows:

- Industrialization and urbanization disrupt the traditional relationship between generations as well as the relationship between spouses, children, and other kins.

- Industrialization and urbanization change the family and kinship ties and transform the family by converting it from a unit of production into a unit of consumption.

- Kinship practices often undergo drastic changes. The number of kins with whom regular contacts is maintained drastically goes down.

- The distant kins and even tertiary kins are ignored and replaced by friends, neighbours, fellow workers, club members, and so on. Thus a 'fictive' or 'pseudo' chacha (uncle), mousi (aunt – other's sister) and so on take the place of the real ones. Not only this, even in the realm of friendship 'transient friends' may be the rule rather than permanent or long-lasting friends.

- Industrialization and urbanization give rise to multiple new occupations. Occupational differentiation and spatial mobility may compel people to ignore 'not so close' kins. Such kins may also not be easily available and accessible.

- Industrialization contributes to the reduced mutual dependence of people, thus promoting individualism. Because of availability of hospitals, medical and life insurance, pension, hostels for working men and women, and a host of welfare and social security measures, people tend to become self-dependent and may feel concerned only about their close or primary kins.

- Because of new means of transport and communication, people are willing to travel long distances for better education, employment, and a better quality of life, affecting kinship ties and practices inspired by rising aspirations.

Critical Thinking Questions

- Why has the study of kinship been so important?
- Are biology and marriage the only basis for kinship?
- How and why are kinship practices changing in the modern world?

****

7

Economic Organization

Chapter Outline: *Introduction; Economic organization; Economic System, Primitive Economy and Primitive Economic System; Distribution and Exchange; Types of Exchange; Reciprocity; Redistribution; Reciprocity and Redistribution Compared; Market Exchange; Tribal Markets; Money, Trade,and Market; Market as Social Institution; Property; Peasant Economy; Technology; Division of Labour; Production Relations and Mode of Production; Work; Organization of Work; Work and Technology; Work, Technology, and Society; Formal and Informal Economy; Economy in Capitalism and Socialism*

Learning Objectives
- Is money really the measure of all things?
- What are the different ways by which societies get their food?
- How have humans adapted to their environments?

Money is to the West what kinship is to the rest.

–Marshall Sahlins

Human activities concerned with the satisfaction of basic needs of survival – the need for food, shelter, clothing and so on – are termed as 'economic activities'. Every society produces, distributes, and consumes or uses goods and services. Every society therefore has an economy, that is, a system of managing these processes of production, distribution, and consumption of goods and services.

Natural environment is the main resource from which all necessary goods for the fulfilment of needs is derived. Even in modern industrial societies, most of the raw material used for manufacturing of goods and items of utility have to be obtained from natural resources. In societies using simpler technologies, people have to exploit environmental resources to extract food and material for shelter, clothing and so on.

But humans cannot exploit the environment bare handed; certain means or tools have to be used. Hence the use of some kind of technology is a must, howsoever simple it may be. Any device that makes the exploitation of available natural resources for procuring the things of utility easier, is technology. Economists have often accused anthropologists of confusing between economy and technology, as in the past anthropologists made technology as the basis for the classification of economies. They used the basic techniques of food production as an index for its classification.

Economic Organization

All person-to-person relations are broadly termed as 'social organization'. No single person is capable of fruitfully engaging himself or herself alone in an economic activity. People must organize themselves into groups to collectively engage in the extraction of food from natural resources. No technology can replace human resources as they are essential means. The nature of physical environment and the level of technology available are the main deciding factors as to how people can organize themselves in order to engage themselves successfully in economic activities. We call this as 'economic organization'. Economic organization is that part of the social organization which is specifically directed to achieve economic ends. Organization of human resources for economic ends is as important as technology.

Economic System

The term 'economic system' is used for that part of a social-cultural system that deals with the production, distribution, and consumption of goods and services within a particular society. Economics deals with things of use, with tools, and instruments used to produce or procure food and other basic utilities. It also deals with the relationship of goods with people in the process of production, distribution, and consumption.

In the study of a particular society from the economic point of view, anthropologists are interested in understanding the relationship between the economy and the culture prevailing in the society. One aspect of this inter-relationship is that culture defines or shapes the economic ends sought by individuals and the means of achieving them. We use the term 'economic system' when we are studying the economy of a particular society in all the economic respects. The manner in which the processes of production, distribution, and consumption of food and other items of utility are managed in societies and cultures constitutes their economic system.

All societies have economic systems, whether or not these systems involve the use of money. All societies have customs and rules specifying access to natural resources and transforming or converting those resources by organized human effort (labour) into necessities and utilities. All of them have customs for distributing the goods and services thus produced.

Primitive Economy

The modern science of economics was developed to study and analyse economic systems where machine technology produces an abundance of goods, where the economic system is based on the use of money, and where the market is the prominent distribution mechanism. But for anthropologists, who have been studying other cultures since long, machine technology and market based economic systems constitute only one of the many ways that humans have devised for utilizing scarce means. There are a large number of people spread around the world whose economies are so immediate and technologies so simple that the problem of survival is paramount.

Modern Western economic system is different from others and has a special relationship between machine technology and pecuniary orientation. This relationship gives rise to certain institutions found in no other culture. Its unique focus of economic effort on production for profit has repercussions on all other aspects of life. In this economy, the organization of work and the allotment of resources are not concordant with kinship and community but rather are determined by the network of contracts fostered by industrialism. Market exchange or the sale of commodities at a price determined by the law of supply-and-demand was the basic fact around which this network of contract functions. In such a system, everything needed for the fulfilment of individual or social wants, like resources, work, and skills, all became the subjects of contracts.

In societies where social groups which are family or lineage based, where kinship rather than contract are granted the highest regard, and where land, work, resources, and ingenuity are institutionalized very differently, different concepts and exercises are required for their analysis. In these societies, the principles of economic and social organization are quite different. Markets, if it is present at all, are of only peripheral significance. Money, though widely used in them as special-purpose money, does not have the exclusive function of expressing value as the sole purpose, as money used in industrial economic systems does.

The substantive differences among these economies have been recorded by anthropologists and they consider them equally worthy of paying attention and systematic comprehension. Anthropologists have been using the term 'primitive economic systems' or simply as 'primitive economies' for them. They consider the exotic lives and thoughts of these people and their economic behaviour as different patterns of economic organizations worthy of serious attention. The word 'primitive' in the term 'primitive economy' simply indicates the basic level of technologies associated with these systems.

Until 1940, the descriptions and categorization of these societies on the basis of their economic pursuits constituted the subject matter of the study of primitive economies. It was since 1940 that the emergence of a specialized branch of study within social-cultural anthropology called 'Economic Anthropology' with theoretical intent and a 'broader perspective' that this term gradually started losing its significance.

Primitive Economic Systems

Several classifications of economic organizations have been made ever since Adam Smith talked about hunters, pastoralists, and cultivationists or agriculturists. In any human community, the first and most essential requirement is to feed itself. In some of the primitive societies, it is everybody's main preoccupation. Apart from food, the environment must also provide for shelter, clothing, and essential tools.

Technology is the aspect of culture which encompasses all the tools, artifacts, and techniques that a society uses to meet its material needs. The term can be usefully examined in terms of four basic categories:

a. Food getting or food procurement
b. Shelter
c. Manufacturing
d. Transport

The 18th century anthropologists and some later ones, ranked different categories of food procurement strategies in an evolutionary order of progress. Thus, food gatherers or hunters; herding and pastoralism; and horticulturist and agriculture were the categories of food getting and procurement. These strategies of food procurement constituted the basis for the different types of primitive economic systems. Environment was the common resource for all humans to procure food, the most basic of the basic necessities for survival.

Distribution and Exchange

The goods which are produced must reach the members and groups in a society before they are ultimately consumed. In most of the primitive societies, whatever is produced is all consumed. They also do not have many options to choose from in their consumption. Hence, unlike modern societies, we cannot talk about consumption patterns and consumer economies in the case of primitive economic systems. That is why these economic systems are categorized as production–consumption economies, while modern economic systems are called as production–consumption–and–surplus economies.

Exchange

The method by which goods and services reach the members and groups in a society is by means of economic exchange. Whatever is produced must reach all members and group. This requires a system of distribution and exchange of commodities and services.

In both simple and modern societies, people exchange a variety of items such as axes, secret spells, sheep, goats, and cattle or presents, gifts and so on. The study of such exchange systems has assumed prominence in modern anthropology. The most well-known and thoroughly studied example of the Kula ceremony, found off the coast of New Guinea, was meticulously analysed by Malinowski (1922). This society typifies many non-market exchange systems such as absence of haggling over exchange rates, uneconomic nature of commodities exchanged, and people gaining prestige by participation in these exchanges. There are a great variety of exchange mechanisms operating in different societies and they have been variously categorized.

Anthropological theories of exchange are equally varied as their ethnography. According to Mauss, the psychology of gift or present-giving originated in exchange as it entails the obligation to return and reciprocate. Malinowski viewed Kula as a kind of peace pact. Some exchange patterns, it is argued, serve to build up political following and thereby to secure territory and access to much-needed resources. These views express exchange as means for gaining personal utility or satisfaction.

According to another view, derived from Malinowski, Mauss and Levi-Strauss, exchange itself is an end as it establishes and mediates the distinction between self and others. According to this view, exchange is a fundamental condition of social life and is not reducible to the means for self-interest.

Some anthropologists have laid stress on the meaning which the participants themselves give or attribute to exchange avoiding Western debate on the subject. This perspective provides an altogether different form of explanation. It emphasizes on looking for cultural metaphors, which are foundations of exchange. In exotic contexts, it is an international act that has wider impact and effects.

According to Durkheim, exchange necessarily involves some degree of economic specialization. This means that in societies where all the people engage in similar economic activity and produce the same kind of goods, we cannot expect any kind of exchange between them. But in actual ethnographic experience, we find that even among the poorest-of-the poor living in societies at the technologically lowest level of existence, food is considered more than just something meant to be eaten. While eating is a biological, necessity feasting is not. Feasting is a social activity. Thus, to anthropologists, economic value is not the only significant attribute of goods. Goods produced have economic value in so far they serve the basic necessities of life. They are also significant and important in terms of their social value as they generate and sustain social relations.

Types of Exchange

A broad categorization of the exchange mechanisms operating in primitive economic systems can be those using some medium (money) for effecting an exchange and those where no such medium is used, that is, monetary and non-monetary exchanges. Market and trade are the only kinds of exchanges where some medium of exchange is used. There are a great variety of nonmonetary exchanges. Barter, gift exchange, ceremonial exchange and ritual exchange are the main types included in this broad categorization.

Barter Exchange

Direct give-and-take or exchange of commodities is termed as 'barter'. Very often, it is inter-tribal and not intra-tribal. It is based on traditionally accepted standardized equivalences. There is no bargaining. Barter can be considered as a non-monetary and most primitive form of trading. It is purely need based and does not generate any kind of social relationship.

Three types of barter exchange have been identified:
1. Face-to-face barter
2. Silent barter
3. Money barter

In face-to-face barter, two individuals or groups exchange their commodities in a face-to-face interaction.

In silent barter, the two neighbouring communities leave their goods at a specified location, expecting the other group to visit the place silently, take the goods lying there, and leave their own goods on some other specified spot for the first group to take them. Such barter is practiced among the Chukchi of Siberia and Alaskans.

In money-barter, a consumption good is used as the least common denominator of value. Rice-money among the Ifugao of Philippines is an example.

Gift Exchange

Gift giving involves exchange of goods between persons and is an essential element in every inter-personal, social relationship. It is just not a matter of economic consideration or value, though the practice of gift giving and the commodities exchanged do serve economic ends. Gift giving is not only for status assessment, though gift giving implies a claim to prestige as in Kwakiutl and Haida. Giving and receiving gifts means involving oneself in mutual indebtedness, thereby enhancing and reinforcing social cohesion and solidarity.

According to Mauss, three kinds of obligations are involved in gift giving. These are obligation to give, obligation to receive, and obligation to repay (counter gift). Whatever is given is not returned immediately. The giver becomes a loser, only to be a gainer at some other time.

All gift giving is based on an integrative principle of reciprocity. Where gift giving is the dominant form of exchange, its economic importance is obscured. The spirit, emotions, and social relationship between the givers is realized as important. Sometimes two neighbouring groups may indulge in mutual gift giving to purchase goodwill and maintain cordial relations.

Ceremonial Exchange

Many institutionalized exchanges are categorized as 'ceremonial exchanges'. They entail an element of religiosity or are in the form of ritualized gift giving. In traditional societies, the investment in gifts during ceremonial or ritual occasions appears to have no direct material benefit to the individual; rather, it can even cause indebtedness. Exchange of presents and feasts in wedding or funerary gifts in West Africa or gifts given to priests or religious functionaries are all included in this category of ceremonial exchange. The most widely described examples are Kula and Potlatch.

Kula

Kula is an extensive inter-tribal exchange in a ring of islands in the Trobriand Islands of New Guinea. It is basically a ceremonial exchange establishing trade relations among alien people residing in a group of islands spread over a large area in Pacific. Two kinds of articles are exchanged, each type moving in different direction. A 'soulavo' is a long necklace of red shells and moves in clockwise direction while 'mwali' bracelets of white shells move in an anti-clockwise direction. Every year, people from the kula ring of islands move out for Kula voyage on meticulously prepared boats loaded with the produce of their island and ceremoniously visit all the islands in the ring, one by one. They carry the gifts in accordance with the direction of their movement (clockwise or anti-clockwise). These voyages are treated as pilgrimages. Every participant has two kinds of partners – those from whom to receive bracelets and give necklaces and those from whom to receive necklaces and give bracelets.

These ornaments are non-commercial and non-utilitarian but are regarded of great prestige value. This exchange of ceremonial gifts or institutionalized exchange is non-economic but contains within itself an elaborate trading system among the Kula partners. Like all other ceremonial activities, it has an expressive aspect as participation in it is an indication of social status. It involves other activities as well such as canoe building. Though valuables themselves are not traded and have only institutionalized ceremonial significance, there is a lot of trading during Kula expeditions. Also, possession of Kula partners in foreign lands provides protection from the dangers of robbery. It builds a high degree of mutual trust and commercial honour among the partners. Kula is not done under stress or need as its aim is to exchange articles which are of no practical use.

Potlatch

The Potlatch of Kwakiutl Indians of the North-West coast of North America is another example of institutionalized ritualistic exchange. In Kwakiutl society, social ranking is a primary interest. Potlatches are feasts associated with ceremonial occasions such as marriage, birth, death, or house-building in which many kinds of wealth is distributed by the Chief to the people and to the Chiefs from other villages who are his guests. The number of guests present and the amount of goods given away or destroyed establishes the wealth and prestige of the host Chief. In a competitive Potlatch between two men competing for the same symbolic privilege, one of the rivals might destroy great quantities of property such as canoes and blankets and, in former times, even slaves. During these feasts, the host boasts about himself.

Thus, Potlatch involves an overt competition. It is a public demonstration of distribution and callous destruction of wealth, competitive spirit and prestige consciousness being the two principles. Feasting makes a common occasion to make such demonstration of one's capacity to give.

Among the Haidas, several types of Potlatch can be identified. There are, for example, funeral Potlatch, house building Potlatch, face saving Potlatch and vengeance Potlatch. Its institutionalized character makes it a form of ceremonial exchange.

Integrative Exchanges

'Who should get what?' is a question tackled differently in different societies and cultures. Men in religious or political hierarchy normally get preference over the others. All the factors of production must be integrated into a system so that the requirements of society can be dependably produced and allocated. In non-Western societies, production is simple but allocation usually very complex. This complexity of allocation does not lie much in quantity as in diversity of principles involved.

Karl Polayani, the economic historian, studied allocation cross-culturally without disrupting the science of economics and without becoming its slave. He initiated a theory of allocation and a classification of institutions of allocation that includes the market but is not limited by it. Polayani mentioned three basic models of allocation – reciprocity, redistribution, and market. Every empirical economy exhibits at least one of these three as the dominant principle of integration, although all the modes may be present in a particular society.

There are three basic types of societies – egalitarian societies, ranked societies and stratified societies. The economies of egalitarian societies are organized through reciprocity, those of ranked societies through redistribution, and those of stratified societies through market exchange.

Reciprocity

Reciprocity involves exchange of goods between people who are bound in non-market, non-hierarchical relations with one another. The exchange does not create the relationship, but is a part of the behaviour that gives it content. The most common systems of reciprocity are those based on kinship obligations.

Literally, reciprocity implies a principle of mutuality. It is a common mode of exchange of goods and services among people with very simple technologies. These are the systems of economics without any economic surplus. The social relations expressed by such economic transactions are friendship, kinship, or status relations. The reciprocal systems of exchange are usually predominant and more important as a mechanism for the movement of goods and services among people where relations are structurally symmetrical. They are typically either independent from or equal to one another in wealth, social status, and political power.

Marshal Sahlins has categorized three forms of reciprocity – generalized reciprocity, balanced reciprocity and negative reciprocity.

Generalized Reciprocity

It includes gift giving without any immediate or planned return. Rather, the giver may not even expect a return. Philanthropy is one outstanding example of this. All societies have some kind of generalized reciprocity which is not entrenched in altruism but in their awareness of social interdependence. Sharing a big game is also a form of generalized reciprocity. Sharing is more common when resources are unpredictable. Some foods may be shared more often as their availability is unpredictable. The degree of food sharing may increase during the periods of shortage and scarcity.

Balanced Reciprocity

All gifts received have an obligation to return. The exchange is generally motivated by a desire or need for certain objects. Such trade transactions between neighbouring groups may be crucial for survival.

Balanced reciprocity means willingness to give and also giving up hostility or self-interest for mutual benefit. It tends to generate cordiality, friendliness, and sociability. Formal friendship, group alliance, peace-making, and marriage transactions are different forms of balanced reciprocity. Kula exchange is an example of balanced reciprocity.

Negative Reciprocity

This is an attempt to take advantage of others to get something for nothing or for something less than its worth. The goods may be obtained by use of force or by compulsion. In such cases the two sides are totally opposed to each other. Material gain by one at the expense of the other is the only motive. It only generates discord and conflict.

Redistribution

Polayani defined redistribution as a systematic movement of goods towards an administrative centre and their re-allotment by the authorities at the centre.

In a society operating on redistribution, the structure of relationships between the participants is asymmetrical. Often some individuals or groups, generally in a minority, have more power than those who are in the majority. As a system of economic exchange, it is characteristic of societies with some systems of ranking and stratification but which are not organized for market exchange. There is also a marginal economic surplus. These are economies of marginal cultivationists and herders, and societies with a central source of authority, or some individuals or groups wielding greater power or greater say.

In this type of exchange, goods move towards an allocation centre upwards and move out again downwards. The process, in effect, provides legitimacy to the central authority and ensures cordial relations between the rulers and the ruled. It nurses harmony. Among the State organized modern societies, the tax systems is an example. In early civilizations, the Aztecs of Central America and the Mayas of Mexico in South America followed this system. In Polynesia and Africa, this system is common among chiefdoms.

All forms of social stratification require some sanction for their retention and continuity. These mechanisms may be social, political, theological or economic.

Redistribution mechanism appear in a society with a ranking system created by economic surplus. Hence, an economic device is needed to sustain it.

Reciprocity and Redistribution Compared

As dominant integrative principles of exchange of non-market societies, reciprocity and redistribution can be fruitfully compared. The two are not opposed to each other. Both of them may co-exist, with one of them being predominant. Both are characteristic of non-market economic systems.

Reciprocity requires only two sides, one which gives and the other which receives. It is horizontal in character. Redistribution requires a social centre. It is characteristic of groups with an authority centre, such as a chief or a king.

Redistribution may be a matter of law, custom, or a special decision. In most hunting–gathering societies, a central authority needed to redistribute the goods is lacking, so reciprocity is more likely to occur. Also, the phenomenon of redistribution requires a marginally surplus economy. It is from this surplus that people pay tributes to the centralized authority. Hence, it is associated with production systems which are able to create economic surplus. Potlatch, among the Kwakiutl Indians of the northern Pacific coast in America is a good example of redistribution, though its purpose is to proclaim and confirm a particular status. Also, the difference is that among Kwakiutls, it is an expression of competitive spirit while redistribution promotes and has its basis in the spirit of cooperation. In redistribution, people willingly part with their meagre economic surplus to pay tributes to the designated authority for the maintenance of peaceful surroundings by their rulers, which enables them to carry on their economic activities. There is no element of coercion. Those in authority redistribute the wealth collected by them. In doing so, everybody is not the recipient of the payback every time. The authority uses its discretion to decide who shall be the beneficiaries of redistribution. This right of exercising this discretion and the willing acceptance of the people establishes the legitimacy of the authority. This implies a democratic intent rather than a coercive feudalistic system.

Thus, from the total egalitarianism of hunting–gathering non-surplus economics, to the development of a weak administrative centre as a consequence of marginal economic surplus, these societies were not mature enough to behave like centralized authority of stratified social systems as they needed a redistributive allocative system to maintain them.

In societies where all people engage themselves in food production activities and produce for themselves, the only way movement of goods in exchange is possible has to be horizontal in character and exchanges need to have their basis in assistance and mutual benefit. The reverse movement of goods and materials takes place between parties of equivalent status. In redistribution, the flow of goods is always vertical, both ways.

Market Exchange

The term 'market' can be used in a wide variety of settings, from a physical location to an intangible set of transactions such as those associated with currency exchange. However, all markets share the same basic characteristic that they are a medium for exchange between buyers and sellers, where transactions between the two parties can be conducted to the satisfaction of both. The concept of mutually satisfying exchange, as suggested by this definition, lies at the heart of the transactions that take place in the market.

There are several different views of markets depending upon the perspective chosen. To early economists, a market was determined in terms of a balance between supply and demand; the result of market transactions was a price, which was agreed between the buyer and supplier.

As a result of technological innovations, this situation has changed in many markets. The concept of buyer and seller meeting as partners to exchange led to the question of buyer and seller relationship predominating in the concept of market. It was held that since the interests of both clashed, the concept of market was visualized as an arena of competition between the buyer and seller and between the sellers themselves to attract the buyers. But subsequently there was a tilt towards the other extreme, that despite the opposing interests of sellers who are interested in extracting more profit and buyers in saving their hard-earned resources, the two constitute a co-operative community in market activity.

Most primitive economic systems do not have markets as medium for exchange. Karl Polayam has talked about the market system of exchange owing its emergence to a particular level of technology where resources and techniques of production were able to generate economic surplus supporting bigger groups, larger in size and able to expand still further. He also associates markets with economic specialization, proliferation of craftsmanship, and enlarged scale and complexity of the society.

According to Polayari, as a consequence of these changes, primarily brought about by technological advancement, a new mechanism was developed, known as 'market and trade' whereby goods produced reach the expanded contours of the society. In this process, exchange assumes great importance.

The market system is essentially a money-based system. A market exists where an economy has developed to a point where food items are in surplus and also where craft and labour specialities can offer what a lay person cannot do.

Tribal Markets

Tribal markets refer to the actual physical sites where goods change hands through sale and purchase; this buying and selling is not always done through money as the medium of exchange. In tribal markets, wherever money is used, it is special purpose money. Reciprocity, redistribution, and barter predominate tribal markets. Goods bought and sold are not always locally produced food articles or other products – products not a produced locally are also transacted. There is a strong social undercurrent that passes through tribal markets which serves the purpose of fulfilling the social obligations, maintaining contacts with people, and developing new relationships. The exchange of goods is the economic feature behind which social relationships are attempted to be maintained. Buyers and sellers constitute a cooperating community in the market activity. Tribal market, being periodical or intermittent in nature, is a sporadic phenomenon.

Market systems are widespread among peasants. In American tribes they are free, open, and self-regulating. In Myanmar (earlier Burma), among the Shans, there is a system of rotating markets with central markets and several subsidiary markets. In several parts of Africa, there are markets lacking investment in expensive facilities. In New Guinea (Salisbury), there are different kinds of exchange of goods. Each kind is limited to its particular circuits. One category of goods exchanged are subsistence items, others are only luxury items, and still others are items conferring status and prestige.

Money

When market exchanges work with money, price become the basic process in organizing an economy and the price setting mechanism is characterized by bargaining behaviour.

The market exchange concept is inevitably tied to the concept of money, which in itself is quite impersonal in character. Money becomes a commercial commodity. Among the small-scale communities, money may have social, moral, or even emotional connotations.

According to economists, money can be used for three or more purposes. It allows exchange of goods and services in varying quantities. Moneyless exchange of commodities is called barter.

Money is also used as a standard of value. Every exchangeable commodity in the modern economic system is given a money value.

Money is also used as a means of payment. In modern Western societies, a single concept of money, with its numerous material manifestations (notes, coins, cheques, drafts, and so on), perform all the functions. In other cultures, different material items are used to functionally distinguish money. The modern Western money which performs all the functions with a single set of cultural items is called 'general purpose money'. Any cultural item which performs one or two functions but not all the three is called 'special purpose money'.

In economies lacking general purpose money, the commodities valued and exchanged are separated into self-contained categories.

Trade and Markets

Trade involves buying and selling of commodities. It implies continuity of relations even after the transaction is over, a common affair in peasant societies. Barter may be treated as a form of primitive trade where transactions do not permit any continuity of relations between the two sides.

Anthropologists and sociologists usually analyse market and trade transactions quite differently from economists. For economists, trade and markets are a way of distributing goods through a pricing mechanism so that individual preferences may be satisfied. For anthropologists, trade and markets provide an index or mirror of social organization. Anthropologists try to know how people organize and conceive of trade and markets and how these are linked to the other activities in the society. Generally, trade reflects the technological condition of a society. In non-complex societies, the traded goods are usually small, durable, and portable, while the velocity of trade is very low.

Anthropologists have distinguished several patterns of trade, such as silent trade (described earlier as silent barter); ports of trade – found near east African coast, where permanent market centres are located in neutral zones to promote intergroup trade; institutionalized trade – it has a variety of non-market transactions encompassing extensive trade network; and market trade – found in societies of most diverse types.

According to Polayani, historically, trading represents the development stage of the civilization, with market and money being its important elements. Emergence of trading involves proliferation of specialized craftsmanship, break-up of localism – development of roads and transport systems, and permanently organized markets. Transport and communication are the main factors in the development of trading activities. All trade is characterized by the impersonal character of economic relations and their association with regulatory mechanisms.

However, Polayani distinguished between primitive trade and civilized trade. According to him, primitive trade is characterized by the exchange of utilitarian articles without much regulations or intricate rules. It is not associated with any type of accountancy system as it operates non-literate societies. Most of the transactions are verbal. Price is usually not a basis of transactions. It is characteristic of peripheral and irregular markets.

On the other hand, in civilized trade, commodities are specially produced for trading. There are intricate regulatory mechanisms. Civilized trade is associated with urban centres, literate populations, and developed accounting system. Trade in civilized societies becomes an instrument of inter-regional and inter-national relations.

Anthropologists have stressed the characteristic of continuity of trade relations or trading partnerships. Trading partnership is a lifelong affair. It can be asymmetrical when partners are of unequal socio-economic or ethnic status, or symmetrical. Having a trading partner is an intra-community feature. Inter-community trading is represented by gift trade, administered trade, and market trade.

Market as a Social Institution

For anthropologists and sociologists, a market is not only a place of interaction between the buyers and sellers or between producers and consumers with regard to goods and services, but a market may also be looked at as a social institution which is constructed in culturally specific ways.

Sociologists want to study economic institutions in a larger social environment unlike economists who usually study the functioning of the economy, independent of the social context. They are of the view that markets are organized by social groups or classes and that markets are also influenced by other social institutions such as family and kinship. This sociological idea is often expressed by the statement that economies are socially embedded. Perhaps, the tribal market is the best example of this statement. Not being regularly held and usually a weekly event or held on festivals or special occasions and known in many parts of India as 'haat', it is a meeting place for the local population. It serves a variety of purposes. People assemble here not only for barter or exchange or any other economic transaction, but also for social interactions, to meet relatives and friends, for marriage negotiations, gossip, and so on. They discuss their mutual problems and explore the possible solutions. The market also serves to strengthen the ethnic bonds. Several of these functions are also held also in non-tribal markets and hence this kind of market may be understood as a social institution.

Property

The notion of property is closely associated with ownership, which is deemed to be exclusive. Ownership means the right to use or destroy or sell certain material effects which may be land, house, cattle and livestock, tools and weapons, and so on. A slightly modified view lays stress on material aspects rather than on ownership aspects. According to this view, property consists of those things, material or otherwise, over which persons have rights. Ownership is transferable either by inheritance or sale or gift.

The ownership of property is called private or incorporeal when its right to use or enjoy is exclusive and absolute. In many simple societies, there are complicated shared rights over land, livestock, and other material objects and, at times, also over non-material objects such as magical spells and knowledge of rituals. The term 'corporate property' refers to the vesting of ownership in a body of people considered as a single entity, having a corporate personality in a legal sense.

In simple, small-scale societies, the notion of property is closely related to the display and expenditure of wealth rather than its accumulation. The 'big men' of Melanesian societies gain prestige and social status by throwing mass scale feasts by slaughtering a large number of pigs, accumulated over time. This display of generosity (also known as 'levelling mechanism') is an expenditure of accumulated wealth. Similarly, the Naga chiefs excel in giving feasts for acquisition of the prestigious role of chieftainship.

As indicated by Lowie, conceptions of property have always been changing in accordance with the development of technology. We cannot employ modern conception of property to primitive societies. Among food gathering and hunting tribes, we cannot speak of any kind of property in the absence of any economic surplus. The herders cannot be the owners of land. Thus, in primitive societies, instead of accumulation of only material, property consists of certain privileges which may include the privilege to distribute and destroy.

Common sharing of property has many instances in primitive societies. Very often economic resources like land, livestock, and pastures are shared jointly. There is a unique instance of multiple possessory rights among some of the societies in New Zealand, Melanesia, and West Africa where several persons use the same thing for different purposes. On a piece of land, for instance, a person can own the trees growing on the land which is cultivated by another person. Whatever the form of property may be, two things are common to this notion – firstly, it is always subject to certain rules of inheritance. Secondly, the rights to use are transferable by inheritance or sale or gift.

In collective or communal ownership of property as owned by a joint family or a lineage group, the right to use remains vested in the group as the group is regularly replenished by fresh recruitment and it never ceases to exist. In hunting-gathering groups, all the members constituting a group have equal access to the economic resources. This situation is sometimes called a state of 'primitive communism' where the idea of ownership and any concept of property does not exist. These societies, therefore, are also called 'egalitarian societies'.

Peasant Economy

Before talking about peasant economy, it will be fruitful to know as to who are peasants. This is a term which has been used to refer to a social type and also as an adjective for certain features of various rural productive systems.

In contemporary social sciences, the usage of this term is derived from the Eastern European experience in late 19th and early 20th century, according to which 'peasants' are defined as people who organize production almost exclusively on the basis of unpaid labour in a nuclear family or a close kinship group. They either produce only for their own consumption or sell some of their product in the market solely in order to meet their culturally-defined consumption requirements. This assumes that they are almost self-sufficient in production and consumption.

As producers mainly for the subsistence of the household, they are distinguished from other kinds of cultivators due to their participation in larger social and political entities such as the State. The horticulturists produce for the subsistence of the local group and are the owners of the land which they cultivate. But peasants have little control over the land they use for cultivation though they produce to support non-producing populations.

The characteristic of a peasant economy is that a part of its agricultural production is taken away by a politically dominant and non-food producing class. The peasant must pay for the use of land either in cash, or a percentage of harvest or the donate agricultural labour to the landowner or as a tribute to the State.

As modern peasants are required to pay for their own seeds, tools, and animals, they must participate in market economies over which they have no control. In modern agricultural practice, the use of costly chemical fertilizers has added to their burden. They are thus distinguished from modern farmers and primitive horticulturists. Their identity as a social type, though ambiguous, has its basis mainly in their more distinctly defined economic category. Some of the peasants in contemporary societies have taken to cash crops. In Maharashtra, the potato, onion, and grape cultivating peasantry and the sugarcane producers of the sweet belt have taken big strides and have directly or indirectly involved themselves in world markets. In growing cash crops, they tend to maximize their profits. Their culturally defined consumption patterns have changed. They have acquired considerable leverage in the power game of the state politics.

Technology

Anthropologists have often been accused of confusing technology with economy. This is because in the past technology has formed as the basis of classification of economies by anthropologists. The earlier anthropologists found technology as a more convincing index in terms of basic techniques of food procurements or getting subsistence. They categorized five basic forms of technology and thought them to be the same as five basic forms of economy. This was more so because the 19th century anthropologists, much interested in the study of social–cultural evolution and influenced by the idea of progress, found the realm of technology as the most suitable for depicting progressive development of economies. Morgan's contemplation of the cultural history of humankind in a progressive order of savagery, barbarism, and civilization, was based mainly on technological parameters with social and cultural concomitants.

Technology is an aspect of culture and has its basis in the conception of humans as homo faber. It has its origin in the thinking and problem-solving ability of the developed human brain. Through human dexterity, it finds expression in the form of tools, weapons, implements, and many such objects made and used as devices to produce foodstuff, shelter, and clothing necessary for survival. The tools, weapons, implements and all the cultural devices are categorized as 'material culture' as their manufacturing requires the use of some material (maybe stone, wood, bone, or metal) and constitute the products of material culture. Technology is the only aspect of culture susceptible to objective evaluation.

The traditional matters of interest to anthropologists investigating the general aspects of primitive economy largely centred around the study of technological processes, that is, the description of the technical devices used in the economy, how the material used in the technological devices is obtained as well as the different categories of tools, implements, and weapons manufactured. These technological aspects of economic living led them to construct techno-economic levels of an economy. In this manner, the study of technology moved along with the study of economy. Today, anthropologists are very clear that technology is a broad aspect of any culture and is associated with economy. In primitive societies it is more so.

Division of Labour

No man or woman can live for themselves alone, especially in the arduous conditions of many primitive societies. The bonds of economic co-operation form the foundation of social life. This reflection has led social anthropologists to analyse different ways in which people tend to co-operate with one another in their day-to-day lives.

This type of analysis was first undertaken systematically by Durkheim in his famous book, The Division of Labour in Society. His primary concern was sociological rather than economic.

Marxists start with the assumption that humans are material makers and that they produce things of value only through labour. The organization of this capacity provides the base for the super-structural parts of social life. In this view, a relation exists between modes of exploiting labour and other sectors of society such as religion, ideology, and kinship. In his view, the primary concern is economic.

Durkheim was interested in knowing the forces binding communities or the bonds of social cohesion. He came out with a thesis that social cohesion could be sustained in two ways. Firstly, through mechanical solidarity – a state of affairs in which all or most of the members of the co-operative group (whether hunters or cultivationists) follow the same rules. Conformity to a common set of rules is the paramount value. This conformity is achieved through the fear of punishment (secular or supernatural).

Secondly, through organic solidarity – a more civilized type of co-operation. Here the bonds lie not in conformity to rules, but rather in individual or group specialization – some people producing one kind of goods, others producing different kinds. These goods are often reciprocally exchanged so that like the constituent organs of an organism, everyone is dependent on one another. This joint activity contributes to the smooth running of the whole community. Repressive sanctions tend to be replaced by restitutive ones. The fulfilment of contractual obligations and not conformity to the rules becomes the binding force.

There are several factors upon which different kinds of tasks may be allotted to different kinds of people. Four criteria are particularly important. They are sex, age, ascribed status, and aptitude for a special skill. The physiological difference between sex and age are almost universal in character as they involve physiological distinctions. But other factors are socially and culturally determined as they vary from society to society. In many cultures, including those of Western societies, class distinctions affect the kinds of occupations in which a person may engage. The caste system of India is also based on ascribed status.

There are many societies whose technologies call for a division of labour among craftsmen working as iron smelters, wood carvers, or canoe builders and women engaged in pottery, basketry, weaving, and so on. However, these people do other things too. In modern economic systems, specialization of labour has been carried so far that the identification of a particular individual with a product is not possible.

Production Relations

This refers to the relationship between people in the process of production as any productive process involves relationships between those involved in the process. Production is not possible otherwise because humans cannot produce outside of a social structure, whether it is a nation or a family.

Production relations may be described as those relations that people form with one another in order to fulfil their material needs. Marx believed that different forces of production lead to different relations of production. Marx and Engels used the term to refer to the socio-economic relationships and meant the sum total of social relationships that people must enter into in order to survive, to produce, and to reproduce their means of life, for example, a capitalist's exclusive relationship with a capital good, and a wage worker's consequent relationship with the capitalist; in the pre-capitalist era, a feudal lord's relationship with the fief or a serf's relationship with the lord; a slave master's relationship with the slaves; and so on.

'Mode of production' is a central concept in the Marxist analysis. This is understood as the way a society is organized to produce goods and services. Mode of production has two major aspects:

- Forces of production
- Relations of production

'Forces of production' or productive forces include manpower or human labour power. It also includes means of production, that is, tools, productive machinery, infrastructure, technical knowledge, materials, plants, animals, and land. 'Relations of production', that is, social and technical relations of production, include property, power and those controlling productive assets and relations between social classes.

Allan G. Johnson in *The Blackwell Dictionary of Sociology* (1995) writes, 'Since production is a social activity, any mode of production must also include a set of social relationships – the relations of production through which the forces of production are used and decisions are made about what to do with the results. Karl Marx's own conception revolved around the key idea that people produce not only 'linen and flax' but in so doing also produce definite social relations. The social relations of production are the basis of the Marxist analysis of society.

Production Relations in Indian Agriculture

In the light of this understanding, let us examine the changing modes of production in Indian agriculture.

Let us look at the caste-based system of production represented by the jajmani system. In the traditional caste system, land ownership was vested in higher castes only. This system of production developed an elaborate system of exchange of goods and services. The landed higher castes were called 'jajman' (patron). The service providers, who practised specialized occupations and belonged to lower castes, such as carpenters, barbers, blacksmiths, oilseed pressers, landless untouchable castes, poor Muslims, and so on, were called 'prajan' or 'kamin' or by some other names as per regional languages. The landless service castes provided their services and in exchange received a share in the harvest. The jajmani relations were permanent and hereditary in nature. In the post-Independence period the, zamindari and jagirdari systems were abolished by the Indian State. With this, the jajmani system also declined.

A number of traditionally landless castes received the land recovered from the erstwhile zamindars and jagirdars. With the advent of democracy and adult franchise, some leaders mobilized the untouchables and backward castes politically and the entire gamut of relationships in the production system underwent a drastic change in most parts of the country. In many regions, technological innovations such as the safety razor and hand pumps freed castes such as barbers and bhishtis (water-carriers) from jajmani obligation. With the introduction of new tools and mechanized agriculture, manual labour did not remain the only input in agriculture. This altered the very nature of relationship between the land holders and agricultural labour. With the increasing avenues of transport and communication, rural to urban migration increased manifold. Those who remained in many villages were either landless or had small and unproductive land holding. They insisted and got wages in cash. So agriculture labour became a cash-based wage transaction and that is how mode of production in Indian agriculture changed.

Work, Organization of Work, Work and Technology

The sociology of work goes back to the classical theorists in sociology, Marx, Weber, and Durkheim, who considered the study of work to be central to the field of sociology.

In sociology, work is anything that a person undertakes with the goal being productive in a way that meets any human need. It includes both the physical as well as mental work that does not necessarily involve any remuneration. An occupation is a type of work which is performed for the purpose of monetary gain. For individuals, work gives an identity, even a defining identity. Work gives a person a sense of pride and self-satisfaction that he or she is not financially dependent on anyone.

Work, Technology, and Society

Since the human society moved away from a food gathering–hunting economy to an industrialized economy, the relationship between technology and work has changed radically. Technology has been impacting work structures in different ways.

Though the relationship between work, technology, and society has been interpreted by a number of sociologists and anthropologists, the discussion still revolves around the scholarship of Marx who studied the emergence of industrial work under the influence of mechanical engineering. Marx understood technology as a productive force. Later, after internet was introduced, work structures changed drastically.

Today, technology is being used by the human society to explore, connect, study, and to do work. The beneficial and detrimental effects of technology depend on the way we use it and the goal we aspire to achieve. Some of the important effects of technology on the society are:

- Easy accessibility of information through technology has changed the way people think and behave. Internet has revolutionized the human society and any information can be transmitted to any part of the world in seconds, though this has its own hazards because of its potential for misuse.

- Technological aids have radically improved the learning process.

- Advancement in agricultural technology has facilitated 'green revolution' in many parts of the world including India and liberated many populations from starvation. This had a profound impact on human societies.

- In several developing countries, increased use of modern technology has caused unemployment among traditional workers, thought it has increased employment avenues for higher skilled workers. Automation is like a double-edged sword.

- Technology is also responsible for increasing air and water pollution, creating serious threats to our environment and the health of the society. Decreased physical activity is also causing health problems like obesity, depression, and several lifestyle diseases.

The developed countries are passing through an unprecedented transformation in all aspects of social, cultural, and economic life. Questions surrounding the relationship between work and technology remain as vital and relevant as ever.

Formal and Informal Economy

As contrasted with the informal economy, the part of an economy of which the government is fully aware and which is regulated by government authorities, particularly in the areas of contract and company law, taxation, and labour law, is known is 'formal economy'.

The formal economy:

1. Has an organized system of employment with clear written rules of recruitment, agreement, and job responsibilities.

2. Has a standardized relationship between the employer and the employee which is maintained through a formal contract.

Formal economy may also be described as a portion of a nation's economy which includes businesses that are formally registered, taxed, licensed, and regulated.

Informal economy, as contrasted to formal economy, is often described as 'informal sector' and sometime even 'grey economy'. It is that part of any economy which is, in most of the cases, neither taxed nor monitored by any government agency. In most of the developing countries, the informal sector makes up a substantial portion of the economy.

The term 'informal sector' is said to have been coined by Hart (1971) in a study of Ghana to describe urban employment outside the organized labour market. Tabour class working in the informal sector was described as 'unorganized labour'.

The informal sector includes a great diversity of occupations characterized by self-employment. In a developing country like India, small shopkeepers, vendors, rag-pickers, washermen, fruit and vegetable sellers, and so on constitute the informal economy. A majority of population earns its livelihood while working in the informal sectors. They are poor and lack security, both legally and economically. During the Covid pandemic of 2020, the worst hit were those earning their livelihood in the informal economy. In most of the cases these workers are not organized through trade unions and are vulnerable to all sorts of harassment and exploitation by the police, local musclemen, and a host of other agencies. In many cases they carry a stigma because of their occupations and described by the law-enforcing agencies as troublemakers.

The informal sector is very important to the economically vulnerable sections of the society because it provides critical economic opportunities for the poor. When the economically marginalized sections of the rural society migrate to the city, they are easily absorbed into it and their earnings increase.

Economy in Capitalism and Socialism

Besides being economic systems, capitalism and socialism are also political ideologies with social–cultural ramifications. They also influence social institutions and a web of relationships in the respective societies. A capitalist economy may be understood through the following points:
- Private entities control the factors of production such as capital goods, natural resources, and labour.

- Market forces are supreme and they decide everything. The production and consumption of goods and services depend on demand-and-supply.
- The economic activity is based on individual initiative.
- The government plays minimal role in the production process.
- The transactions are based on free market economy with hardly any State control.
- The main motive in this economy is to earn maximum profit even if it is at the cost of the weaker sections of the society.
- The society is characterized by gross inequality of income of individuals.
- The private sector dominates the production of goods and services and distribution.
- The price of goods and services is largely determined by the forces of demand-and-supply.

Contrasted with the capitalist economy, a socialist economy looks more humane as the market forces are not allowed to play with the interests of people. Here, the government is the main player. The following are the salient features of a socialist economy:

- The government controls production of capital goods and natural resources.
- The government has a complete control over the factors of production.
- The main motive of this economy is not profit but welfare of the people.
- The prices of essential commodities are controlled by the government.
- The private sector plays a limited role in the production and distribution of goods and services.
- Inequality of income is kept to the minimal.
- The government controls every sector and there is hardly any competition between commercial entities.

Several countries in the world, including India, have been following what is popularly called a 'mixed economy', with both public and private sector playing their roles. With the disintegration of the Soviet Union and the East European socialist countries moving away from socialism, China and Cuba are the only countries following socialist economy. Even China is described as a country following the principle – socialist at home, capitalist abroad.

Critical Thinking Questions

- How do technology and environment influence strategies for procuring food?

- How does culture shape the value and meaning of money?

- Why is gift exchange such an important part of all societies?

****

8

Political Organization

Chapter Outline: *Meaning and concept of political organization; Concept of power and authority; Forms of social distribution of power: Marxist, Elitist,and Pluralist; Locus of authority; Systems of authority: Unicentric authority system,multicentric authority system;Kin based segmentary societies; non-kin based organizations; village councils;Centralised authority system; State and stateless societies;Primtive states;Chiefdoms and kingdoms; Leadership;Elements of democracy in primitive societies;The forms and functions of government;Primitive governments;Concept of law, law and justice in primitive societies;Sanctions of primitive law;Justice;legitimacy and the state; Civil society.*

Learning Objectives

- What are the different types of political organizations?
- What are state and stateless societies?
- What are the elements of democracy in simple and complex societies?
- What constitutes a civil society?

Meaning and Concept of Political Organization

All societies, if they are to remain viable over time, must maintain social order. Hence every society has to develop a set of procedures for making and enforcing decisions. It must also develop some mechanisms for resolving disputes and regulating the behaviour of its members.

A political organization is about power. The salient characteristics of a political organization are:

- It focuses on power – what it is, who has it and 'how it is related to other cultural patterns and social institutions in a society' (Nanda and Warms, 2009).

- It refers to the way in which power is distributed in a society. This is to control people's behaviour and maintain social order
- It acknowledges that all societies are organized politically but formal mechanisms vary from society to society.
- It explains how societies deal with disruptive and destructive behaviour of their members.

Maintaining a coherent social life is a prerequisite of every society.

'There could be no coherent social life unless the social relationships which bind the people together were at least to some degree orderly, institutionalized and predictable. The only alternative to power is chaos. To maintain an orderly system of social relations, people have to be subjected to some degree of compulsion; they cannot, all the time, do exactly as they like' (John Beattie, 1964).

All interpersonal relations are broadly categorized as 'social organization' or sometimes referred as 'social system'. But this concept of 'social organization' is a very generalized one. Interpersonal relations exist and persist in a number of specific contexts. One such specific context is called 'political' in which:

1. Efforts are made to set up territorial limits of a community and the mechanism adopted to protect it from internal disintegration and dissensions and also from the evil designs of similarly organized outsiders or others.
2. The word also refers to the activities which are directed to and meant for the group or the community as a whole.
3. It also concerns the distribution of rights and privileges among the members of the group.

All such activities, behaviours, procedures, and mechanisms are recognized as 'political'.

The term 'political organization' thus refers to a kind of a social organization. It is a sub-system of a social organization and defined as a system of regulation of relations between groups or the members of different groups within a society and between other such societies.

A political organization may be defined as that part of a culture which functions explicitly to direct activities of the members of a society towards community goals or public affairs.

All the objectives mentioned so far assume making of certain decisions and their compliance where power is implicit. All politics is concerned with power. It is power game or a struggle for power. But unbridled use of power is anarchy. For the maintenance of the internal order and external peace, certain checks, controls, rules, and norms must be evolved regarding the modes of use of power. According to Harold Lasswell, the knowledge about who controls whom and what, how, and by what right, is crucial to an understanding of a political system.

All human societies must coordinate and regulate the behaviour of their members by mechanisms of making and enforcing decisions. There are two ways in which societies organize and regulate themselves. One is called a political organization – the structured ways in which legitimate power or authority is used to co-ordinate and regulate behaviour. The other is law – including the enforcement mechanisms of the decisions made.

In most societies, the authority to make decisions that affect public interest is placed or located in some part of the social system such as kinship, economy, or religion, such as persons holding the positions as heads of families, lineages or clans. Rulers may also base their claim on divine ancestry. At times, the supernatural intervention may be an important aspect of the decision-making process. In such societies, persons having access to supernatural power have important political roles.

Concept of Power and Authority

Power is an aspect of social relationship. An individual or a group does not hold power in isolation; they have it in relation to others. Power is, therefore, power over others. According to Max Weber, 'Power is the chance of a man or a number of men to realize their own will in a communal action even against the resistance of others who are participating in the action.'

All politics is about power. Politics occurs when there are differentials in power. Any social relationship which involves power differentials is political. Bertrand Russell defined power as the ability to compel forcefully the behaviour of others. In a society, power is widely distributed. Each person in the capacity of performing various roles, wields some power.

The concept of power involves influence, authority and coercive control.

Influence is a form of power which entails the provision of models or ideals. Coercive control, through commands, is believed to be enforceable by sanctions such as withholding of rewards (or economic gains) or desired conditions and various other control measures.

Authority is the kind of power which orders and articulates the actions of others through commands which are effective because those who are commanded regard the commands as legitimate. It differs from coercive control. Coercive control elicits conformity with its commands through its capacity to reward or punish. In practice, authority and coercive control exist together in many combinations.

Authority is, by definition, legitimate. The legitimacy of authority is ultimately a matter of belief concerning the rightfulness of the institutional system through which authority is exercised.

Max Weber has distinguished three types of legitimate authority:

- Traditional authority
- Legal–rational authority
- Charismatic authority

Authority is the socially approved ability to orient the behaviour of others. Legitimacy is the essence of authority. Power and authority are both universal. While power is a purely physical concept, authority is a socio-legal or jural concept. Yet, power without authority can serve only a limited purpose; authority without power can achieve nothing.

Power is often looked upon as illegitimate by those over whom it is enforced. It is regarded as a coercive control rather than a legitimate authority. Authority can also lose its legitimacy when it becomes ineffective in the maintenance of order and a fair distribution of roles, rewards, and so on.

There is one more revealing distinction between power and authority. While power is exercised by many over the few, authority is exercised by few over the many.

Forms of Social Distribution of Power: Marxist, Elitist, Pluralist

Three different power models help us to understand societal and political power.

Power elite model or elitist model says that there exists a small group of very powerful people who make just about all of the important decisions in the State or society. This power elite join hands with those through whom they control levers of power. They may come into power through democratic means.

Pluralist model states that power is distributed among several groups. These groups may be a coalition of likeminded people, unions, professionals, and lobbyists – mainly business lobbyists.

The Marxists form of distribution of power takes an entirely different view. The Marxist sociology asserts that power should be regarded as structural relationship existing independently of the will of the individual. In this context power has the following features:

- Power cannot be separated from economic and class relations.
- It involves class struggle and not simply conflicts between individuals'
- The analysis of power cannot be undertaken without some characterization of the mode of production.

Locus of Authority

As authority is exercised by a few over many. Who these 'few' are in different societies becomes a relevant question. These are the persons (or person) or groups in whom the authority is vested and they constitute the 'locus of authority'. In some societies, authority may be concentrated in the hands of a small minority, in others it may be widely distributed throughout the society. In every society, the demographic and socio-economic factors become the basis for the determination of the locus of authority.

Systems of Authority

Varying situations occur in different societies regarding locus and functioning of the legitimate authority. According to Radcliff Brown, 'Political Organization is concerned with the maintenance of social order within a territorial framework by the organized exercise of coercive authority through the use of physical force.' This definition employs two different criterion. First, a reference is made to the end to which political activity is directed. Second, the means by which it is achieved are brought in, that is, the organized exercise of authority backed by force. Social anthropologists have been able to create typologies of increasing precision by employing three kinds of criterion:

Firstly, the degree of centralization of authority: Social anthropologists inquire whether there is some central authority that is acknowledged by all the component groups in the society. Or, there may not be a head of the society where the society consists of a number of distinct groups or segments and the relations between them itself make up the political system.

Secondly, the degree to which political function is specialized: That is, is there a person or are there persons vested with specific authority, with right to issue commands in a certain territory, backed by threat of using physical force?

Thirdly, the basis of allocation of political authority: That is, whether the system is hereditary or dynastic or elective or some combination of them.

It is seen that except for the first criterion, the other two do not permit any rigid classification. In the category of politically non-centralized societies, four types of political systems exist:

1. Simple food gathering and hunting communities: The social units are the co-operating group consisting of families of closed kins. They have no formal groups of any kind. There is one leader in whom all authority is vested. Authority has very limited scope in these societies.
2. Societies comprising separate village communities: Each village has a village council of a few elders who work as political functionaries.
3. Societies having age-sets: All political functions are performed by different age-sets. Each-age set has a leader or a manager to look after the functioning of the age-sets.
4. The societies in which political functions are performed through groups organized as unilineal descent groups which function as corporate groups.

On this basis, Evans Pritchard and Fortes have talked about three kinds of authority systems which are also associated with different socio-economic characteristics and techno–environmental adaptation. They have named these authority systems as unicentric, multicentric, and centralized authority systems.

Unicentric Authority Systems

This type of authority system is characteristic of food gatherers and wanderers consisting of small, mobile, nomadic groups known as 'bands'. The size of the population of these bands is very small, ranging from 30 to 50 persons. In very rare cases, the group may exceed 100 when they are inhabiting a comparatively richer hinterland. Each band consists of two or three related, extended families. All the members of the band are kins.

Their political relations equate kinship relationships, that is, their political system and kinship organization get fused together. They choose their head from the elderly persons in the group. The head is considered most knowledgeable, experienced, and a person with qualities of head-and-heart, appreciated by all. But the head is for namesake; though authorized by tradition to take decisions, all decisions are taken by consensus.

Since they do not own property nor have non-kins in their group, there are hardly any disputes. Only occasional sex rivalry may give rise to some disputes which are collectively settled by the pressure of public opinion, which is very effective in such small groups of related persons. However, customs provide the strongest basis for the settlement of any dispute or the resolution of any problem regarding their movement and resources. These bands have their traditionally-defined territories and sometimes they may encroach on the territories of others. But such encroachments never lead to any fighting because they are cautious due to their small numbers and also because most of the bands are related by the bonds of marriage. Bands are exogamous groups. Bushman of Kalahari desert in Africa, the Semangs of Malaya, the Eskimos of Siberia, and the Kadars of South India are some of the tribes who belong to this category.

Multicentric Authority Systems

These are the political systems where authority is not located at one point as in the heads of bands, but it is differentiated and diffused at many points. There are three different patterns of political systems existing in this category: (a) People having segmented social structure, (b) A tribe divided into villages and each village functioning as an independent polity through a constituted village council, and (c) A society divided into various age-sets and each age-set performing traditionally allocated political functions.

The first one of segmentary societies is a kinship-based multicentric authority system while the other two types are non-kin multicentric authority systems.

Kin Based Segmentary Societies

Societies divided into clans and lineages, and bigger lineages being segmented into smaller lineages, all being uni-linear descent groups, are called societies with segmented social structure.

In these societies, all these groups (clan lineages and sub-lineages) have heads who command and exercise authority within the limited sphere of their groups. There is no overall authority in a commanding position over the community as a whole. However, there is institutionalized interlinking and no clash of authority between the groups. All heads of small or big lineages enjoy equal status. No one is the first among equals. Generally, pastoralists, horticulturists, and marginal cultivators with larger populations have such political systems. The Nuers, Masai, and Nandi of Africa, Tiv of Nigeria in Africa and Kuma of Melanesia are some of the examples of this type of a political system.

Among the Nuers of Sudan in Africa, apart from clan, there are at least three categories of lineages. Clans are divided into medium sized lineages and each medium sized lineage is segmented into smaller lineages. All these units function as corporate groups. Their political functions are traditionally allocated.

Among the Tiv of Nigeria, the lineage system is based on segmented opposition. Each lineage at every level is associated with territory. Smaller lineages of two brothers federate into a bigger lineage of their common father. They also combine their territories.

War and fighting are controlled in self-interest. If two people fight, the third joins the one to whom he is most closely related. If both are distantly related, the third may not join but makes an effort to stop the fight. Those who do not bind one another on the ground of not fighting with each other, do not interfere either. Disputes within the lineages are settled by lineage elders. Those between the lineages are settled by fighting or by meetings and activities verging on diplomacy.

In case of divorce, the elders of the lineages concerned meet with one another to work out a modus vivendi. Every dispute is settled and every war is fought on the basis of a power system, not on an authority system. It is an order of a sort and can be called 'ordered anarchy'. It enables a person to predict what will happen. But it is not really government and certainly not a State.

Non-Kinship Based Organizations

Age-Sets

Another example of a multicentric political system are the societies which are divided into age-sets. These political systems are not very common and are comparatively rare. The Hopi Indians of North America, the Yako of Nigeria in Africa and the Ibo of West Africa are some of the people having this kind of a political system.

The division of society into institutionalized sets of different age groups, where they have a formal system of entry and exit of the members. At the time of entry, a new entrant is ceremoniously initiated. Customarily, different age-sets are allotted different political functions. Each age-set has its captain or head. There is no overall authority at the head of the tribe as a whole.

Village Councils

In another non-kin, multicentric political system, the society is divided into a number of villages as independent political units, each having a council constituted by the village elders who collectively perform all the political functions. The council heads of all the villages may meet together either in an emergency situation or in the event of inter-village disputes. The Pueblo Indians of West Coast in North America have this kind of a political system.

Evans-Pritchard has named all these multicentric authority systems as headless or a cephalous system, since there is no overall common authority in any of them which functions for the society as a whole. According to Evans-Pritchard and Fortes, one person as the leader or head and as overall authority is possible only in two situations. The first in a situation when the group is 'too small so that the leader is in direct face to face contact with all the members of the group' and second 'in a situation when the group becomes too large and power is centralized at one single source as in centralized authority systems.'

Centralized Authority Systems

The centralized political systems are invariably associated with advanced cultivators and animal husbanders, and economic specialization, that is, economies capable of supporting larger populations.

The people at the apex of the society, being economically and socially in an advantageous position, there is centralization of the authority in the superior-most class of the society. The size of the population and the conditions of economic specialization themselves create many problems and disputes. The society acquires a heterogeneous character with the inclusion of a class of serfs and prisoners of war. Race, language, culture, and religion introduce an element of heterogeneity in the population.

In these socio-economic conditions, kinship-based and diffused multicentric political systems become dysfunctional. The part-timer kins become a non-entity. An unambiguous and unmistakable authority system with a centralized control-and-command comes into existence with whole-timer organized and trained functionaries as organized bureaucracy of the modern State. It is with a changeover to this type of centralization of authority that a State-like phenomenon might emerge. States have centralized authority systems, territorial administration and defence systems, judicial apparatus of some kind for the resolution of disputes, and some kind of fiscal apparatus.

By State we mean a body of persons authorized to make and enforce rules that are binding on everybody in the group under its jurisdiction, to settle disputes arising between them, to organize defence against external enemies, and to impose taxes or other economic contributions on the members of the group. A State is neither a community nor the population. It is an association within a society.

Calling a State as an association means a specific organization of society. It is more appropriately conceived as a major part of the apparatus of civilization. It is a broader concept than government, governance being one of the many other functions of State. Some States may be based on the principle of nationalism or nationality and some other States may claim to stand for a distinctive creed (the theocratic States). Functionally, political as well as economic interests are not bounded by any such considerations.

State and Stateless Societies

The political system is a universal phenomenon. The three major functions of any political system are:

1. Maintenance of social order.
2. Reduction and resolution of conflicts and disputes.
3. Ensuring cohesion and integration of the society.

There are societies where there are no explicit institutions to undertake these functions. In these societies, these functions are performed by the implicit nature of the social system and not by the dedicated, exclusive, political organs. David Easton calls them as 'stateless political systems'.

Characterized by lack of an obvious, unmistakable control mechanism of authority transcending the maximal level of lineage segmentation, all unicentric and multicentric political systems can be categorized as 'stateless political systems'.

Morton Fried defined State system as, 'A complex of institutions by means of which power is organized on a basis more extensive and therefore more superior than kinship, by delegating it to persons of proven ability to facilitate stability and balance, to maintain order and to see that its decisions are implemented and members follow them or else get punished.'

The dichotomy of stateless and state political systems rests between the two extremes of completely ordered system and near anarchy. Stateless systems, according to Fried, are characterized by the absence of centralized and identifiable authority structure, where functions are diffused among a number of acknowledged people who are more like the first-among-equals rather than superior to anyone. State and stateless political systems are differentiated by a few essential characteristics such as population, territory, economy, and the presence or absence of:

1. Judicial and legislative sub-systems
2. Mechanism for enforcement of rules
3. Fiscal sub-systems

The nomadic and subsistence economies like those of Yir-Yoront (Australia) and pastoral herders like Nuer, Masai, and Nandi, where all members have to work to procure food daily, cannot function as a State whereas surplus economies with diversification of functions, social stratifications, and delegated authority and other duties forming fiscal, legislative, and judicial sub-systems function as State political systems.

State Societies

It is quite possible to analyse a political organization without any recourse to the concept of State. Indeed, as Linton remarked, 'The failure of political scientists to realize this until quite recently handicapped the development of political theory beyond the realm of European types of government. For a long time, thinking in terms of State did more harm than good because it diverted attention from broader institutional aspects of political process as they are woven through the entire web of social life. Yet, the State is so overpoweringly important in modern civilizations and is steadily becoming more so, that it cannot be ignored.'

Anthropologists have also given recognition to this while distinguishing between state and stateless organized societies. The concept of State embodies three elements:

1. A territory
2. An actually organized population
3. A centrally organized government with strong coercive powers.

The government is conceptualized as 'an executive instrument of political organization'. The personnel of government are specialists and functionaries who perform the State's business; they are the headmen, chiefs, kings, and council members of their various domains.

A political system may use one or more of the three major units of social organization as the basis for its structure, that is,

1. Genealogical or kinship units
2. Geographical or territorial units
3. Associational units

Primitive societies generally rest most heavily on kinship principles. Lineage clans, phratries and moieties may each have their headmen responsible for the regulation of affairs within their kin groups. They may act within or outside for the tribe in public affairs.

As every community is distinguishable as a territorial entity, all political systems – primitive and modern – use geographical unit as a basis of organization. The smallest such unit is the household, the next largest is the camp among the nomadic people or the village among the sedentary people. The next largest is the band, comprising several related, extended families. Then there is the tribe – the largest group with a common language and culture. A tribe may incorporate certain alien groups too. Tribes occur among pastoralists and horticulturists, economically integrated by reciprocity and redistribution. Like bands, they too are basically egalitarian as there are no important differences among the members in terms of wealth, status, power, and prestige.

Tribes may ally on a permanent basis with other tribes to form a confederacy. This is usually done on a voluntary basis for mutual defence against aggression. In a confederacy, each tribe remains self-determining in political matters to a great extent.

All these forms of territorial organizations were achieved by one or the other primitive society.

The use of special associations as a principle of political organization is relatively weak in primitive cultures but even then, quite widespread. The heads of secret religions fraternities form the tribal council among many Pueblos. The military fraternities of Indians in the plains performed major governmental functions. Many of the secret societies of Africa and Melanesia also performed governmental functions. In other parts of Africa, the age-sets do likewise. The constitutional structure of USA ignores the associational principle but churches, labour unions and manufacturers' associations have secondary political functions of which lobbying is but one form.

Thus, State societies may be classified as primitive States and modern States.

The primitive States have chiefs as locus of authority. Chiefs may be war chiefs, peace chiefs, ceremonial chiefs, talking chiefs with hereditary dynastic rule and privileged clans being the ruling clans.

Modern States may be classified as city States, feudalistic States, modern democracies, nation-States and new States. Another phenomenon is characterized by highly structured, organized, and identifiable government with a bureaucracy and party system of democracy, which may be:

1. Two-party system
2. Multi-party system, with nationalism as an ideology, constituted authority, and locus of authority being in an elected government.

Primitive States

State systems have chiefs, kings, or councils with authority over certain spheres of social activities covering the entire society. Primitive States are usually multi-community political units, each headed by a chief or a council. The chief or the ruler rules with the help of self-elected followers and uses his authority through them. According to Radcliff-Brown, through this type of a system, the State maintains internal order by redressal of conflicts and ensures security during aggression and war.

The ruling class has unlimited access to basic resources. In chiefdoms, ranking is based on kinship; in State societies, kinship does not regulate relations between different social classes. Political organization is characterized by a high degree of functional specialization. The components of State are no longer kinship groups. Use of force is the monopoly of the centralized authority.

Using social complexity as the basis, anthropologists have defined four major types of political organizations. They are bands, tribal societies, chiefdoms, and States. Each of these types tends to be correlated with a particular mode of making a living, population size and density, economic system, and patterns of social ranking.

Chiefdoms and Kingdoms

In tribes, all segments are structurally and functionally similar. But in chiefdoms, there are many parts structurally and functionally different from one another. A ranking system ensures that some lineages and individuals in them have higher or lower social status than others. In Polynesia and north-west coast of America, rulers, nobles and commoners may be distinguished from one another by genealogical closeness to the chief. There may also be geographical units within a chiefdom, each having their own chief or council.

A chiefdom has a centralized leadership that consists of an office of the chief, as opposed to individual or self-determined leadership of 'big men' in Melanesian societies. The rise of a centralized governing centre, that is, the chief and his political authority, is closely related to its distributive exchange patterns and is the primary support of the chief's power and prestige. An economic surplus provides members of the chiefdom a greater security than is possible in a tribe. A centralized authority prevents an outbreak of violence between segments of the society. Complexities of social life sharpen the need for leadership and delegation of responsibilities. A chief is differentiated from a headman by the degree of authority. His functions and powers are variable in different societies.

In North American tribes, one paramount chief is unusual. There may be a peace chief, a war-chief for military operation, a talking chief, and so on. In some societies, the primary responsibility of a chief is not necessarily to govern. In Trobriand Islands, the chief enjoys high status of leges because of his 'divine' powers. He controls the fertility and rains through magic.

The Council

The council is a universal instrument of government. No tribe or nation does without it. In small, primitive tribes, a council comprises a democratic gathering of adult males. Some kings and dictators may ignore it for some time and show his might to the people, but it is difficult for them to successfully ignore it for long.

Leadership

Leaders in foraging bands are older men whose experience, knowledge of group traditions, success in hunting, and so on are the source of respect by the others. Leaders have no way to enforcing their views in bands. Decisions are usually made with the concurrence of all adult men in the group.

Like bands, tribal societies also have leaders but no centralized leadership and no formal offices that are a source of political power. In primitive societies, a leader is one who enjoys some superiority over others. He may be wise, clever, experienced, brave, and a man of character who enjoys the confidence of the others. Among many American Indian tribes, there are different kinds of leaders for different purposes for different kinds of activities. The Cheyenne had war chiefs and peace chiefs. Other tribes may have war leaders, hunting leaders and/or ceremonial leaders. The notion of a 'big man' commonly conforms to the notion of leadership in most of the tribal societies.

An effective leader is said to be group oriented, who fulfils 'group needs', and oils the wheels of human interactions. The concept of leadership is egalitarian in its assumption, manipulative in its orientation. There are also leaders who do not have a consensus, but try to impose their will.

Under certain ecological and social conditions, a more substantial kind of leadership may emerge in tribal societies. In areas with predictable climate and relatively abundant resources, strong authority roles of true chiefs emerge.

Elements of Democracy in Primitive Societies

Democracy is an emotive term which implies the freedom of the individual to participate in the decisions affecting his or her life. This requires that the individual should be directly and regularly involved in the political process. Democracy can also be seen as a system in which every individual has an equal opportunity to participate in the political process and an equal responsibility in the governance of the society. From this viewpoint, Western societies cannot be considered truly democratic. The widespread social inequality in all Western societies prevents this form of political equality.

Morgan and other social evolutionists of his time held the view that primitive societies and classless societies are true democracies as primitive people do not appraise or evaluate individual differences. They are of the view that stratification and centralized authority are civilized notions. In primitive societies, according to them, atomistic existence prevails and therefore there is a bias towards democratic functioning.

The Forms and Functions of Government

The study of government lies at the heart of political science, yet there is little unanimity in the discipline as to how it should be studied and the types and forms of governments that exist. The term itself has many distinct meanings.

According to Finer (1974), there are four distinct meanings of the term 'government':

1. Government refers to the process of governance, that is, an authoritative exercise of power.
2. The term can be used to refer to the existence of the process that leads to a condition of ordered rule.
3. Government is often meant to address the persons who fill the positions of authority in a society.
4. The term may refer to mean the manner, method, or system of governance in a society, that is, the structure and arrangement of offices and the relationship between them, and between the government and the governed.

A government protects members of the political community against lawlessness within and enemies without. It also makes decisions on behalf of the people or community in matters which concern them all and in which they have to act together.

The existence of some institutions of a sovereign government is a distinguishing feature of the State. The study of such sovereign governments has been the major preoccupation of political science.

But all governments are not sovereign governments. Governments in the sense of an ordered rule may exist in the absence of a State. A number of anthropological studies have revealed the existence of primitive societies in which conflicts are resolved by various social processes without recourse to the coercive power of a formalized State. Indeed, in any society there are many social situations where potential conflict is avoided by a non-coercive social process.

Primitive Governments

In a number of primitive societies, fighting or war is recognized as a legitimate means of obtaining redress for an injury. But in these societies, the conditions are not as imagined by Hobbes, that is, war as a means of dominating others.

Whether societies can or cannot be said to have a government or law is an interesting question which contemporary anthropologists have tried to answer in different ways. Much depends upon how we define government. Many modern scholars of the subject assume that government must be carried out through the type of organization we call the 'State'.

We see that some of the primitive societies have this kind of organization while others do not. Hence, the question is whether they can be said to have a government. The textbook definition of government says, 'It is a complex combination of three functions viz. legislative, executive, and judiciary functions.' The authority of a State extends over a fixed territory.

Primitive societies did not recognize territorial authority. According to this view, primitive people do not have a country with laws that apply to everyone within it. They suppose that in the early stage of the human society, while people recognized their duties towards their kinsmen, they did not recognize a ruler whom they must obey because they are in his territory. The first form of society according to anthropologists was a 'tribe'.

Henry Maine (founder of 'Comparative Jurisprudence') maintained that the changes from tribe, based on blood relations, to the State, based on local contiguity, was so important that he called it a sort of a revolution. The people who believe that they are all kins do not have the type of political structures we call 'State'.

The State itself, in its simplest form, entails the recognition that one body of kins has an exclusive claim to provide the ruler from among themselves.

Forms of Primitive Governments

Anthropologists, using the word 'primitive', do not imply by it anything about the characteristics of the persons who constitute these societies. It is the ways of doing things which can be described as primitive or otherwise. Many anthropologists have classified as 'primitives' the people who are pre-literate, having no tradition of writing. This makes a useful broad division because when people cannot keep records or send written messages, the range over which any government can exercise power has to be relatively narrow.

Neither of the words 'pre-literate' or 'small scale' go well with 'government'. While examining the question 'Do all primitive societies have government?' we are again confronted with the interpretation of the word 'primitive' as some writers of the 19th century thought that many of the institutions, which are fundamental to Western societies, developed fairly late in the history of humankind so that we cannot expect them in societies which had not advanced along with civilization. Government and law are among these, and if politics is defined as that which pertains to government, then according to this view, primitive societies pursue no activities which could be called as political or labelled as politics.

Modern anthropologists and sociologists hold the view that the sphere of politics is associated with the struggle for power, which is a universal phenomenon. In every society, there are conflicts which must somehow be reconciled if the society is not to split and break apart.

The fact that a political system, entailing some form of authority structure, is a universal phenomenon means that there is some form of governance present in every society. Functionally, this means making of rules, their enforcement, and some system or mechanism present for the redressal of people's grievances.

As a body or as an association of persons with well-defined rules, a government may not be present in all societies. Morgan, Maine, and others have denied the existence of governments in primitive societies. Goldenweiser and others have tried to show that sub-clans and tribes are always intimately correlated with spatial aspects. Government exists when there are specialized functionaries or officers designated to take, implement, or execute political decisions by delegated authorities under the law. Politics is more than government and government is less than law.

In primitive societies, all the three functions of government are not clearly defined and demarcated. Legislative function is seldom recognized. For the functioning of governance, certain established procedures of implementation of rules are found everywhere.

A government protects members of the political community against lawlessness within and enemies without. It also makes decisions on behalf of the people or community in matters which concern them all and in which they have to act together.

Concept of Law: Law and Justice in Primitive Societies

Law may be understood as a body of norms whose violation is met with sanctions which are publicly acknowledged, socially approved, and (at least in principle) consistently applied.

'The formulation of law has long been considered a hallmark of State-level societies. Many of the fundamental institutions of civilization are bound up with a concept of law: sovereign authority to create law, courts to try disputes, a police power to prevent and punish illegal acts. Yet does the absence of a sovereign authority, courts, or a written legal code imply the absence of law (Robert Winthrop, 1991)?'

As an aspect of sociological discussions which are concerned with the question of maintenance of order and stability in society, social control, consisting of certain mechanisms employed to maintain order, is used. Social control may also be used to categorize discussion of social institutions which contribute specifically to social stability. These institutions may be legal, religious, or political. This is an area of study in sociology which examines the nature and causes of both stability and change.

Talcott Parsons (1951), elaborating on the prevailing concept of social control in sociology, holds the view that the study of social control is the analysis of those processes which tend to counteract deviant tendencies. 'Every social system,' according to Parsons, 'has a complete system of unplanned and unconscious mechanisms which serve to counteract deviant tendencies.' This counteraction of deviance conception of social control is widely accepted in two social science disciplines – sociology and social anthropology.

Deviance is a universal phenomenon. It is a negative concept and refers to only the acts or behaviours which are punishable under the law. In every society, 'law' concerns deviant behaviour. It is a counteraction or reaction against deviant behaviour. It is a mechanism of social control. Social control is a wider social phenomenon, law is simply an agency of social control.

Conceptions of what is law are culturally and historically specific. When modern Western scholars study laws and legal institutions of other cultures, they try to discover the norms and institutions that are analogous to their own, either in form or functions. There is a wide range of opinions about what is law or what it should be, but mostly covering two major views. One view is that law is an expression of cultural values and moral consensus. The second view is that it as a conscious and rationalized framework of power. In ethnographic findings, it is usually both.

According to Max Weber, evolution of law was marked by a movement from formal irrationality to rationality. In this sense, rationality meant a logically coherent system of principles and rules, while legal irrationality was the use of means other than logic or reason for the decision of cases such as ordeals and oracles. Arbitrary decisions and personal whims of the men in authority constituted substantive irrationality.

At present, social scientists approach law with a distilled and selective recombination of many of observations of the 19th century and the early 20th century scholars, using new methods and new information. Modern scholars use statistical techniques and quantitative methods in their study of legal systems and institutions. Approachability, cost of justice, and efficiency are regarded as more valuable considerations than the nature of justice and the value being promoted in the judgments.

Primitive Law

Defining the law of primitive people, Hoebel (1974) observed that primitive law constituted the social norms whose neglect or infraction is regularly met (in thereat or in fact) by the application of force by an individual or group who have the socially recognized privilege of acting this way.

In every society, certain acts are considered so disruptive that force or the threat of force is applied. The control of deviant behaviour is therefore a major function of law in all societies. This also resolves conflicts of disruptive potential to community life. In modern States, wrongs against the State (called 'crimes') are differentiated from grievances that individuals have against one another (called 'torts').

In structurally simpler societies, disputes between individuals are handled by the community in the interest of maintaining order. Involvement of the whole community or a go-between (at times having the authority to impose their decisions on others) are the various means and ways to resolve differences peacefully. In other cases, the threat from supernatural powers is a more potent factor in curbing deviance.

In whatever manner we may define it, law concerns behaviour or conduct of people, means and ways of controlling their behaviour, and certain rules. The rules may be ethical rules, customary rules or norms, or the rules supported by the supernatural as divine rules.

All the types of rules develop control mechanisms. There are two types of control mechanisms. The informal control mechanisms involve traditional or customary rules and beliefs – the rules which are uncodified. Disputes are settled in face-to-face, that is, interpersonal contact. The mechanisms are usually in the form of social pressure involving gossip, public opinion, public ridicule, or avoidance in the form of social boycott, non-co-operation, fighting or war.

The formal control mechanisms consist of systematically codified sets of rules known as laws. They are operative in complex societies. Individuals and institutions emerge to interpret these rules. Anthropologists and sociologists speak of three basic features of law:

1. A legitimate authority to use power.

2. Allocation of rights and duties and delegation of authority.
3. Element of regularity or predictability.

Modern law is enacted or codified law. The non-literate societies do not have law in this sense.

Sanctions of Primitive Law

In the absence of formal institutions and use of coercive force, a question which anthropologists have discussed elaborately is, what makes primitives to obey their laws? In other words, what are the sanctions for breaking primitive laws? One view has been that in the absence of any formal enforcement mechanism, primitives obey laws spontaneously. However, Malinowski contradicted this view, maintaining that there is no society where rules are followed automatically or spontaneously without any fear or compulsion. According to him, in primitive societies, people are complete slaves of customs to the extent that they do not need any coercive institution.

R.R. Marret (1912) held the view that it is difficult to recognize anything like law in primitive societies because no one dares to break the rules there.

There is some truth in each of these assertions. In primitive societies, the public opinion is so organized, uniform, and undivided that it is very effective and compulsive. The laws in primitive societies are equated with ethical norms and the fear of supernatural associated with their violation. This makes people follow the laws. Besides, public ridicule acts as a positive sanction. All this gives the impression that primitive people obey laws spontaneously, willingly, and completely. But Malinowski came out with a remarkable explanation when he said that primitives obey laws out of sheer self-interest. According to him, the withdrawal of co-operation, social boycott, and the fear of ex-communication create conditions for individuals in which they just cannot survive. The question of survival and economic interest is one of the major self-interests. In addition, while taboo and fear of the supernatural are important negative sanctions, in primitive societies positive sanctions count far more than negative sanctions. That is why coercive mechanisms have very limited role in them.

According to Radcliffe-Brown, the positive sanctions involve prizes, approval, and citations. They all underline what one is expected to do. The element of social approval rather than fear provides the people strength to be more effective. On the other hand, negative sanctions are not always definitive and well regulated. Often they are unorganized, hence not very effective. The effect of sanctions is a more important consideration than its form. No one can deny the effective importance of ridicule, avoidance or denial of favours – the sanctions that are very subtle and informal.

The spirit of law is positive, not negative. It exists, primarily, not to punish but to channelize behaviour towards socially acceptable goals thus preventing the breach of laws.

Justice

According to Friedman (1976), the function of the legal systems is to distribute and maintain an allocation of values that the society believes to be right. That is, allocation invested with strict discipline commonly referred as justice. This is done by redressal of injuries, resolution of disputes, and meting out punishments. These processes uphold the desired values and norms of the society by punishing individuals breaching the norms.

In centralized authority systems and modern State societies, there are separate judicial sub-systems with delegated authority to carry out this function. These sub-systems have offices staffed by knowledgeable, competent persons of integrity. In simpler societies with non-State political systems, there is a wide range of procedures adopted to settle disputes and resolve conflicts between individual and groups.

Self-help or revenge, blood-for-blood, and an eye-for-an-eye are the recognized procedures in most of the non-State political systems. A principle of collective responsibility by which the kinsmen of two individuals may avenge the injury caused to one of them. Thus the onus of redressal of injuries lies on the individuals concerned or their kinsmen. Another common practice involves feuds which occurs when the principle of self-help gets out of hand. Though feud or threat of feud is a type of counteraction found throughout the world, it is found to be a faulty jural mechanism.

In certain cases, in some of the societies, involvement of the entire community in resolving disputes may also take place. In some duels, the participation of the entire community in the judgment is common – the community decides exile or execution of the wrong doer. In this process, an informal leader takes the entire community into confidence and gives an approval to the wronged person's kins. This amounts to the process working like an unorganized court.

In some of the African tribes, apart from these jural procedures, there is a process called 'moot'. This is a typical feature which is not a court, nor does it consist of officials, but produces a consensus within the community. It is a gathering similar to a townhall meeting. Among the Tiv of Nigeria, such gatherings take the form of street-corner meetings where the verdict of the people is given about a dispute.

Certain corrective measures may also be at work in resolving disputes. For example, ex-communication, community dinner, blood wealth, or other forms of penalty imposed, work as efficient corrective measures.

Very few chiefdoms and kingdoms have indigenous courts where systematic proceedings take place and disputes are resolved. Among the Bantus of South and Central Africa, for instance, there are indigenous courts of a panel of chiefs (at times more than 20). Litigants present their case and disputes are heard by the court. Evidences are produced. By tradition, the most junior among the judges announces the judgment. In Bechuanaland (now Botswana), the indigenous courts are much more elaborate in procedure and similar to any of the courts of the modern societies.

Legitimacy and the State

Legitimacy of the State is very important because without it there would be conflict and disorder. State legitimacy is a key aspect of the State–society relations. State repression and violence, which occurs in many conflict-affected contexts, results in negative experiences of citizens with the State. This leads to a legacy of mistrust and rejection of the legitimacy of State institutions.

State legitimacy derives from a number of sources, foremost of which is the performance of public institutions. Citizens must have a sense of satisfaction that the State protects their interests. If they lose faith in the State, there would be tension, conflict, and violence. It may also result in the emergence of terrorism.

In the present world we find a number of non-State actors taking to violence and terrorism. In pluralistic societies, sometimes minorities, especially religious minorities, are discriminated, oppressed, and marginalized and their faith in the State as a non-partisan entity gets eroded. For such sections of the society, the State loses its legitimacy. This is not a good sign in any society, especially democratic societies.

Civil Society

'Civil society' is one of the most used and abused concepts in current socio-political thinking. Civil society (from the Latin Sociatas Civilis) is not a new concept. It entered European discourse in the 15th century. Contrary to modern use, it did not denote a natural, or pre-State type of a society. The concept of civil society, though highly popular and much revived in recent years, remains intensely contested and debated. As Susanne Rudolf (2000) rightly points out, civil society is defined variously by different theorists, and a minimal definition would include:

1. The idea of a non-State autonomous sphere
2. Empowerment of citizens
3. Trust building associational life
4. Interaction with rather than subordination to the State.

According to the conventional notions prevalent in the social sciences, civil society refers to the space in a given society that:

1. Exists between the family level and the State level.
2. Makes interconnection between individuals and families.
3. Is independent of the State.

Elaborating further, Ashutosh Varshney (2002) says, 'Many, though not all, of the existing definitions also suggest two more requirements: that the civic space be organized in associations that attend to the cultural, social, economic, and political needs of the citizens and that the associations be modern and voluntaristic, not ascriptive.'

Going by the first requirement, trade unions would be a part of civil society, but informal neighbourhood associations would not. The modernity of civil society is, of course, qualified since not all modern political systems have civil societies. In the opinion of a number of scholars of civil society, the communist polities were not civil society (though this has generated lot of debate) despite the fact that they were modern; attacked ascriptive statuses, hierarchies, and privileges; undermined religion; and instituted a secular order. This was largely because the State penetrated all sites of organizational life: hospitals, universities, theatre, and literary societies. The idea of association is central to the concept of civil society. Associations empower citizens, each of whom, in isolation, could not confront the State as agent and participant, not create consequences within society.

Hegel is the pivotal figure in shaping contemporary understanding of the idea of civil society. Hegel's question concerned the possibility of creating and sustaining a community under modern conditions. It was in response to this problem that he introduced the distinction between the 'State' and 'civil society'. His solution tries to integrate the individual freedoms specified by the natural law tradition (from Hobbes to Rousseau and Kant) with a rich vision of the community, existing under conditions of modern exchange.

As Joseph Femia (2002) points out, modernity was crucial to the development of the concept of civil society. 'Customary models of authority were progressively undermined by the commercialization of land, labour, and capital; by the growth of the market economy; by great scientific discoveries, such as the Copernican system; and by the Protest Reformation, which destroyed the corporate unity of the Catholic ecumene. The break with the past traditions and customs, as the binding forces of society, engendered the search for new principles of moral unity. Because of the detachment of individual human beings from their defining social matrix, from the primordial givens of existence – kith, kin, membership in the Universal Church – there emerged a tendency to conceive people in terms of their humanity alone' (ibid).

When we look at the ramifications of civil society in India, we may refer to the much-acclaimed work of Ashutosh Varshney, Ethnic Conflict and Civic Life in the context of Hindu–Muslim relations. He calls for the strengthening of civil society and integrated civic networks. Towns where Hindus and Muslims continue to be integrated – in business, political parties unions, professional associations of lawyers, teachers, doctors and students, and clubs – riots remain either absent or rare despite the attempts by the vested interests. 'An integrated organizational and civic life makes the State behave better than intellectual and political exhortations that it do so,' (ibid).

It follows that citizen action in India has to take two forms – (a) continue to pressure the State of its dereliction of constitutional duty, (b) pressure the State to focus on building integrated civic structures. The first has been the primary strategy for citizen action in India so far (of course by concerned citizens). Such action is necessary, but not sufficient. Varshney then proceeds to conclude by saying that citizen initiatives should follow a two-track strategy, combining (a) and (b). Civil society, which by-and-large tends to be local or regional, is the missing variable in available theories, to which researchers of ethnic conflict should pay increasing attention. Associational civic engagements are necessary for peace in inter-ethnic urban settings.

Critical Thinking Questions

- In what ways does social distribution of power takes place? Does it satisfy human needs?
- Do you think that the simple or primitive societies are the basis of democracy in modern societies?
- In present time how is legitimacy is obtained by the State?
- Can civil society alone protect the rights of citizens?

****

9

Religion

Chapter Outline: *What is religion; Notion and definition of religion; Origin of religion(psychological theories, EB Tylor, James Frazer, animatism/manaism, sociological theories) ; Functions of religion ; dysfunctions of religion, modern sociological view: primitive religion ; Functionaries of primitive religion ; Totemism ; Taboo; Divination ; Rites of passage ; Religion, majic and science ;Religion and symbolism; Religion and economy ;Religion and politics ;Monotheism and polytheism ; Sects and cults ; Classical theoretical perspective(Durkheim, Weber, Marx) ;Secularism and secularization ; Religious revivalism and fundamentalism ;Religious/communal conflict and violence*

Learning Objectives

- What is meant by the universality of religion?
- What are the theories about the origin of religion?
- What is religious symbolism?
- What are the range of religious beliefs?
- What are the changing faces of religion in the present times?

What Is Religion?

It is generally accepted that all societies have beliefs that can be grouped under the term 'religion'. These beliefs vary from society to society. Religion may be defined as any set of beliefs and practices pertaining to supernatural powers. Because of global diversity, achieving a universal definition of religion is difficult. K.G. Guest (2018), in a brilliant analysis of religion, says that all local expressions of religion combine some, but not necessarily all, of the following elements:

- Beliefs in powers or deities whose abilities transcend those of the natural world and cannot be measured by scientific tools.
- Myths and stories that reflect on the meaning and purpose of life, its origins, and human's place in the universe.
- Ritual activities that reinforce, recall, instil, and explore collective beliefs.
- Powerful symbols, often used in religious rituals, representing key aspects of the religion for its followers.
- Specialists who assist the average believer to bridge everyday life experiences and religion's ideals and supernatural aspects.
- Organizations and institutions that preserve, explore, teach, and implement the religion's key beliefs.
- A community of believers.

Social scientists, social anthropologists, and sociologists have been uninterested in questions of any religion's ultimate truth or falsity. Instead, they understand that religious worlds are real, meaningful, and powerful for those who live in them. Thus it may be said that religion is just a matter of faith for those who believe in it.

Religion, often referred to as concerning faith and beliefs, speaks of imaginations, of fantasy, of things and affairs not having any concern with realities that surround us. Yet its universal presence as a category of culture and the emotional esteem attached to it by its followers everywhere and in all human societies, makes it a subject of immense importance to study.

Despite the positive knowledge that death is inevitable, fear of death and fear of the dead constitute the core of all supernaturalism. Supernaturalism as a term stands for many kinds of beliefs and faith in the existence of a world beyond the world of our experience, peopled by the powers, forces, or entities based on human imagination.

The element of chance and the need for a mechanism to avoid failure of aspirational fulfilment is one of the strongest incentives for supernaturalism. In every culture, despite all the technological achievements, there are always areas of inadequacies. No culture is a perfect coping device. The areas of inadequacies leave behind unfulfilled desires and aspirations of the people. Also, despite all rational explanations, there are unpredictable events and hazards posing challenge to the survival of the people. Positive knowledge of science and technology has its limitations. The world of beliefs and faith is elastic in nature.

When positive knowledge fails, human to human and human to nature rational organizations are rendered futile, then humans establish their communication with the cosmos. All supernaturalism is human to cosmos relations and communication. The procedures of communication are mystic, beyond reason and formed on faith. The commonly observable procedures are invocation, sacrifice, worship and so on.

There are four forms of expression of supernaturalism in human societies and cultures which have been attested ethnographically. These are religion, magic, totemism, and taboo. While the last three are commonly preponderant in primitive, non-literate societies and culture, the first one, that is religion, was considered for a long time as a product of civilizational level of living and a later historical development. It was only when Tylor came out with convincing proof that primitive societies have their own versions of religious activities not very different from the civilized societies that a category of primitive religion became the subject of anthropological discussions.

Notion and Definition of Religion

The four kinds of supernaturalism expressions mentioned previously are differentiated much in terms of the nature of supernatural powers and their functions. Some kind of mysticism and other-worldliness is common to all of them.

Supernatural powers are conceived as personalities, bodies, and entities with human characteristics who can listen and sympathise, but unlike human beings, nothing is impossible for them. Humans in this world establish unique and mystic relations with them through a wide range of acts and performances categorized as 'rites' and 'rituals' and adopting specific cultural procedures such as prayers, worship, and sacrifices. This is what we call it religion.

Yet, it is difficult to define religion in specific terms. There is such a wide variety of belief patterns, rites, and rituals that it is difficult to bring all of them within the limited capacity of words and build a common definition.

Origin of Religion

The scientific study of religion has had relatively little development. Most of the basic data required for the objective, comparative study of religion is available to us from the records of the early travelling missionaries and during the last century by scholars of social sciences. Information on exotic religions provides many examples of apparent diversity. Similarities in religions are, in part, reflections of the essential uniformity of human nature. Variations are seen to be chiefly due to extrasomatic factors, external to humans.

The 19th century scholars of religion were mainly concerned with the questions of the origin and evolution of religion. The antiquity and universality of religion led many anthropologists to speculate about its origin. Several theories of the origin of religion were presented, its subsequent evolution culminating in monotheism.

These early theories of origin of religion and its evolution into monotheism were discarded in the 20th century when the question of the origin of religion ceased to be a matter of interest. The prevalent view has long been that theory of the origin can only be a speculation as verifiable data is beyond reach. All the theories of origin of religion can be categorized into two groups of theories.

The first category is of those theories which treat religion an outcome of some kind of intellectual fallacy. The evolutionist scholars have given importance to the psychological characters such as fear of the dead, love for the dead, and have tried to show that religion originated from the cult of the dead.

The second category is the sociological explanation where the origin of religion has been expressed as a consequence of societal need and social factors have been considered most important.

Psychological Theories

One of the oldest theories of the origin of religion is the theory that religion originated in fetishism – the worship of inanimate objects and animals by coastal people of West Africa, which developed into polytheism and then into monotheism. This theory was prevalent until the middle of the 20th century when it was replaced by psychological theories. Psychological theories had to contest with theories of the nature–myth school.

Max Muller

The nature–myth school was predominantly a German school and was mostly concerned with Indo-European religions. According to this thought, the gods of antiquity and gods anywhere and at all times were no more than personified natural phenomenon– the sun, moon, stars, dawn, spring, mighty rivers, and so on. The most powerful exponent of this school was Max Muller, a German scholar at Oxford. He was a linguist of exceptional ability. In his view, humans always had an inclination for the divine – the idea of the infinite deriving from the sensory experiences. All human knowledge comes through the senses and all reasoning is based on them; and this is true of religion also. Things like sun and the sky gave humans the idea of infinite and also served as symbols for it.

Max Muller was chiefly interested in the gods of India and of the classical world, though he did interpret some primitive material and believed that his explanations had general validity.

Herbert Spencer

Anthropology has obtained some very important methodological concepts from Herbert Spencer. He devoted a large part of his book The Principles of Sociology to a discussion about primitive beliefs and practices. Though he interpreted them not much differently from E.B. Tylor and his book was published after Tylor's Primitive Culture, his views were crystallized much before his book appeared in print. The primitive humans, according to him, acquired the notion of duality from their observation of phenomenon such as the sun, moon, stars, and clouds which come and go. They are visible and invisible, hence the logic that if other things could be dualities, so could humans. Human's shadow and reflection also come and go. But it is dreams which are the real experiences of primitive people which chiefly gave them the idea of their own duality. They identified the dream with the self which wanders at night and the shadow of self which appears during the day.

E.B. Tylor

Tylor coined the word 'animism' for his theory of the origin of religion, which is very similar to that of Spencer, though the word 'anima' implies, according to him, the idea of 'soul' rather than of 'ghost'. In anthropological literature, there exists some ambiguity about the term 'animism', as it is sometimes employed in the sense of the belief of the primitive people that not only creatures but also inanimate objects have a life and personality and they have souls. Tylor's theory covers both the senses.

According to Tylor, primitive human's reflections on experiences such as death, disease, trances, and visions and, above all, dreams, led them to conclude that all these are to be accounted for by the presence or absence of some immaterial entity – the soul. Both Spencer's ghost theory and Tylor's theory can be regarded as two versions of a dream theory of the origin of religion.

Later, according to Tylor, primitive humans transferred this idea of soul to other creatures and even to inanimate objects, which aroused their interest. Tylor wished to show that primitive religion was rational and that it arose from observations, however inadequate, and the logical deductions derived from them, howsoever faulty. This constituted a natural philosophy.

James Frazer

Frazer's entire monumental work, The Golden Bough, is devoted to primitive superstitions. According to Frazer, humankind everywhere, sooner or later, passes through three stages of intellectual development, from magic to religion and then to science – a scheme he must have taken from Comte's phases (the theological, the metaphysical, and the positivistic). His contemporaries also believed that magic preceded religion. Eventually, Frazer says, some people discovered that magic did not really achieve its ends, they fell into another illusion that there were spiritual beings who could do it. In course of time, still shrewder intelligences saw that spirits were an equally bogus idea and that dawned the emergence of experimental science.

These intellectualist theories can neither be refuted nor sustained as no evidence exists about how religious beliefs originated. These evolutionary assumptions are rather vague hypotheses. Yet, whatever has been said about the essential rationality of primitive people is worth retaining. It is true that they may not have arrived at their beliefs in the manner these scholars supposed, yet the element of rationality is there in spite of inadequate observations, faulty inferences, and wrong conclusions.

The animistic theory in various forms retained wide acceptance for a long time so much so that animism became a synonym for primitive religion in anthropological literature.

Animatism and Manaism

The great advance in ethnography in the last decades of the 19th century and in the early 20th century provided later writers abundance of information of better quality. While Frazer differed from Tylor in claiming a pre-religion stage of magic, other writers also took the same view. Wilhelm Schmidt, for example, expressed the opinion that ghosts and spirits were the ideas too sophisticated for 'crude men', so there must be a stage earlier than animism, a 'mana' stage in which the idea of luck, of the canny and uncanny, was the sole constituent of the supernatural.

Other writers like Codrington, R.R. Merrett, and Andrew Lang vehemently opposed the view that gods could have developed out of ghosts and spirits. They pointed out that the conception of a creative, omnipotent, and ethereal god is found among the most primitive people and is probably explained as a belief of the primitive humans that the world around them must have been made by some superior being. The superior being of these people, according to Lang, is not thought of as spirit at all or evolved out of reflections on dreams and ghosts.

Modern Sociological Theories

The primitive beliefs and rites may help people to cope with their problems and misfortunes, removing despair which inhibits action. Religion is valuable if it serves the purpose of giving comfort and a feeling of security, confidence, and relief. The sociological theories of religion hold that religion is valuable in the contribution that it makes for social cohesion and continuity.

One of the most far-reaching and comprehensive sociological treatment of religion is Fustel de Coulanges's The Ancient City. He was a French historian who had considerable influence on his pupil Durkheim. In The Ancient City, it has been held that the ancient classical society was centred in the family in its widest sense, that is, the joint family or lineage. What held this group together as a corporation and gave it permanence was the ancestor cult in which the head of the family acted as a priest. He claimed that all customs of the period can be understood in the light of this central idea of the dead being deities of the family.

Another influence, strongly marked in Durkheim's theory of religion, was that of Robertson Smith. Clans-men, according to him, were conceived to be of one blood and so also their totems of the same blood were the god of the clan. Sociologically speaking, the god was the clan itself, idealized and divinized. Fundamentally, Fustel De Coulanges and Robertson Smith put forth something like a structural theory of the genesis of religion stating that it arises out of the very nature of the primitive society.

For Durkheim, religion is a social that, is, an objective fact. He expressed his contempt for the theories which tried to explain religion in terms of individual psychology. A religion, he said, 'could not originate' in any fallacy or illusion. Had it been so, it would not have been so universal and so enduring.

Durkheim believed that three characteristics gave religion objectivity:

- Firstly, that religion is transmitted from one generation to another.
- Secondly, that in a closed society, it is general. Everyone in the society has some sort of religious beliefs and practices. This gives them an objectivity which places them over and above the psychological experience of any individual.
- Thirdly, religion is obligatory, even if there is no coercion. To Durkheim, religion is a collective, autonomous, and objective phenomenon. He elaborates his thinking by saying that religion is a social fact which arises out of the nature of social life itself, being bound up in simpler societies with other social facts.

Thus, Durkheim starts with four cardinal ideas borrowed from Robertson Smith – that primitive religion is a clan cult and that the cult is totemic; that the god of the clan is the clan itself, divinized; and that totemism is the most elementary or primitive area; that this is the original form of religion. By that he meant that it is found in societies with the simplest material culture and social structure.

He defined religion as, 'A unified system of beliefs and practices related to sacred things, i.e., the things set apart and forbidden. These beliefs and practices unite into one single moral community called a church and all those who adhere to them.' On these criteria, totemism can be regarded as a religion as it is hedged around by taboos and it is a group manifestation.

To prove his theory, Durkheim heavily depended on data from Australian aborigines and used the data from North American Indians as a check. The Australian aborigines were hunters and collectors, wandering about in small hordes in their tribal territories seeking game, roots, fruits, and so on. A tribe was composed of a number of such hordes. Besides being a member of a little horde, person was a member of a clan. As a member of a clan, he shared with other members a relationship with a series of natural phenomenon, mostly animals and plants. Durkheim held that these animals and plants represented their clans and by having a mystic relation with them and worshipping them as clan gods or clan ancestors, they simply worshipped the group. Thus, according to Durkheim, there could not have been a simpler religion than this. Thus religion originated as a worship of the group. Its genesis lay in primitive man's dependence on the group.

Durkheim criticized the efforts of the evolutionists to seek the origin of religion in psychological sentiments of love or fear as ridiculous. Religion, he said, was an outcome of certain harsh realities of life – the people's dependence on society.

Functions of Religion

Anthropological studies of religion have been mainly concerned with the origin and evolution of religion in earlier phases. Later, the emphasis was changed to its functional interpretation. The earlier scholars like Tylor and Max Muller saw religion as a response to human's intellectual needs. Psychological and emotive factors such as sense of love or fear predominated various theories of origin advanced by them. They also constituted a negative approach as most of them held some sort of intellectual fallacy or confusion in human thinking which was responsible for its origin.

The functionalist perspective changed the emphasis from human needs to social needs. Functionalist analysis is primarily concerned with the contribution religion makes to meeting the basic needs of society. From this perspective, society requires a certain degree of social solidarity, value consensus, and integration between its parts. The function of religion has to be assessed in terms of the contribution it makes to meeting such social prerequisites.

Malinowski's View

Functionalist tradition of studies in anthropology was well-established by Malinowski, though his ideas on function were greatly influenced by Durkheim's thinking.

Like Durkheim, Malinowski also used data from small-scale, non-literate societies to develop his views on religion. His own fieldwork in Trobriand Islands off the coast of Guinea made him realize that religion is intimately connected with various emotional states which are states of tension. The fear of crop failure in the absence of rain, or thunder and lightning are the type of real life situations which inculcate an element of tension and anxiety. These situations create stresses and strains and if allowed to persist for long, are likely to frustrate all action. For the single-minded participation of individuals in production and other important activities, a tension free mind is a must. Thus, according to Malinowski, religion becomes instrumental in building up a sense of confidence in individuals to participate in their regular activities as normal persons. In this manner, religion functions as a tool of adaptation. Its function is to relieve the human mind from fear and the other emotional strains, instilling a sense of confidence in and works as an anxiety reducing mechanism.

Radcliffe-Brown's Views

Radcliffe-Brown, another British social anthropologist, describes the functions of religion differently. He lays emphasis on the fact of human dependence on the group. Hence, according to him, the survival of the group is necessary for the survival of the individual. Adherence to the norms of behaviour is essential for social survival. It is the fear of supernatural control that brings about this adherence to the norms. Religion instils or creates a sense of fear against non-observance of social norms. Its function, therefore, is the contribution it makes to the social activity which is designed to perpetuate society.

The views expressed by the two stalwarts of functionalism in British social anthropology appear to be opposed to each other, but there is some element of truth in both in the views. Both of them have relied heavily on Durkheim's theory of religion. Raymond Firth, another British social anthropologist, has overstressed the tranquilizing function of religion in crisis situations.

Thus, by integrating society and overcoming anxiety, fear, and frustration, religion makes this world more comprehensible to humans when positive knowledge fails to deliver the goods.

Talcott Parsons

Parsons's view is not much different from an anthropological viewpoint when he says that human action is directed and controlled by norms provided by the social system, but the cultural system provides more general guidelines for action in the form of beliefs, values, and systems of providing meaning to everyday events. The norms which direct action are integrated and patterned by the values and beliefs provided by the cultural system. Religion, as a part of the cultural system, and religious beliefs provide guidelines for human action by establishing general principles and moral values. As a part of the cultural system, religious beliefs give meaning to life.

Dysfunction of Religion: Modern Sociological View

The functionalist perspective emphasizes the positive contributions of religion to the society but closes its eyes to its negative and dysfunctional aspects with its preoccupation with harmony, integration, and solidarity. Functionalists have neglected many instances where religion appears as a divisive and disruptive force. They ignore the internal divisions within a community over the question of religious dogma and worship, much apparent in modern, multi-ethnic, and multi-religious societies. Some of the modern sociologists like Charles Glock and Rodney Stark find it difficult to reconcile with the general theory due to the considerable evidence of religious conflicts. Marxism regards religion as the opium for the masses and an instrument of oppression.

Primitive Religion

'Primitive religions are species of the genus religion and that all those who have any interest in religion, must acknowledge that a study of the religious ideas and practices of primitive peoples which are of great variety, may help us to reach certain conclusions about the nature of religion in general and therefore also about the so-called higher religions or historical and positive religions or the religions of revelation' (E.E. Evans-Pritchard).

Evans-Pritchard's quotation apart, stressing on the importance of the study of primitive religions also brings into focus the distinction between what may be called as 'natural' and 'revealed' religions. Primitive religions, in isolated and widely separated parts of the world, are independent developments without any relations or connections between them. They become valuable from the point of view of comparative analysis to study the essential characteristics of religious phenomenon for making general, valid, and significant statements about them.

Primitive religions are the religions of the pre-literates, lacking any text. They constitute such varied aspects, apart from beliefs and practices, as magic totemism, taboo, sorcery, and witchcraft. To European scholars, all this appeared as irrational and superstitious. Religion in traditional, primitive societies is not just a set of beliefs about superhuman powers. It is an idiom, a manner of thought and speech that people must use to explain their world to themselves.

A universal or world religion, on the other hand, is one which is basically independent of any specific social group or type of group and hence it is independent of specific mores to a great extent. World religions emerged only in a few places in the world. The rest are national or tribal religions.

As society becomes more complex and differentiated, some institutionalized liminal statuses emerge in the societies. They are most often the persons or groups that share the characteristics of liminality. They are outlaws or of low social status or of ambiguous nature. It is their very marginality or low status or ambiguity that is paradoxically the source of their power. 'Monotheism' was the word which earlier anthropologists used for this conception.

The mere idea of expansion of belief systems in a wider geography often becomes a cause for exploiting people, at times using coercion for their acceptance by others. In modern religions, doctrines predominate and the ritual content of the religion gets diluted to some extent.

All common religions are genetically related such as Judaism, Christianity, and Islam; and Hinduism, Buddhism, and Jainism. The efforts to describe and define primitive religion by the earlier anthropologists by coining of special terms have brought in more distortions and confusion than any clarity about them. Primitive religion was called 'animistic', 'pre-animistic', or 'fetishism' and the like. At times, exotic terms such as 'mana', 'bonga', 'taboo', 'totem', and so on were picked up from the native languages. Efforts were made to generalize about primitive religions on the basis of these terms of local significance.

The Functionaries of Primitive Religion

Religion, basically being a public affair, individual communion or contact with the supernatural is not the normal practice in different societies and cultures. Almost all the societies have part-time or full-time religious or magic practitioners who invoke gods, goddesses, spirits, and ghosts for their people. Anthropologists have reported at least four major types of practitioners or functionaries – shamans, sorcerers or witches, mediums, and priests.

Shamans

Usually a part-time specialist, a shaman has a fairly high status in his community and is often involved in healing. A shaman is socially recognized as having special supernatural powers that are used for and on behalf of the clients for a variety of activities such as, curing divination, sorcery, and recoding fortunes, among others. Among inlet coastal communities of South America, shamans make an annual spiritual trip to the bottom of the sea to persuade the sea goddess to ensure abundant animals for one more year. They are also frequently called upon to cure illness. They do it by discovering the supernatural being who has been offended by the breach of some taboo to cause the illness.

Shamanistic activity has important therapeutic effects on individual clients who are often relieved of illness through the cathartic effects of the ritual. Shamanism also has important integrating functions in the society. Through a wide variety of symbolic acts, shamanic performances bring together multiple beliefs and religious practices. Such performances usually involve participation by the audience. These performances are healing in the sense that they help individuals or the community as a whole who are under the impact of anxiety due to various disturbing events affecting them. The word 'shaman' itself is derived and got established in anthropological literature from the nomadic herders and the marginal cultivators of the Central Asian tribes.

Sorcerers and Witches

While shamans enjoy high social status, sorcerers and witches are from the low social and economic status groups in their societies. They may belong to both the sexes. They acquire their roles not out of their choice or desire, but because others think that they are suited for these roles. Since sorcerers use certain objects and materials for their act, they can be easily traced and located. Often suspected sorcerers are killed for the malevolent activities they supposedly perform. On the other hand, since witchcraft is supposed to be in the form of thoughts and emotions, it is hard to prove someone as a witch; there may be a lot of witch hunting with no result.

Mediums

Only the females tend to be mediums. They get into a trance suddenly and become possessed by spirits. When in a trance, they start behaving peculiarly and it is in this state that they are asked to heal and divine secrets. They function as part-time practitioners.

Priests

Enjoying very high status in the society, priests are generally fulltime male specialists who officiate at public events. They are thought to be in companionship with superior or high gods beyond the reach and control of ordinary persons. Only societies with economies producing a food surplus can afford to have priests. Their fulltime occupation itself indicates that priesthood is a specialized profession requiring some amount of training. The office of the priest is obtained either through inheritance or political appointment. Priests acquire a special identity by putting on special clothing or displaying a peculiar hairstyle. They have to go through an arduous training programme which includes fasting, praying, and learning of rituals and the dogma of their religion. Before functioning independently, they have to serve as apprentices under established priests. They are not paid for their performance but are supported by the funds created by public donations.

There are marked differences between the shamans and the priests. While shamans are called upon to cure maladies which brings popularity to them, priests are only expected to bless the sufferers. In the event of a shaman's repeated failures to effect a cure, he is very likely to lose his following and clientele. Priests, however, do not have a clientele. They are expected to perform the rituals meticulously for everyone. Even if gods fail to respond to his prayers and rituals, he keeps on enjoying the confidence and the faith of the people and retains his position. Thus, from shamanism to priesthood, there is the trend of changeover from magic to religion or religious complex and then to modern religious practices.

Societies may have more than one type of religious practitioners. A complex society may have shamans as curers or healers and priests as performers of rituals. This division in areas of religious performances simply addresses the complex problems which arise with the increasing complexities of social life. It is also a matter of economic convenience. Nomadic or semi-nomadic food collectors only have shamans as practitioners. Those with two types of practitioners (shamans and priests) are agriculturists or pastoralists, with political integration beyond the community. Societies with all the four types of practitioners have agriculture and political integration beyond the community and social classes.

Totemism

The word 'totem' is an anglicized word derived from the word 'todam' used by North American Indian tribes. It refers to a widespread, but by no means universal, phenomenon among primitive societies where groups, usually clans, are associated with some animal or plant species, the members of which have mystic relationship with them. The people regard these animal or plant species as their common ancestors and these animal or plant species as their 'totems'. To kill or destroy the totems is tabooed, that is, banned. The people tend to express their relation and concern for their totems by a variety of cultural practices such as periodic collective worship of the totem, artistic representation of the totem by painting or engraving it on their body parts and on the walls of their houses. They may also, at times, organize cultural ceremonies when they take part in dances, putting on masks featuring their totem on their faces, wrapping the skin of the totem animal or the leaves of the totem plant around their bodies and mimicking the sound of their totemic animals. The practices are so varied and so differently distributed in different regions that none of these practices can be singled out for the purpose of defining totemism.

In 1910 Goldenweiser wrote a brilliant essay, mentioning all these practices to synthesize all available information on totemism. According to him, while referring to totemism we mean that a tribe has a social organization, usually of the clan pattern, which is associated with a form of supernaturalism consisting of certain typical attitudes towards species of animals or plants or classes of natural objects. Although killing or eating of the totemic plant or animal species may be taboo, it may take place on ceremonial occasions and the death of the totemic animal may be ceremonially mourned. The totem and totemites may be supposed to share physical and psychical trail and the totem may be looked upon as a sort of a guardian angel of the totemites. Totemic emblems may be worn as charms. Special ceremonies may be performed to pray for the increase of the totemic species. In most cases, the clans are named after the totems.

A great confusion prevailed among anthropologists until Goldenweiser, wrote his celebrated essay. Some of them had tried to show that the association of groups with animal or plant species had nothing mystical about it and regarded it simply a sort of device of naming the group by them. There were yet others who had sought its roots in economic motives. According to Frazer, totemism represented a sort of cooperative division of labour in certain groups, elevating the status and protecting one kind of edible animal or plant. Again, on the basis of Australian evidence, it may be responsible for conception.

Durkheim, again on the basis of Australian evidence, saw in it an emblem or symbol of the collective representation of the social mind. However, Goldenweiser pointed out that given the considerable variation, no ominous solution or explanation of totemism was possible.

In India, quite a number of tribal societies practise totemism, particularly the tribes of Central India tribal belt. The totemic people in India are all organized into exogamous clans. In Australia, Bantu Africa, and North America, the whole society is organized into totemic groups, very often exogamous groups. Even dangerous species such as leopard, crocodile, and cobra are among the totemic species of animals. In some African tribes, individual totems are also found. Mythical belief of totemic descendance is found in Australia and Melanesia, but rarely in Africa. Ritual avoidance of totem is a common experience. In Australia, on specific occasions, totem may be ceremoniously killed and eaten. Durkheim found that among the Aruntas of Australia, it was much a symbolic representation of the group. He regarded totemism as the earliest form of religion.

Divination

Magical practices directed to obtain useful information from a supernatural authority is found in many societies. Divination is considered magical as it is a mechanical procedure for choosing one of a set of alternative solutions when none of them seem to be better or worse than any other. It helps in decision making in the absence of any objective information in favour of any of them. In the event of an indecision or disagreement over a group decision, divination is the most convenient and self-satisfying procedure. In the absence of any scientific information about alternative courses available, it helps to choose one particular course. In the process, it infuses a sense of confidence in the individual or the group about the course chosen since the chosen course is believed to be divinely ordained.

Sorcery

Magic performed with anti-social or malicious intention is sorcery. The intention is always to harm others. Bone pointing is a magical technique in Melanesia. The sorcerer ritually imitates throwing a magical stick, either an arrow or the spine of some animal, towards the individual who is intended to be harmed or killed. There is also some dramatization in the process. The sorcerer performs the actions with an element of expression of hatred or anger. Thrusting, twisting, and pulling are the physical acts associated with emotion which are considered essential to achieve results.

Sorcery, like the other forms of magic, achieves its results indirectly by affecting the individual's emotional state. The effectiveness of sorcery depends on whether the victim is aware that a magical ritual is being performed against him or her. The person against whom sorcery is intended or targeted is made aware about it by indirect sources. He or she remains tense and psychologically disturbed. There is physiological breakdown to begin with. The person may start losing appetite and slowly starve to death. This is deemed as the success of sorcery.

Sorcery is an art or knowledge which is institutionally professionalized. Warner cites the Australian example of sorcerers using a pointed magical bone which is raised towards the targeted person That person gets affected out of fear. He or she may have their speech affected and develop nervous tension leading to unconsciousness.

Witchcraft

Like sorcery, witchcraft is a magical device to harm another person through supernatural means. But unlike sorcery which is a cultivated art, witches are believed to have certain inherited or inborn supernatural powers inherent in their body itself. They tend to enhance their efficacy by consuming rubbish and performing culturally disapproved acts.

Witches are held responsible for evils in the event of calamity or disease since it is believed that these events take place because witches are active. As a result, witch-hunting starts. That is why belief in witches goes hand-in-hand with witch-hunting. Efforts are also made to undo their impact.

Writing about African Azande, Evans Pritchard describes that they believe that witches are persons with in-born supernatural capabilities, but themselves do not have any knowledge of it. A victim knows that a witch is likely to be someone who is acquainted or has a grudge against him or her. Witches are supposed to attack those whom they hate.

A person who thinks he or she has been bewitched consults an oracle. By oracular techniques, the oracle determines or confirms the identity of the attacker. If the witch's activity has not yet resulted in death, the victim or his/her relations may approach the witch and politely ask them to withdraw their witchcraft. The suspected witch usually agrees in order to avoid trouble. But if the victim died, the relatives might avenge the death by killing the witch, provided the chief agrees and his oracles confirmed the original diagnosis. Many survivors also make magic against the witch. The magic is known as vengeance magic.

Thus witchcraft is the practice of harming others at a distance through magical means. It is as old as humankind and universal. It explains evil by stating that someone is out to get one, that is why evil be fed one.

Rites de Passage

Rites of passage are rituals which mark the transition of an individual from one social status to another. In almost all societies, occasions such as conception, birth, puberty, marriage, death, and so on are important and critical events and are marked by religious rituals.

These rites tend to have three phases – separation, transition, and incorporation. Separation involves the break of the individual from his or her old group or status. The rituals concerning this phase symbolize the loss of the old status. Shaving of the head, change of name, change of clothing, and so on symbolize this phase. In the transitional stage, the individual, though cut off from the old status, is yet to be incorporated in the new group and acquire new status. In the third phase he or she is finally incorporated in the new group with new status. The rituals and symbols of this phase are those of rebirth.

Initiation rites prevalent in many African tribes or elsewhere are one of these types. The initiation rituals use many kinds of religious symbolism. Similarly, funerary rites from our own and other societies indicate that death is a rite of passage. In this, the rituals of the first stage involve demonstration of grief by family and friends mark the loss of the person. Separation also involves ceremonial burial or burning of the remains of the dead person. In the transition period, the soul of the dead is very scary as it can take the form of a ghost. In the final stage, which marks the culmination of the whole process, the deceased is incorporated into a new status as one of the ancestors of the family. After the rituals of this stage are over, the deceased is no longer dreaded.

In societies where there are age-sets with marked political functions, the entry and exit of the members from one age-set to the other is elaborately ceremonialized.

Religion, Magic, and Science

Magic is another form of supernaturalism which is differentiated from religion since it has different kinds of supernatural powers and belief and therefore requires a different kind of approach to supernatural powers. To understand magic, its distinction from religion becomes a must. Yet, in ethnographic experience, most of primitive religions are a mix of magic and religion.

Magic believes in the world of supernaturals consisting of forces in control of humans. Unlike magic, in religion the supernatural powers are conceived as entities having consciousness and with human characteristics who can listen and act in a decisive manner. But in the concept of magic, supernatural powers, though capable of fulfilling all human desires, are believed to be in total control of persons who have knowledge of magical procedures and are capable of manipulating them according to their wishes and desires. Unlike religion, in magic humans are not subject to the mercy or sympathy of the supernatural. They are in command and control of the mechanically-operating supernatural forces and an manipulate them for events and situations to work in their favour. Prayers, persuasions, offerings, have no place in magic. Instead, the verbal pronouncements or the formulae are the commands to the supernatural forces to make them behave in the manner desired by the magician.

Magic involves specific ritual procedures which, if done correctly, will produce a specific and predictable result. Frazer studied magical procedures in minute detail and came to the conclusion that magic is like science in a number of ways. Like science, according to Frazer, there are things used, things done, and things spoken. The things spoken are like the formulae of the scientists. Also, analysing magical practices of a large number of primitive people, he concluded that like science, magic is also based on certain immutable laws. One such law, as in science, is the 'Law of Similarity' which states that similar acts or causes yield similar results. Another law is like the law of inertia in science which states that two objects once in contact are always in contact. Frazer called this law as the 'Law of Contiguity' or simply the 'Law of Contact'.

One form of magic can be categorized as 'imitative magic' or 'homeopathic magic'. In imitative magic, the procedure performed resembles the results desired. Imitative magic may go back to thousands of years to upper Palaeolithic times. In cave paintings of those times, pictures of bleeding animals suggest that imitative magic was used by them to ensure success in hunting.

Magic based on the law of contact may be categorized as contagious magic. However, according to Frazer, there are many magics in which such a clear-cut distinction is not possible and both the types of laws are synthesized in them. To such magic, Frazer gives the term 'sympathetic magic'.

Like science, magic is also a specialized knowledge requiring a lot of precision. It cannot be everybody's job. It requires a specialist performer who must be approached by people with their problems and desires. Thus, unlike religion, magic has a clientele. It is individualistic and not public. There cannot be a church of magic. At times, its activities are secretive because of the possibility of a more potent counter-magic to undo it.

But despite all these similarities, why is magic not science? Frazer gives the clarification that there is nothing wrong with the validity of scientific laws used by magicians. They are as valid as they are in science but for their misapplication – Frazer calls that as illegitimate application of scientific laws by the magicians. This emergence of illegitimate application is because of the illogical understanding of these laws. Similarity is confused for identity.

Identical acts can never cause similar results. Similarly, in the law of contact, once in contact always in contact is all right, but the scientist uses this law with the condition that the law is valid unless the two are removed or separated. Magic skips over this conditionality and applies this law even when the physical contact is removed. If legitimately applied, these laws yield science, if illegitimately applied, they yield magic or 'the bastard sister of science'. He calls magic as pseudo science.

Thus, according to Frazer, all magic is false. If at all it is ever to be true, it will be science and not magic. Yet, people continue to have faith in magic because sometimes people's desires are fulfilled by chance – not by the consequence or efficacy or success of magic but because of the interplay of the chance factor and the credit for this success goes to magic.

The role of the magician is yet another factor. Magicians never accept the failure of their magic. They always find some mistake in the accuracy of the procedure adopted or attribute the failure to the success of some counter-magic.

'Unlike science which measures outcomes through empirical and experimental means, magic invokes a symbolic cause–effect relationship. Moreover, like religion and unlike science, magic has an expressive function in addition to its instrumental function. Magical rainmaking strategies, for example, may or may not be efficacious, but they serve the expressive purpose of reinforcing the social importance of rain and farming to a community' (Encyclopaedia Britannica).

Religion and Symbolism

Clifford Geertz holds that there are two reasons for which anthropologists study religions. Firstly, they wish to perform an analysis of the meanings embodied in the symbols which make up religion. Secondly, they want to relate these symbols to social structural and psychological processes.

A symbol stands for a general or a particular concept. The things, categories and ideas, or events evoked as a concept may be only imaginary but may bring about thoughts, feelings or intentions, and complex messages among the decoders of the symbol. Parsons (1961) speaks of typology of four types of symbolization – constitutive, moral evaluative, expressive, and cognitive.

According to him, constitutive symbols are often latent and are patterns of the most general kind in their implications. Religious symbols are constitutive in character. Moral evaluative symbols are integrative. Expressive symbols have to do with goal attainment and in their aesthetic forms express relatively pure purposiveness. Cognitive symbolization is largely adaptive. Concrete symbols are often of mixed types, constitutive or religious symbols frequently have cognitive, expressive, and moral evaluative implications. Religious ideas are always expressed through, symbols which carry meaningful and integrative message for the society of which they are a part.

Ritual constitutes the behavioural concomitant of religion. It is always a patterned activity of numerous rites which are defined as acts which are directed to the supernatural. Rituals are patterned acts involving manipulation of religious symbols to contact gods and spirits. They constitute a highly expressive form of symbolism. Ravana and Mahishasur, symbols of evil, are killed and burnt ritually and ceremoniously every year in Dushehra and Durga-puja celebrations. Ritual inculcates, enhances, and fortifies the faith of the people in the powers of their world of belief. It is this element of faith which integrates or binds people in a community of common faith.

Religion and Economy

In the formal science of Economics, religion has no role to perform. Economy is defined as the management of basic needs of life and relies basically on the human effort of organizing with the help of technology to extract essentials from the environment. Economics is basically a question of human–nature relationship.

Whatever may be the means and modes of production, food is the most basic necessity. Procurement or production of food is often surrounded by many kinds of uncertainties on which humans have no control. To assure regular food supply, humans have to take a recourse to religion. Many complex magico-religious rituals are organized by hunting and fishing communities to assure their success in hunting and fishing expeditions. To horticulturists and even advanced cultivators, suitable climatic conditions and timely occurrence of rains is a must. Religious offerings, sacrifices, and prayers are ritually organized to invoke supernatural powers to sustain people's confidence.

Lower the level of technology, higher the domination of religion in the economy. In modern economies, governments arrange to maintain enough buffer food stock for a year or two to feed the population. Yet, despite technological efficiency, the unseen hands of destiny are always feared. Despite overall improvement in the Indian economy, people in the country still remember what failure of monsoon means. The scientists can only predict the general prospects of the monsoon and some precautionary measures can be adopted to minimise the negative impact. But if the monsoon has failed, nothing can bring about a normal one. Faith in supernatural powers and organization of mass scale religious rituals are the only recourses open to the people. Even in American life, the annual thanksgiving ritual at the arrival of a new harvest is an example of the role of religion in the economy in a highly technological economy.

Religion and Politics

Religion and politics are composed of separate threads, yet they are woven into the tapestry that is society. Sometimes carefully separated, each forming its own design, but often inter-twined. joining church (religion) and State in one pattern.

The sword of the ruler and the priest's robe are two different objects, and a person may have one or the other. But if he is skilled enough and if his culture permits, he may seize the sword and don the garb of the priest and may become an awesome power to cope with. The essential doctrine of separation of the church (religion) and the State in European and American administration is a defensive reaction to that power.

Shamans, priests and spiritualists control the actions of supernatural. Headman chiefs and kings are specialists in controlling the actions of individuals and groups. A politician uses religious means for political purposes when he or she acquires control over religious power.

A priest is apt to use political means to promote religious ends when he has the capability to do so. This occurs sometimes in the primitive world, but it occurs very often in the modern world that the rivalry between the church and the State becomes sharp. In primitive States, a working agreement between the two often exists.

In modern times, theocratic States do exist to promote religious ends. In some of the modern States, creation of vote banks on the basis of religion leads to dangerous consequences of creating fault lines in the society. In modern politics, politics and religion often get mixed. This creates an explosive social situation. A quotation from Praful Bidwai (The Times of India, 25 October 1991) makes the point clearer:

> Religion has never been a politically integrative force or an adequate criterion for the definition of National Identity in modern

period. Religion's potential as a unifying force, underpinning nationalism was long exhausted. Indeed, for the most part, in the entire process of formation of nation-States, first in Europe and the white settlements and later in the former colonies, religion has undoubtedly been at work in disintegrating nations in various stages of crystallization. Pakistan was a remarkable success in equation of religion and politics, but there too, religion could not furnish a durable basis for a new nation-State. Elsewhere in Asia and Africa too, religion has been less of a cementing force than a destabilizing force. The particular case of Indonesia in South East Asia is remarkable, if not unique, for its strong and relatively stable relations between communalism and nationalism, between ethnic, national and religious identities. In their own way, different religions have under-pinned separatist movements aspiring to New Nationhood.

The way religion and religious identity are being used as a political tool by various political parties in India is playing with fire. They do not seem to have taken any lessons from the past.

Monotheism and Polytheism

There has never been a single idea of god. Different human societies are divided on the existence of one or multiple gods. Monotheism refers to the belief in one god and oneness of god. Among the major religions Islam, Christianity, Judaism, and Sikhism are strongly monotheistic religions. The case of Hinduism has been debatable. In the pantheon of gods Hinduism may look as polytheistic but scholars are of the view that the number of gods/ deities are merely manifestation of one Supreme Being.

Sects and Cults

Sects and cults may be understood as derivatives of popular religions. Sects and cults are closely inter-related concepts. A sect is a type of religious group that is distinguished by having broken away from a large religious organization. It is a more organized closed group adhering to a minority religious code. Beliefs and practices of sects are orthodox. Quakers and Mormons in Christianity, Sunni, Shia, Bohra, and Khoja in Islam and Vaishnavism, Shaivism, and Shaktism in Hinduism are some examples of sects.

Cults may be explained in terms of more spontaneous and open movement, often revolving around a particular religious leader and lacking a formal authority and structure. Its membership requirements are also not strictly defined. Thus a cult may be seen more as a politico-religious concept. Membership of a sect is largely based on birth and transmitted from parents to the next generation. This is not the case with a cult, which is largely an individual's choice.

Classical Theoretical Perspectives: Durkheim, Weber, Marx

Though a number of ideas and theories have been advanced on religion, the sociological approach to religion is strongly influenced by Emile Durkheim, Max Weber, and Karl Marx. Through their writings, they reshaped the study of religion moving from the theological and cosmological orientation of the earlier scholars to the role of religion in society. That was a major departure from the past, making way for sociological explanations.

Durkheim (1858-1917)

Durkheim was a towering scholar in French sociology and was a proponent of the functionalist school of thought. According to this school, society functions as a whole and each part of the society has a specific role to perform, contributing to the better functioning of the society. In his celebrated work The Elementary Forms of Religious Life (1912), he explored the ideas of the sacred and the profane. While sacred stands for holy, profane represents unholy. He asserted that society practises religion by regarding certain things as sacred and others as profane. According to Durkheim, totemism represents the simplest form of religion, which he explained through his study of the Australian aboriginal tribes.

Weber (1864-1920)

He was a German sociologist, philosopher, and economist. He looked at religion from the perspective of its contribution to the development of industrial capitalism in Western Europe. While Marx considered economics as the factor shaping society, Weber thought that ideas, especially religious ideas, were equally important. Weber's well known work Sociology of Religion is regarded as the first sociological attempt to compare the world's religions. On the basis of this comparative study Weber inferred that Asian religious beliefs and ethical systems were a barrier to the development of capitalist economic growth in the way it developed in Western Europe. In his most celebrated work, The Protestant Ethic and the Spirit of Capitalism (1905) he said that the value of self-denial and self-discipline which developed in West European Protestantism provided the ethic that played an important role in the development of capitalism. 'Weber found evidence of the ethical and psychological framework necessary for the success of industrial capitalism. He did not dismiss the role of economics in shaping the social dynamics of western Europe' (K.G. Guest, 2018).

Marx (1818–1883)

He was a German political philosopher, economist, and socialist. He had an entirely different perspective on religion. He was highly critical of the role of religion in society. In his celebrated work Capital (1867), he radically criticized capitalism and the capitalist economic system. He did not do a detailed study of religion. He described religion as opiate/opium for the masses as it makes the exploited masses and working class numb and dull and diverts their attention and energy from their oppression, deprivation, and exploitation and makes them believe that God shall give them all comforts in the life after death. Thus, he considered religion as a system of social stratification and inequality that hinders social change and promotes the perpetual state of injustice in the society. The role of religion is exploitative and destructive. Marx described religion as 'the sigh of the oppressed'.

Secularism and Secularization

Being a sociological concept, secularism stands for an ideology and has strong ideological connotations but the popular usage of this term in India does not conform to this ideological position.

Let us take up the ideological implications of this term in purely sociological terms. On a theoretical plane, as Emile Durkheim puts it, all that is there in the world – beliefs, myths, dogmas, actions, persons, and beings, are either 'sacred' or 'secular'. All that is related with religion is covered under sacred. According to this definition, all traditional societies arc basically sacred societies because they are governed, in crucial segments of social life and in varying degrees, by laws of religion. Religion controls the activities of the members of these societies. Among the characteristics of secularism, the following are the most important ones:

1. Separation of authority between the church (religion) and the State
2. Emphasis on 'this world' as opposed to the 'other world'
3. Rationalism and scientific outlook

Secularism implies that the State will not be governed by the church, that is, by a religious authority such as a bishop, pundit, mullah, or khalifa.

The doctrines promoting social inertia such as fatalism and divine retribution have no place in secularism. A secular mind is characterized by rationality. A secular (modern) society is not against religion and it has to fight superstition and intolerance as well as bigotry and obscurantism.

Societies are not born secular. The societies that are practicing varying degrees of secularism had to undergo transformation from a traditional (religious/sacred) society to a secular society. The process of secularization played its part in this transformation. Secularization is a process of social change through which the public influence of religion and religious thinking declines and is replaced by other ways of explaining reality and regulating social life. A number of Western societies are examples of this process where religion still survives but is largely confined to the private domain of individuals.

Secularism was inserted in the preamble of our Constitution in 1976. Two explanations of secularism have been operating side by side. The first is the Western concept of the separation of religion and politics, especially separation of religion and the State, which virtually relegates religion to the realm of the private. The second is the sarva dharma sambhava (equal respect to all religions). Secularism in the Indian context is opposed to communalism ideologically. It signifies religious non-discrimination and equal liberty for all citizens, believers and non-believers. A secular polity is one in which the State does not discriminate between citizens on the basis of their religious conviction. It grants equal civil rights to all citizens, respects the religious liberty of each and protects even the liberty of those who are atheists or agnostics and do not believe in religion and god.

Secularism today is facing a crisis worldwide. Gurpreet Mahajan (2003) points out that the critics of secularism in India make two arguments: (a) the concept of secularism – separation of religion and politics – is alien to Indian society and way of life, hence it has no place in the Indian context; (b) separation of religion from politics is an idea that comes from the Protestant ethic – as a 'gift of Christianity' – and has limited applicability. The advocates of secularism regret the fact that the Indian State is not sufficiently secular as it allows the use of religion in the public domain. According to them the intermixing of religion and politics can play havoc with the peace and prosperity of the country as is amply clear from the prevailing conditions in our neighbouring countries, Pakistan and Afghanistan.

Secularism is understood as antithesis of communalism. This view also promotes the protection of minorities from a dominating majority.

Indian society, since its beginning, was able to set traditions under which an integrated social, cultural and political life was possible in a multi-religious, multi-ethnic, and multi-lingual framework. Imposing its own cultural and religious ideas and symbols on others has been alien to the Hindu tradition and true Hinduism. This is amply demonstrated by one of its greatest exponents, Swami Vivekanand.

The process of secularization operates through three factors:
1. Education
2. Legislation
3. Social reform

Education, when imparted on scientific and rational lines, gives rise to rationality in the thinking process. If we take the case of India, education was imparted through religious institutions pathshalas, madrasas, and seminaries attached to temples, maths, mosques and churches. When the scope of acquisition of formal education was widened and secular educational institutions were opened, it brought about a sea change. The change in the content of education and medium of instruction was largely responsible for this. That is why the role of formal education in social transformation is critical.

Legislative action is also crucial factor in the process of secularization. But mere legislative action, not supported by proper motivation and social environment, may not achieve the desired results. Many developing countries may be cited as examples of this situation. Take the case of India. Our country became secular by legislative fiats without the backing of sufficient infrastructure for the emergence of true secularism. In our country's desire for secularism and national unity lurk a variety of challenges like parochial, narrow minded, obscurantist, and unscientific beliefs that threaten to tear the fabric of our 'secular' country apart. Casteism, tribalism, linguism, communalism, and religious extremism are painful facts of our day-to-day existence.

Secularism is a way of life. It is not a slogan but an article of faith. Social movement for social reform is a potent weapon for the promotion of the process of secularization. It does mental conditioning and prepares the people to accept social change. Whatever degree of secularism our society has achieved and absorbed owes a lot to various social reform movements launched from time to time.

Two subsidiary factors in the secularization process are urbanization and industrialization. Both these factors owe a lot to technological innovations. As the area of scientific knowledge and technology widens, the area of religion shrinks. This does not mean that religion and science are incompatible. As S.C. Dube (1974), an eminent scholar, pointed out, 'On a higher spiritual and moral plane, religion is not necessarily inconsistent with the idiom of science and the ethos of progress. Moreover, urbanization and industrialization help loosen the grip of "in group" feeling and present newer alternatives to humans. Further, it promotes rational cause–effect explanations and the hold of religious beliefs over different aspects of life declines, although interest in religion as a phenomenon persists. It sheds much of its collective and communal overtones and becomes largely a personal concern.'

The State of India sought to promote the secularization process by:

1. Abolishing such symbols of ritual inequality as untouchability, the practice of which has been declared a penal offence.
2. Throwing open all religious places and institutions to all classes and sections of the people.
3. Reform of the Hindu Personal Law, eventually aiming at evolving a common/uniform personal law for all communities in the country.
4. Forbidding all such places as shops, public restaurants, hotels, and places of public entertainment from discriminating against any citizen of the State.
5. Throwing open all educational institutions to members of all communities.
6. Secularizing the content of text books by including material which could be helpful in the promotion of a scientific–rational outlook by deleting material likely to poison the readers' minds, which smacked of traditionalism, obscurantism, and religious orthodoxy.
7. Developing a sound economic base to eradicate poverty and ensure an equitable distribution of wealth among the people.

Secularism is one of the basic elements in the process of modernization. If our society is to become modernized to cope with the worldwide changes, we are left with no other option but to adopt 'secularism in practise' by speeding up the process of secularization.

Religious Revivalism and Fundamentalism

Religion and its practices have never been static. People of different religions have been trying to infuse energy and zeal in their religious practices from time to time, depending on social, economic commitment to the group, as well as restoring the past 'glory' of the religion or the religious ideology.

Religious revivalism refers to mass movements which are based upon intense religious upheavals and seek to restore the purity and core values of the religion which, according to them, had suffered or eroded with the changing times. For instance, religious revivalism called the Methodist movement occurred in Christianity in Europe in the 18th century. In India, the Arya Samaj movement is an example of religious revivalism among the Hindus. It tried to abolish untouchability, make the rituals simple and inexpensive, and minimize the role of the priests. It motivated the Hindus to give up idol worship and adopt rationalism in religion, as much as possible. However, its reformist zeal suffered when, through the shuddhi (purification), it began converting outcasts as well as Muslims and Christians who had earlier come out of Hindu fold and adopted Islam or Christianity for different reasons. The shuddhi movement resulted in communal tensions and riots and dented the reformist image of the movement.

Fundamentalism is frequently used in the same breath as revivalism and communalism. But fundamentalism is more closely associated with the notion of religious fanaticism. It is an attempt to go back to the 'fundamentals' of a religious tradition in a glorifying, non-critical, and absolutizing way. 'It is unquestioning faith in the infallibility of a doctrine, usually religious, accompanied by a readiness to act in its defense and/or promotion.' The word is most widely used in modern times in relation to Islamic faith. However, fundamentalism is not restricted to Muslims alone. There is a rise of militancy with a similar attitude of intolerance in other religions, too.

Fundamentalism is sociologically important because of its unique place among religions, and also because it easily extends itself into the political realm. Whatever the religious colour, fundamentalists are opposed to modern ideas and denounce all forms of intellectual arguments. 'Though strictly speaking fundamentalism is more a characteristic of the religions of the (divine) books like Judaism, Christianity and Islam. However, what can today be observed is an attempt to "fundamentalise" Hinduism as well, by reducing it to certain basic scriptures like the Vedas, Upanishad, Gita and certain "unifying" myths like the martial and militant version of Ram' (Gabriele Dietrich, 1995).

If we take a close look, we find that fundamentalism associates itself with political conservatism along with heavily patriarchal values. At the same time it associates 'itself with aggressive forms of capitalism which can be seen among the Christian fundamentalists in the "electronic church" in the USA' (Dietrich, ibid).

Fundamentalism has closer links with religion than communalism. While communalism claims to speak the language of secularism (secular jargon) and nationalism, fundamentalism tries to argue about the fundamentals of religion. It may, therefore, at times open up inter-religious arguments but usually tends to be frightened of inter-religious dialogue. Under the present pressure of communal politics which creates a feeling of Hinduism, Islam, Christianity, and so on being in danger, fundamentalist forces are gaining ground in all the religious communities. Occasionally, fundamentalism can also be a response to the uprooting effects, accelerated by capitalist development, as the socially reformist beginnings of Bhindranwale, the present face of Sikh fundamentalism. Jamaat-e-Islami in India represents Muslim fundamentalism because it continues to over emphasize, as core ideology, certain fundamentals of Islam which do not seem to be compatible with modern times. The fundamentalist elements in Pakistan and the Taliban of Afghanistan are the worst forms of Muslim fundamentalism threatening to take their societies into medieval or ancient times or dark ages.

According to some scholars, fundamentalist movements appear to be in response to the rapid changes occurring in the modern world.

Religious/Communal Conflict and Violence

Religion and religious identity have played a role in several conflict zones of the world. Religious beliefs and religious identity provide the moral ammunition to justify and carry out violence. In India, hate speeches and statements in print media, social media, and TV channels instigate religious conflicts and violence.

Violence between religious communities in the form of riots and acts of terrorism draw our attraction in a dramatic manner but the underlying and root cause of this violence is the spread of communalism. As Bipan Chandra (1984) remarks, while the communal riots give credibility to the basic communal ideological precepts among the ordinary people and enlists further support for communal politicians, it is the communal ideology and politics, which the communal politicians and ideology preach in normal times, which form the real basis on which communal tensions and violence occur. 'Communal riots and other forms of communal violence are only a concrete conjectural manifestation of communalization of society and politics. Communal ideology leads to communal politics and psychology differentiation, distance and competition along religious lines' (Chandra, ibid).

Communalism and communal violence are the products of the overall social, economic, and political situation of the society. Communal violence has usually been an urban phenomenon where the deprived and poor people have been involved. But more than religion, it is the communal propaganda, rumour mongering, and communal mobilization that have been responsible. Any type of violence and lawlessness provides an opportunity to the interested people to indulge in loot and plunder, largely for economic reasons. Significantly, the dirty work of violence is left to a certain type of communalized militant youth, especially belonging to the deprived classes, and sometimes to tribal groups, while the ideological work is performed with great subtlety. This may be an 'intelligent' tactic on the part of the communal leadership to divert the attention of the traditionally deprived sections of the people from their problems. It may also be a ploy for blocking the deprived sections of the society from finding a rightful place in the power structure and challenge the control of the those in power.

Critical Thinking Questions

- How should we understand religion and religious beliefs?
- How is religious faith transformed into fundamentalism?
- How is religion exploited for political goals?
- What is the relationship between magic and science?
- What is the relationship between magic and religion?

****

10

Caste and Caste Systems

Chapter Outline: *Introduction and definitions; Varna model and jati model of caste; Functions of caste system; Jajmani system, its decline and consequences; Untouchability; Perspectives on the study of caste system: Ghurye, Srinivas, Dumont,and Beitelle; Ritual aspect or binary opposition between pure/impure (pollution); Caste system as viewed by contemporary social anthropologist; Caste: cultural and structural view; Caste mobility and sanskritization; Changes in the ritual and economic aspects of caste ; Caste system and its transformation; Caste and politics; Caste and non-Hindus(Muslims, Sikhs,and Christians); Dalit identity and consciousness; Future of caste system.*

Learning Objectives

- How can caste system be seen as a model of social stratification?
- How is caste status an ascribed status and caste system a closed system?
- What are the changes coming into the caste system?

Introduction and Definitions

Historically, India has been existing as a nation for millennia with closed groups divided by caste, creed, and language. Caste and caste systems are such a significant feature of Indian society that when thinking of India, it is hard not to think of caste. Many scholars see India's caste system as the defining feature of Indian culture.

Caste has come to be associated with a social science concept. The phenomenon which we now call 'caste' was named by Western observers at an early stage of the colonial period. The phenomenon of caste has probably aroused more controversy than any other aspect of Indian life and thought.

Caste is such a complex phenomenon that it is difficult to define it precisely and every definition pose some problem or the other.

Caste is deeply ingrained in our social system and in the minds of the overwhelming majority of people with the concomitant features of discriminations of all sorts. Except for the tribal communities, caste system or caste-like social organization may be witnessed in almost all segments of the Indian society. Whether status sub-divisions or caste-like groupings among the non-Hindu communities, especially Muslims, should be called 'caste' is a matter of academic discussion.

In theory, the caste system defines a division of labour and in practice many occupations are caste-specific, especially in the services and artisan sectors such as barbers, washermen, blacksmiths, goldsmiths, weavers, butchers, carpenters, leather workers, scavengers, and so on. If we go into the history of caste studies, we find that 'Census reports, together with the gazetteers and the encyclopaedic "Caste and Tribes" volumes covering almost all parts of British India contained copious information about thousands of different castes. This corpus of "official ethnography" is still useful as a repository of facts and (often) fictions about castes but it reveals little about how the caste system actually worked in any particular place. When modern sociological and anthropological research on India began in the late 1940s, it was based on intensive ethnographic fieldwork, mainly in rural India' (C.J. Fuller, 2003).

On the basis of dozens of definitions, caste may be understood and explained as a form of social stratification which involves:

1. A system of hierarchically ranked levels
2. Closed
3. Endogamous strata
4. Ascribed membership
5. Restriction of contact between castes
6. Mobility theoretically impossible.
7. Social-economic-political disabilities of lower caste groups

'It reflects economic inequalities; by virtue of the occupations typically followed by, or permitted to members, caste stratification is ultimately rooted in non-economic criteria. In its purest form, in Hindu India, the caste principle is religious – castes are ranked in accordance with the degree of "ritual purity" ascribed to members and to their activities' (David Jary and Julia Jary, 1991).

Historically, the most developed form, and some would argue the only true form, of caste stratification occurred in India in association with Hinduism. The origins of this system are obscure. They probably lie in the twin bases of ethnicity and occupational specialization. The system which the Brahmins perfected was founded on five main divisions, four caste groups (varna) and an outcaste group (pancham varna), the fifth varna or the untouchables. The four caste groups were the Brahmins, the priestly class having religious authority; the Kshatriyas, the secular and military ruler and landlord caste; the Vaishyas, the mercantile middle class, and the Shudra, the servants and slaves class. The untouchables performed only the most degrading and ritually impure/polluting tasks.

Caste has been described as the fundamental social institution of India. As Andre Beteille (1996) points out, 'Sometimes the term is used metaphorically to refer to rigid social distinctions or extreme social exclusiveness wherever found. But it is among the Hindus in India that we find the system in its most fully developed form, although analogous forms exist among Muslims, Christians, Sikhs, and other religious groups in South Asia.'

In order to avoid any confusion, scholars have tried to understand caste through two models – the varna model of caste and the jati model of caste.

Varna Model

The origin of caste (varna) cannot be traced to an exact point of time or source. There are several theories which deal with the origin of the caste system. The divine origin theory explains the divine origin of caste system. It involves a certain amount of sacrament and thus it is believed that it is an arrangement made not by human beings, but by divinity. The 'Purush Sukta' a hymn of Rigveda tells us of the emergence of four varnas after the Purusha (Brahma) resorted to self-destruction so that a proper social order could come into existence. The Brahmins came out of the mouth, the Kshatriyas from the arms, the Vaishyas from the thighs, and the Shudras from the feet of the primordial being, the Mahapurush.

The racial theory of varna takes into account the term 'varna' which means skin colour, an important criterion of racial classification. The racial theory suggests segregation of people according to their social affiliations. Several scholars like H.H. Risley agreed with this theory. But in the virtual absence of any scientific data or evidence like fossil records, the racial theory suffers from several lacunae and unexplained areas.

Another theory is the guna theory about the origin of varna makes some sociological sense. It is based on the view that there are three basic gunas (charismatic attributes or endowments) found in the personality of each person. These are the sattva guna, the rajas guna, and the tamas guna. The sattva guna refers to the purity, lack of attraction towards worldly things, and devotion to knowledge The rajas guna represents the steadfastness to truth, duty, justice, and self-sacrifice for the larger interests of the society. The tamas guna refers to obsession with worldly things, satisfaction of biological needs, and hence 'beastly' tendencies. It is believed that all these guna are present in every person but one of the predominates and hence becomes the chief marker of the person's personality. Thus, the predominance of sattvik guna entitles one to be a Brahmin, the rajas a Kshatriya and the tamas a Vaishya. Those who possess only tamas guna were Shudras. Thus a Brahmin's duty was to acquire knowledge and preach, a Kshatriya was entrusted with the job of administration and protecting and defending the land, the Vaishya was supposed to do cultivation, trade, and commerce, and a Shudra was obliged to serve the other three varnas. In hierarchical order, the Brahmins occupied the highest place followed by the Kshatriyas, Vaishyas, and the Shudras. Significantly, these groupings did not enjoy any ascribed status and as the Vishnu Purana tells us, everyone is born as a Shudra and it is only one's karma that entitles one to be a Brahmin, Kshatriya, Vaishya, or Shudra. It further states that the varna system was not closed and inter-varna mobility was possible. During Vedic times, Shudras were not untouchables but were merely a conglomeration or a multiplicity of artisan castes.

The work of Manu throws a lot of light on the state of society of his times as well as the desired and ideal social order. It relates both to secular and sacerdotal spheres of life. He prescribed, in well-defined terms, the duties (dharma) such as varna dharma, ashrama dharma, rajya dharma, grihya dharma, and so on. The Brahmins wrote a number of dharma shastras which may be described as important sociological treatises.

Marriages were also classified according to the varna scheme as 'anuloma', that is, in the natural order of castes, and 'pratiloma', that is, against the natural order of castes. Under the anuloma form, a Brahmin male could marry not only a Brahmin woman, but a Kshatriya, Vaishya, or a Shudra woman; a Kshatriya, apart from marrying a Kshatriya woman, could also marry a Vaishya or a Shudra; and a Vaishya, apart from a Vaishya woman, could also marry a Shudra. Anuloma marriages, though never preferred, were recognized and the offsprings treated as legitimate. But a pratiloma marriage, that is, the marriage of a male from a lower caste to a female of a higher caste, was prohibited and condemned. But both anuloma and pratiloma were practised and sometimes new castes or mixed castes emerged leading to confusion in social hierarchy. Both of these forms of marriage also led to caste mobility.

Jati Model

In an honest and frank appraisal, M.N. Srinivas says that the varna model has produced a wrong and distorted image of caste. The varna model was an ideal form of Indian social stratification. It was more an ideal or desired form of social stratification rather than an actual one. It was a loose and broad categorization of Indian or Hindu society. It had a definite hierarchy where the Brahmins occupied the top rung and the Shudra the lowest in the ladder, with untouchables placed outside its pale. Some mobility was allowed. But the other model, the jati model, has always been an ethnographic and empirical reality. When exactly the jati model emerged is still a matter of debate among the social historians. But one thing is almost certain, that by the Gupta period (around 4th century) it had crystalized and people were living along with it.

With the emergence of the jati model, the system became closed. Jati represented the watertight compartmentalization of society with definite rules. The morphology of the Hindu caste (jati) system can be described in terms of three key characteristics (Bougle, 1908), all of which are underpinned by the religious values of purity (Dumont, 1970). In Social Science Encyclopaedia, J.P. Parry summarises the situation by saying that:

1. There is a hierarchy of castes which is theoretically based on their relative degree of purity. As the purest of all, the Brahmins rank the highest and are, in principle, both distinct from and superior to the caste which actually wields politico-economic power.

2. Since the pure can maintain their purity only if there are impure castes, to remove the pollution that they inevitably incur by their involvement in the natural world, there is a division of labour between castes resulting in their interdependence.

3. Pollution is contagious and a caste must therefore restrict its contact with inferiors in order to maintain its status. This separation takes many forms – a rule of endogamy precluding marital alliances with inferiors, restrictions on commensality, the outcasting of those who transgress the rules lest they pollute the rest of the group, and the phenomenon of untouchability debarring physical contact between 'clean' and 'polluted' groups.

If we analyse these three major features, we get the following characteristics of the caste (jati) system.

1. The Innate Nature: The membership of jati is determined by birth. A man dies in the same caste in which he is born and it is his caste that determines his social status. The caste status is simply an ascribed status.

2. Endogamy: A strict endogamy is one of the most important features of jati. Every jati or sub-jati permits marriage within the group. The system has been so rigid that traditionally, inter-caste marriages were prohibited. Even today, endogamy is followed quite rigidly.

3. Hierarchy: Because of fixed hierarchy, what we see is a hierarchical social structure. A village or cluster of villages or a region maintains a definite hierarchy in which each jati's place is well-defined. But the jati hierarchy, unlike the varna hierarchy, is local or regional in nature. This means that the hierarchical position of a particular jati may vary from region to region while varna hierarchy is fixed throughout India. Thus, in jati hierarchy the place of Brahmins is predominant and the untouchable jatis are placed at the bottom. However, the jatis placed at the intermediate levels may show minor variations in the hierarchy.

4. Commensality: Sharing or acceptance of food and water is governed by detailed rules. Severe restrictions are found in eating and social intercourse. Food has been divided into pucca food (fried) and kuccha food (uncooked) and well-defined rules are followed in the matters of who accepts from whom.

5. Occupational Restrictions: Occupation of each caste is predetermined by birth and every caste is supposed to treat its occupation as a religious duty.

6. Disabilities and Privileges: The Brahmins and other higher castes (dwija or twice-born) enjoy a number of privileges in religious and secular matters while the untouchables suffer from a number of social disabilities.

7. Caste Councils: The existence of caste panchayats (councils) having authority to compel obedience from its members is also an important feature of the caste system. The violation of all sorts of taboos is dealt with by these caste councils. Using its socio-political authority, it can outcaste or excommunicate any of its members.

Functions of the Caste System

Traditionally, the caste system may be seen as performing the following functions:

- It minimises economic competition by determining the occupation of various caste groups.

- By restricting and limiting the range, it helps its members in their endeavour of choosing a life partner. The rules of endogamy are, traditionally, very strict and violations are taken seriously with punishments meted out.

- The economic basis of the caste system is the jajmani system. This is an elaborate division of labour governed by a well-defined system of exchange of goods and services. The higher, land-owning castes and the lower occupationally specialized castes or service castes, are traditionally bound by certain jajmani obligations. The patrons (jajmans) or higher castes who control land exchange the land-produce against the services provided by the other castes.

Caste may also be seen as a social and psychological resource for its members. Because of a sense of solidarity and common consciousness, the members of a caste come to the rescue of fellow caste persons.

Jajmani System

This has been the socio-economic basis of the Hindu caste system and an integral part of the agrarian social structure in India. It is said that the term 'jajmani system' has been introduced in the vocabulary of Indian sociology and social anthropology by Willian Wiser through his pioneering work The Hindu Jajmani System (1936). He carried out this study in the Karimpur village in Uttar Pradesh. In this seminal contribution, Wiser described in detail how different castes interact with one another in the production and exchange of goods and services. Though there are regional variations of this term in different parts of the country the term, 'jajmani system' has become the standard term in sociological literature.

Under the jajmani system, each caste group within a village is expected to give certain standardized services to the families of other castes. In general terms, it stands for the exchange of goods and services between the landed higher castes and landless service castes. These castes have are occupationally specialized, following certain traditional occupations, and are also known as 'artisan castes'. These artisan castes such as blacksmiths, goldsmiths, weavers, oilseed tillers, leather workers, barbers, washermen, musicians, and a wide range of occupationally-specialized groups, along with the traditionally landless untouchable castes providing agricultural labour, constitute the service castes and known as either 'kamin', 'prajan' or similar terms in different parts of the country. The landed higher castes are known as 'jajman' (patrons). These service relations, which are governed by a hereditary tenure, are called the 'jajman–prajan' (patron–client) relations.

The jajmani system is essentially an agriculture-based system of production and distribution of goods and services. Through jajmani relations the occupational castes get linked with the land-owning dominant castes. The land-owning castes maintain a paternalistic attitude of superiority towards the occupational or service castes.

The system operates on the occupational division of labour in Indian agricultural villages, with distribution of services and products under a network of role-relationships and payments. Tradition approves of such an arrangement and mutual interdependence ensures its continuity. Hence, it may also be referred to as a scheme of functional interdependence in the Indian agrarian system based on caste.

The social dynamics of the jajmani system is such that it is not easy for an agriculturist to remove a family attached to his household and secure the services of another. No one else would be willing to act as a substitute for fear of being penalized by the caste panchayat.

David Mandelbaum (1972), a keen observer of village India, emphasised the internal functioning of the jajmani system and says that the jajmani relations essentially operate at family level. A Rajput landowning family has its jajmani ties with one family each from Brahmin, barber, carpenter, and other service castes and the family of service caste offers its services to specific families of jajmans. Jajmani rules are enforced by the caste panchayats.

The jajmani relations are durable and are of hereditary nature. The jajmani relations (or rights) may be regarded as a form of property passing from father to son. These relations are informal and governed largely by local traditions.

Another very important feature of the jajmani system is that though the jajmani relations operate at village level, they are often not confined only to a single village because not all the villages have all occupational castes. Therefore the services of occupational castes from other villages are frequently sought. Moreover, for certain occupational castes such as goldsmiths, blacksmiths, and carpenters, a single village may not be adequate to provide sufficient job round the year. Such castes, therefore, cater to the needs of a number of villages in a given region.

On the whole, the jajmani system carries strong elements of dominance, exploitation, and conflict, as well as conflict resolution. There is a wide difference in the power of landowning dominant patrons and the artisans and landless labourers who serve them.

The jajmani system is an age-old social institution which refers to the inter-caste and inter-family social, economic, political, and ritual ties prevalent in Indian villages. It is one of the most important constituents of social organization of agriculture in India.

Decline of the Jajmani System

Gradual modernization of Indian economy coincided with the decline of the jajmani system. But its rapid decline was witnessed in the post-Independence period. In general, the decline of jajmani system may be discussed under the following heads:

1. Role of the State.
2. Introduction of technological innovations and industrialization.
3. Political mobilization of the Dalits and the Backward Classes.

1. Role of the State: Traditionally, the jajmani system-based village economy was primarily a subsistence economy oriented to meet the consumption needs of only the local population. Due to the localized self-sufficiency and immobility of labour and capital, commercialization and the capitalist transformation of agriculture did not take place. After Independence, deliberate and planned attempts were made to link the village economy with the regional and national markets. In order to facilitate this, the government made huge investments towards the expansion of transport and communication network. The State policies contributed to rapid modernization of economy in Indian villages. Increasing productivity in agriculture was very high on the government's economic agenda to feed the huge, increasing population.

The process of planned development initiated immediately after Independence brought about a capitalistic transformation in agriculture sector. The State also took initiative in providing different inputs like credit facilities, technical knowhow, fertilizer, irrigation, high-yielding varieties of seeds, and so on. Now came a sea-change in the mindset of landowning classes and the entry of market forces encouraged them to generate surplus for the market rather than sustaining the age-old jajmani system. It gave rise to contractual relationship between the landowning classes and agricultural labourers and artisans. The traditional informal ties started giving way to formal relationship as per formal contractual obligations.

2. Technological Innovations and Industrialization: Technological innovations and industrialization also created a situation where there was hardly any need for functional interdependence. With the machine-made goods flooding the market and reaching even remote rural areas, the rural artisan castes were literally made to compete with the machines. Let us take a look at a few ordinary technological innovations. With the growing availability and the consequent increase in the use of the safety razor, the practice of self-shaving became popular, minimizing the role of village barber. With the advent of stainless steel utensils, the importance of village potter declined. And with the availability of hand pumps in the villages, the dependence of higher castes on the bhishtis (drawers and carriers of water to the households) declined. Similar changes rendered the majority of artisan castes jobless. Many of them opted for change of profession or started providing their services against cash payment in a formal economic transaction. This coincided with the rapidly increasing migration of the service castes to the emerging urban centres and industrial townships. Those who stayed behind became wage labourers working on the lands of the landed elite. Village economy started being increasingly integrated with the urban and national economy.

3. Political Mobilization of the Dalits and the Backward Classes: Before Independence, the nationalist movement took a principled or rather a quasi-ideological stand on social equality. The weaker sections – Dalits, tribals and Backward Classes – were promised an equality-based and injustice and exploitation-free new order. The Backward Classes movement had already made its impact on southern and western parts of India. With the promulgation of the Constitution, the State became committed to their upliftment and empowerment. One of the profound changes in contemporary Indian society has been the emergence of a new sense of identity among the Dalits and the other Backward Classes. The democratic assertion of the backward segments of Indian population and their political mobilization in different parts of the country was a serious blow to the exploitative jajmani system based on the monopolistic rights of the landed higher castes controlling

the means of production in the traditional agrarian economy. With the newfound confidence and democratic assertion by the Backward Classes, the jajmani system suffered a serious setback. Yet it also seems to be true that whatever the weaker sections gained, the new economic policy and globalization threatens to take away.

Social inequality occurs when resources in a society are distributed unevenly, typically through norms of allocation along lines of socially-defined categories of persons.

Since independence in 1947, Indian society and the caste system have changed considerably, though unevenly, in both rural and urban areas. Covid-19 definitely gave jerks and shocks to the caste system in several ways, but only future sociological studies will describe these changes.

Untouchability

The notion and practice of untouchability is a direct product of the caste system. Most of the historians are of the view that the earliest Vedic text Rigveda makes no mention of untouchability. Perhaps, it developed with the establishment of the present-day caste system during the Gupta period. In sociology we are not concerned with the debates on this issue among the historians. The sociologists and anthropologists are more interested to know the dynamics of caste-based discrimination manifesting in social, economic, and political exclusion and segregation, and how it is considered as gross violation of human rights in present times.

We have already mentioned how untouchability is the by-product of the notion of purity/impurity or ritual pollution and how the caste hierarchy is based on ritual hierarchy, that is, the degree of ritual purity going downwards up to the zone of impurity/pollution. In order to maintain the ritual purity, the 'pure' castes are supposed to maintain ritual distance, manifesting itself in physical and social distance.

The sections of the society who were made to adopt ritually impure occupations for their livelihood and to serve the rest of the society were considered 'untouchables', whose mere physical touch would make the persons of higher castes impure and polluted, requiring a purification bath. Even in present times, if we look at the settlement pattern in Indian villages, in most of the cases, the castes considered as untouchables are made to live on the fringe of the village while the central place is inhabited by Brahmins and other higher castes and even those relatively lower castes not considered untouchable. The people engaged in leather work, handling dead animals, scavenging, and a variety of other such occupations considered as polluting were considered untouchables. Until some time ago, in several parts of the country, persons of the so-called untouchable castes were supposed to carry a small drum around their necks and beat it to warn others to maintain distance from them. In several other instances, some untouchable castes were allowed only limited or restricted mobility and they could use the public roads only during stipulated hours of the day or night. Things have changed a lot, especially after Independence and the promulgation of the Constitution through which the practice of untouchability has been abolished and made a cognizable or criminal offence. It has almost disappeared from the urban centres, largely because of urban anonymity and secularization of social life; village India lags behind. Untouchability may be seen in practice, in varying degrees, in villages and small towns all over the country in different forms.

The following are some of the widespread practices of untouchability despite the presence of such legislative measures as Protection of Civil Rights Act, 1976 and Scheduled Castes and Scheduled Tribes (Prevention of Atrocities) Act, 1989, amended in 2015:

1. Separate utensils for these castes in tea stalls and eating joints. At several places they have to wash the utensils meant for them to get tea or food.
2. Denial of right to take water from the common source of water.
3. Denial of entry into the houses of upper castes.
4. Segregation in seating arrangement in schools.
5. Denial of the right of their wedding procession with musical bands to pass through the locality of higher castes.
6. Resentment and opposition to the practice of a Dalit bridegroom coming to the bride's place riding a horse.
7. Denial of service from barbers and washermen.
8. Denial of entry into temples.
9. Discrimination in health services.
10. When the state/central governments introduced the practice of providing midday meal to the children in schools, at many places children of upper castes were asked by their parents not to accept the meal if it was cooked by a Dalit person and this creates lot of problems for the implementation of the scheme.

Thus the social, economic and political exclusion continues in varying degrees in villages and small towns. On the basis of past experiences, and to a lesser extent even at present, we may say that to be untouchable did not merely mean to be untouchable but to enter a futile world, devoid of hope. In the past, a number of social and religious reform movements such as the Arya Samaj movement took place, but the practice of untouchability continues in different forms despite the fact that it is a gross violation of human rights.

Perspectives on the Study of the Caste System: Ghurye, Srinivas, Dumont and Beteille

A number of sociologists and social anthropologists have studied the caste system and some of them have done really outstanding and pioneering work and developed different perspectives about it. Among them G.S. Ghurye, M.N. Srinivas, Louis Dumont, Andre Beteille, and some others stand apart. Let us briefly have some idea about their different perspectives.

G.S. Ghurye

He published his landmark and pioneering work Caste and Race in India (1932). Deeply influenced by the Indological and historical approach, he also came under the influence of the 'diffusionist school' of cultural evolution propounded by anthropologists. He put both caste and race on the same pedestal and believed that both were related to each other. He believed that the entire Indian population and society was based on the caste system. Interestingly and significantly, he included tribes too in this system. Following this line of argument, he described tribal population as 'backward Hindus' who needed to be assimilated in the mainstream Hindu society. For this, he did not enjoy the support of many other sociologists and anthropologists. Ghurye maintained that kin and caste networks in India parallel those in some other countries. Moreover, kinship and caste in Indian society served as integrative frameworks. He looked at the evolution of the Indian society in terms of integration and deep relationship between racial groups and kin and caste network.

Being a follower of Indological approach laced with historical approach, he made several speculations. With the rise of empiricism and field-based studies, his over-dependence on text became a target of severe criticism. Despite many of his ideas becoming obsolete and 'Hindu-centric' instead of being totally objective, he will be remembered as the first sociologist to have challenged the colonial notion of caste.

M.N. Srinivas

He added a very significant dimension to caste studies by talking about mobility in the caste system. He pointed out that any social institution may be seen through two views Book view/Textual view and Field view/Empirical view. The textual or theoretical view rules out any change or mobility in the caste system as if it was frozen in time. Through his path-breaking work, Religion and Society among the Coorgs of South India (1952), he presented the empirical situation in which the lower castes were seen emulating the values, customs, traditions, food habits, and so on of the Brahmins to move upwards in the caste/status hierarchy. He termed this process as 'Brahminization'. He gave up this term when confronted by cases from elsewhere in which any higher caste (identified as the local dominant caste) might serve as the reference group to be emulated instead of only Brahmins. He coined the term 'Sanskritization' to describe this phenomenon. Through his perspective on the caste system, he opened new windows for the study of mobility in the caste system in different parts of India.

Louis Dumont

He was an eminent French sociologist who developed a new perspective on the caste system by laying emphasis on the 'ideology of caste system'. He was concerned with the attributes of caste and hence his approach was called 'attribution approach' to the caste system. In his pathbreaking and highly philosophical work Homo Hierarchicus he laid out his understanding of caste and caste system. He described caste as a set of relationships of economic, political, and kinship systems, sustained by certain values which were mostly religious in nature. Dumont maintained that caste was not a form of stratification but a special form of inequality whose essence had to be deciphered by the sociologists. He was of the view that caste divided the whole Indian society into a large number of hereditary groups. These groups were separated by strict rules of endogamy and ritual distance between the groups. Because of an elaborate system of division of labour, each group was assigned an occupation which was hereditary in nature and no group could deviate from it under the force of custom. No two groups could be equal and in this gradation of status/hierarchy one will be superior or inferior to another. He described the caste system as a system of values based on his analysis of the binary opposition between the pure and impure. Dumont's Homo Hierarchicus built a model of Indian civilization based on non-competitive ritual hierarchical system. No other sociologists before him looked at the caste system from this perspective and hence Dumont's contribution to the study of caste system is still considered very significant despite the original publication in French long ago in 1966 and its English translation fifteen years later.

Andre Beteille

His perspective on the caste system was refreshingly new. He moved away from the Indological, theoretical, and abstract model to a model of ethnographic and theoretical analysis. His understanding was largely based on the relationship between caste, class, and power in the context of change. Caste system had undergone substantial change during the British rule but the post-Independence period witnessed the distribution of power in a non-traditional way. His major work Caste, Class and Power: Changing Patterns of Stratification in a Tanjore Village (1966) analysed the change in the caste system in the wake of democracy, land reforms, and empowerment of non-Brahmin castes. He demonstrated empirically that the traditional relationship between caste and power had been radically changed. As an example, at the micro level, village panchayat in the village Sripuram was controlled by non-Brahmins and the traditional elite had been pushed to the background. He observed, 'Power has also become independent of class to a greater extent than in the past. Ownership of land is no longer the decisive factor in acquiring power. Numerical support and strategic position in the party machinery play an important part.' Thus, for the first time, the relationship between the caste structure, the class system, and the distribution of political power was theorized on the basis of ethnographic research.

Ritual Aspect or Binary Opposition Between Pure/Impure (Pollution)

1. The opposition between pure and impure has been regarded by Louis Dumont as the fundamental principle underlying the Hindu Caste System.

2. The principle is implicit in the three predominant features of the caste system which were systematically spelt out by Bougle and later endorsed by Dumont. According to Bougle, the caste system comprises a series of hereditary groups (the socially relevant jatis) characterized by (a) 'hierarchy' or gradations according to ritual status; (b) 'mutual repulsion', implying rules governing contact, ensuring their separation; and (c) division of labour and consequent interdependence.

3. Dumont shows that the opposition between the pure and the impure is implicit in all the three attributes – in hierarchy because the pure and

impure must be kept separate, and in the division of labour because pure and impure occupations have to be segregated.

4. Following from this, the caste system is viewed as a 'whole' which is founded on the necessary and hierarchical co-existence of the opposites (the pure and impure). This represents a viewpoint of caste according to which both the pure and the impure have their rightful place in the system and each has its privileges and co-exists with the other.

5. One way of assigning rank to castes in terms of their relative purity and impurity is to study their attributes and accordingly order them in relation to one another. The attributes of purity include features such as wearing the sacred thread, veneration of cows, vegetarianism, teetotalism, and prohibiting widow remarriage. Pollution is associated with human emissions, death, disrespect of cows, and consumption of meat and alcohol, to mention the principal elements.

6. The attributes of purity and pollution discussed so far may be used to identify the two broad extremes in the caste hierarchy – the Brahmins and the untouchables. But the precise determination of the highest and the lowest among Brahmins and untouchables respectively is conditioned by local interpretations of the pollution concept. Thus, while scavenging and beef-eating would make a caste group untouchable almost anywhere, it may still be able to establish its precedence over some other group through fine distinctions of behaviour. The fact that the empirical referents of the pollution concept are subject to local interpretations highlights the point that caste hierarchy, when viewed as a specific phenomenon, was confined to a given local area. Hence caste (jati) hierarchy shows regional variations.

7. The tendency which results in the hierarchical arrangements of castes in a given locality is often replicated within each caste and leads to the grading of segments, both in the same local community and over a wide territorial area.

8. The operation of local interpretations of pollution explains the regional differences in the evaluation and ranking of castes. However, even within a given locality there is a multiplicity of attributional criteria and the necessity of evaluating them in relation to one another render it difficult to grade all the castes in a fixed hierarchical order.

9. Dumont attempts to show how these attributes may be used to establish a series of divisions, each more precise than the other, between superior

and inferior castes. For example, the vegetarian castes may be placed above the non-vegetarian ones; among the vegetarians those who prohibit widow remarriage would be superior to those who permit it. Similarly, among the non-vegetarians, further dichotomies may be established between beef eaters and non-beef eaters; and among the latter still further gradations may be made between those who eat only mutton or birds and those who eat pig (pork) raised by the lower castes and fed garbage. Dumont argues that such dichotomies, which establish distinctions of relative purity and impurity, reaffirm the importance of the hierarchical principle.

10. At the same time, it is difficult to say that in any particular village, the hierarchy solely depends on the basis of attribution criteria. A vegetarian caste, in some cases, may actually rank below a non-vegetarian caste. It is also not clear how the various attributes of pollution combine together to form an unambiguous hierarchy of values. For example, are the attributes of diet more important than those of occupation? Among certain occupations, such as butchering goats, cutting hair, and tapping toddy, which would be lowest?

11. Such difficulties led Mickim Marriott to propose an interactional theory of caste ranking based on inter-caste relationships as manifested in the 'ritualized giving and receiving of food, and the giving and receiving of ritual services'. He considers food transfers more decisive in establishing rank than the receiving of ritual services, but the two are connected since the services are paid for partly in food.

12. The circulation of food is one significant index of rank because a caste which receives more of the purer kinds of food than it gives to other caste groups may be regarded as the recipient of relatively more ritual honour in relation to the others. Following the same principle, a caste which receives more ritual services from other castes than it gives to them ranks higher. It is lower if it gives more ritual services than it receives or renders these to lower castes.

Caste System as Viewed by Contemporary Social Anthropologists

Since the late 1940s, a number of British and American social scientists have taken a new approach to the Indian caste system. The dominant features of this approach are inspired by contemporary social anthropology. Pauline Kolenda (1984), a keen observer of the Indian scene, in a sharp analysis has tried to identify the important features of this new approach. According to her, the first important feature is the collection of information about the caste system by residing in a village and observing. According to her:

1. Caste as a system operates only within a limited locality, a single village or a few linked villages.

2. A village or local population is composed of a series of mutually exclusive castes, usually numbering anywhere from a handful to a score or more.

3. A dominant caste or a dominant family (or a set of families) typically has preponderant political and economic power over everyone else in the locality. Dominance is rooted in monopolistic control over arable land and in physical force.

4. Each caste has an occupational specialty and offers this to other castes in exchange for food, products, or services. Especially important is the foodgrain provided by the land-controlling dominant caste or families to the landless servants, artisans, and mendicant castes.

   This exchange of food, goods and services is a ritual system concerned with purity and pollution as well as an economic system. Called the jajmani system, it functions so that the highest castes remain pure while the lower castes absorb pollution for them.

5. Castes within a local caste system tend to be mutually ranked according to their respective degrees of pollution in this ritual system.

6. Efforts to improve caste rank in the local caste hierarchy are made by middle and lower castes, especially by means of discarding polluting customs and by emulating the customs of the higher, purer castes.

7. Political power is monopolized by the dominant caste, family, or families, or occasionally by a pair of competing dominant castes. Non-dominant castes tend to support their patrons within the dominant segment. Such support may be important if there are factions contending for power within the dominant segment.

8. Disputes may be settled either by councils within caste segments, or by one or more elders of the dominant caste or family.

9. The caste segment itself is an endogamous descent group. The local contingent of a caste is usually composed of kinsmen, ideally related unilineally, though often actually related cognatically. (Patrilineal descent refers to a line of males related through father–son links, going back to a common male ancestor. Matrilineal descent refers to a line of

mother–child links, going back to a common female ancestor. Cognatic descent refers to a line, related through either male or female links, going back to common ancestors.)

10. Each caste segment tends to live in its own area or locality. Universally, untouchables (who are unclean) live in isolation from those of purer caste, either in a separate hamlet or on the outskirts of the village.

Caste: Cultural and Structural View

Caste is a system of stratification. It represents the basic idea or notion or ideology of social stratification in the traditional Indian society. Sociologists sometimes take divergent views of caste. Two most popular of such views are (a) cultural view and (b) structural view. The differences in these two views lie not in the basic content but in the levels of analysis.

Those who tend to take the cultural view of caste treat it as a system of ideas and values. This may also include beliefs and norms. In this view, the most important factor is hierarchy, which forms the basis of ranking of persons or groups. Among those who are protagonists of this view, the prominent ones are Louis Dumont, G.S. Ghurye, Edmund Leach, and M.N. Srinivas. They look at caste as a social or cultural phenomenon peculiar to the Indian society, more precisely to the Hindu society because among the non-Hindus it does not contain religious ideology despite the fact that they have also developed caste-like stratification. Treating caste as a cultural phenomenon within the general principle of social stratification, they point out the hierarchy of hereditary groups as its basis. These hereditary groups are separated by caste endogamy, restrictions on commensal relations (exchange of food and water) and physical contact. But despite this separation and exclusiveness, they are interdependent because of the traditional division of labour. The underlying principle of this arrangement is based on the opposites of the pure and impure, a sort of binary opposition.

Yogendra Singh further elaborates this arrangement. He talks of universalistic or particularistic categories. The former means that the caste system is regarded as just another manifestation of the universal phenomenon of social stratification while the latter means that caste system may be viewed as a system of stratification, which is unique to the Indian/Hindu society.

Those who take the structural view of caste look at caste at a higher level of abstraction, that is, social structure. Thus, caste for them is a structural reality. Proponents of this view can be found among the Marxist and functionalist sociologists. A.R. Desai, a Marxist sociologist, represents this view among the

Indian sociologists. According to the structuralists, caste as a social structure is comparable cross-culturally. Yogendra Singh again divides the proponents of this view into two categories – structural universalistic and structural particularistic. For the structuralists, the caste system is nothing but the representation of class relations in caste idiom. The religious sanctions behind caste have been interpreted by the Marxists as simply a legitimizing ideology to sustain the existing mode of production. Since the landed castes are mostly upper castes who control the means of production and exploit the 'ritually inferior' landless lower castes, the die is cast in favour of its interpretation in terms of class in the Marxist sense of the term. The majority of sociologists studying Indian society have subscribed to the structural particularistic view of caste. They have treated caste as an institutionalized system of interaction among the hierarchically ranked hereditary groups for marriage, occupation and economic division of labour where enforcement of cultural norms and values is done by caste panchayats or caste organizations. Structural analysts of caste view it as a system of institutionalized inequality. Thus, caste may also be understood as the structural basis of inequality.

Caste Mobility

Sorokin, whose pioneering work on social mobility is yet to be surpassed, says that there has scarcely been any society whose strata were absolutely closed, or in which vertical mobility in its three forms – economic, political and occupational – was not present. At the same time, there has never existed a society in which vertical social mobility has been absolutely free and the transition from one social stratum to another has had no resistance. Contrary to the popular 'book view', caste as a stratification system provides room for social and occupational mobility.

M.N. Srinivas explodes the myth of the caste system as static. He puts forward a dynamic view of caste and contends, 'The caste system is far from a rigid system in which the position of each component is fixed for all times. Movement has always been possible.' He says that the stronger the norms against social mobility, the greater the desire for it. An indication of the widespread desire for mobility comes from an unusual source – the census results. The Indian census reports of 19th and early 20th centuries give us abundant idea of this upward mobility.

The caste system discouraged individual mobility from one caste to another during one's lifetime. Thus, mobility manifested itself as the collective splitting of sub-castes or what Hutton calls the 'fissiparous tendencies of Indian castes'. The process of mobility becomes clearer if we distinguish models of mobility. We consider two referents – the dwija (twice-born higher castes) and the modern, educated elite. The cultural emulation of caste elite as referent or reference group is more important in the process of caste mobility, yet the modern elite is also used as referent. But in most of the cases, both are combined in caste mobility as per the empirical realities.

In his path breaking study, Religion and Society among the Coorgs (1952), M.N. Srinivas explained caste mobility in terms of cultural emulation of the Brahmins by the local lower castes. He then broadened the definition of Sanskritization in his book Social Change in Modern India as:

> A process by which a low Hindu caste, or tribal or other group, changes its customs, ritual, ideology, and way of life in the direction of a high, and frequently 'twice born' caste. Generally, such changes are followed by a claim to a higher position in the caste hierarchy than that traditionally conceded to the claimant caste by the local community.

In terms of varna referents, the Kshatriya model has been the most popular. Surjit Sinha, however, describes it as 'Rajputization' instead of 'Kshatriyization' on the basis of his fieldwork in Central India. The popularity of Kshatriya model is attested by a large number of petitions by the lower castes before the census officials to change their names and hierarchy and recognize them as Kshatriya. The Brahmin model of Sanskritization has been the most difficult because in most of the cases, the Shudra castes found it difficult to be recognized as Brahmins. William Rowe's study of the Noniya in Senapur village in eastern Uttar Pradesh shows the success of a middle level caste in acquiring upward mobility through Sanskritization after achieving economic prosperity. It attests David Mandelbaum's view that a low caste must accumulate wealth and prosperity before adopting Sanskritization as a means of upward social mobility.

Similarly, Pocock has shown successful upward mobility in the case of Kunbi, a traditional middle-rung peasant caste of Gujarat, to the new and more honourable status of the Pattidar. It is generally accepted that untouchability has proved to be such a big barrier that does not allow any upward mobility. However, F.G. Bailey in his study of Bissipara in Orissa has presented a rare example, which shows the success of the untouchables in achieving status elevation through Sanskritization. From liquor distillation, a ritually impure occupation, they moved upwards after acquiring land and laying their claim on Kshatriya status, which was conceded, though grudgingly, by the local Brahmins and Kshatriyas.

In terms of intra-caste mobility, education and occupation have been the most important factors of upward mobility. With the expanding avenues of secularization of education and occupation, a number of individuals and groups within a caste attain upward mobility. Thus, an elite sub-stratum emerges in every caste. We can witness this phenomenon even among the scheduled castes, other backward castes, and tribal communities.

Changes in the Ritual and Economic Aspects of Caste

Traditionally, caste hierarchy has been a ritual hierarchy in terms of a person's status on the basis of the degree of purity or impurity. The secular or material attributes or determinants of status ranking were secondary in nature. These secular attributes were wealth or ownership of land, access to political power, and so on. However, certain processes of change which began during the British rule but acquired momentum after independence have promoted changes in the system of ranking of castes. Urbanization gave a serious blow to the ritual dimension of caste.

With a manifold increase in secularization of inter-caste and inter-personal relations, the ritual and social distance between castes narrowed down. People's concern for improving the quality of life promoted higher levels of consumption. It facilitated the easier entry of secular indicators of prosperity and socio-economic superiority into the caste system. The increased economic development, especially the growth of capitalist mode of agriculture and industrialization, promoted occupational opportunities which were considered 'ritually neutral'. Entry into these new occupations were based on technical skills imparted through modern education. Moreover, new avenues of increasing income and acquiring wealth were introduced. Thus, these new determinants of status pushed the ritual determinants to the background.

In the sphere of inter-caste and inter-personal relations, persons belonging to different castes with different ritual status came together in modern occupational settings and indulged in closer inter-personal relationships, giving a big jolt to the ritual aspect of caste. On secular occasions, the non-Brahmin castes occupied more prominent positions because of their material endowments. The Brahmins could occupy a higher place on such occasions only when they were stronger in material terms. Democratic decentralization of power right up to grassroots level led to an increased participation by all castes in the political process. Besides economic success, access to political power has become another means of status enhancement.

Changes in the Economic Aspects of Caste

When we look at the traditional Indian society, we find that the caste system formed the basis of village economy and the jajmani system was the economic basis of caste system. With the introduction of technological innovations, market economy, and the mobilization of the Backward Classes and Dalits, the jajmani system, which was essentially a system of production and exchange of goods and services, declined. Thus, caste as a system broke down in most of the villages in India though castes survived as social groups with their concomitant caste consciousness.

In the urban areas, because of new occupational structures, an 'occupation free caste structure' emerged. Caste and occupation were delinked because recruitment to the new occupations was based on technical skills which could be acquired through formal, modern education. For example, let's look at the skills needed in the manufacture of ceramics. A person need not belong to a potters' caste to acquire these skills. Jewellery designing can be learned without belonging to goldsmith's caste, and so on.

Lloyd Rudolf (2000) has different ideas. He says that modernity has entered into the Indian character and society, but it has done so through assimilation, not replacement, while Dipankar Gupta (2000) describes this as 'mistaken modernity' which is only skin deep.

A new phenomenon has been observed. A number of caste groups have joined hands to protect their 'class interests'. The examples of Bhartiya Kisan Union (BKU) in Uttar Pradesh and Kshetkari Sangathan in Maharashtra, both of which consist of several caste groups, show that the economic functions of caste have undergone transformation, but caste as a unit of social organization has survived because of its adaptive capabilities.

Caste System and its Transformation

Contrary to its textual view and popular perception, caste has never been static. It has been prone to a number of factors of change which have been occurring over the period of time – from the ancient times to the present. Caste system has always undergone adaptive changes. However, after Independence, the pace of change has increased many times, especially in the ritual and economic aspects of caste. Among the factors of change, right from the British times, the following may be enumerated as the most important:

1. Industrialization and urbanization

2. Westernization

3. Social and religious reform movements
4. Dalit and Backward Classes movement
5. Role of the State

During British rule, the process of industrialization and urbanization played a very important role in the changes in the structure of the society. The process of industrialization placed material and secular indicators and determinants of social status on a high pedestal at the cost of ritual determinants of social status. The process of urbanization accompanied by secularization reduced the ritual and physical distance between the higher and the lower castes largely because of reduced physical segregation between castes and a more secular housing pattern of the urban centres.

The process of Westernization introduced a new social philosophy and value system oriented towards social equality and increased emphasis on rationalism. It also promoted gender rights and gender justice. The Westernized sections of the Indian society reinterpreted Hinduism and had a new look at the caste system. They re-defined the traditional rules of commensality of the caste system and had no inhibitions in taking on new non-traditional occupations. They also did not have any problem of choosing spouse from outside the caste. Thus Westernization promoted the cultural modernization of the Indian society.

Several religious and social reform movements also played their role. The Bhakti movement and the Sufi movement laid emphasis on oneness of humankind and espoused the idea of inequality as man-made, rather god-made. Though they could not eliminate the caste system, they definitely facilitated relaxation of caste rigidities. Several social reform movements such as the Arya Samaj and the Brahmo Samaj movements made a direct attack on the caste system, especially on its ritual aspect of purity and impurity and inequality. Birth of backward castes movements or non-Brahmin movements also gave a direct blow to the philosophy of inequalities and promoted egalitarianism.

Of all the factors that have been enumerated so far, the role of the State was most crucial, especially after Independence. When the Constitution of India proclaimed equality, it derecognized caste inequalities and caste superiorities in one stroke. The practice of untouchability, an integral part of caste system, was made a cognizable offence. Democracy and adult franchise were great steps forward towards social justice, equality, and empowerment of disadvantaged groups of the Indian society. The State sponsored change –

planned, directed, and executed by the State – went a long way in attacking the basis of inequality and injustice due to the caste system. A uniform legal system and equality before law were established.

Caste and Politics

The role of caste in the sphere of politics may be traced back to the British colonial period. In the first half of the 19th century, the British rulers, on the one hand, encouraged Christian missionaries who, besides spreading Christianity, also began projecting it as a reform movement, and on the other hand instituted laws against several socially retrograde customs and practices of the Hindu society like sati, female infanticide, human sacrifice, and so on. These measures were backed and supported by the reforms-minded Westernized Indian elite. These and several such measures were taken as a direct attack on the caste system, caste norms, and Hindu cultural ethos. It gave rise to the tendencies of 'insulation' of caste-minded masses from external influences. This may be considered as the beginning of the role of caste in the political process of the Indian society.

The introduction of modern means of transport and communications encouraged not only spatial mobility but also social mobility. Backed by the new printing technology, caste loyalties and consciousness spread beyond villages, districts, and provinces. The establishment of representative educational and legal institutions and new opportunities for achieving power and prestige added new functions to the caste. The Brahmins, Kayasthas, and Vaishyas immediately grabbed these opportunities because only they were in a position to take full advantage of the new socio-political system. Their previous background helped them to emerge as leaders of the nationalist movement, too. That is why we find that the leadership of the nationalist movement and of the Indian National Congress in virtually the entire Indian sub-continent was in the hands of men from the elite Hindu castes. The same was the case with the Muslim caste groups where the Saiyyeds, Shaikhs, and Pathans monopolized education and politics.

Paul Brass, in his major work, The Politics of India Since Independence (1990), makes the comment that among both the elite and middle status castes, a process of caste succession had begun before Independence and intensified after it, with the adoption of adult franchise by which, in election after election, new leaders from previously unrepresented or under-represented castes began to emerge and the castes themselves began to be mobilized. The intermediate castes acquired increased voting power through adult suffrage and increased economic power through abolition of zamindari.

Intermediate castes with economic resources sought not only political power but educational benefits and urban jobs for their children. As they acquired these opportunities, they came increasingly into conflict with persons from upper caste groups represented in far greater proportion and often in large absolute numbers in educational and political institutions.

The Brahmins were the elite in educational and political spheres because of their historical high status in the caste system. The earliest social movements were mobilized by the non-Brahmin castes against this monopoly. The mid-19th century witnessed the earliest anti-Brahmin movement in Maharashtra. By the turn of the 20th century, such movements surfaced most vocally and strongly in the South, especially in the regions coming under the present states of Tamil Nadu, Kerala, and Karnataka. Thus, the non-Brahmin movement in South India can be seen as the response of the downtrodden, lower castes to the traditional higher caste hegemony. The Western liberal rationalist ideas provided a fertile ground for the new liberating ideology. First, Jyotiba Phule of Pune urged the non-Brahmins not to engage Brahmin priests in rituals. The cause of non-Brahmins was also taken up by Chatrapati Shahuji of Kolhapur. Soon, a non-Brahmin movement came into existence in the state of Madras in the first quarter of 20th century in the form of the Dravidian movement. The Justice Party was founded in 1916, led by Periyar Ramaswami Naiker; the Self-Respect Movement was founded in 1925; and the Dravida Kazagham (Dravidian federation) was founded in 1944. It demanded a separate Dravidian state, to be run on casteless and egalitarian lines. Many Dravida Kazagham members and supporters were atheists, like the members of the Justice Party. They denounced and impugned several socially regressive and retrograde Hindu concepts.

In the regions now in Andhra Pradesh, the Reddys and the Khammas emerged as dominant castes, edging out the Brahmins from the seats of power. The state of Karnataka saw the emergence of Vokaligga and Lingayats as the new dominant castes.

The situation in the North was different from the South. As most of the historians and sociologists believe, there were hardly any 'pure' Kshatriyas or Vaishyas in Madras state, but there was a head-on collision between the Brahmin and the Shudra castes. In the North, a number of castes in between the Brahmins and the Shudra *jatis* acted as a sort of a buffer zone in the political hierarchy. Moreover, in the North there had always been a tendency of upward mobility among the middle level and lower castes towards the higher castes through the process of Sanskritization. Perhaps, that is why the

Backward Class mobilization took roots in North India at a much later stage, from 1960s onwards.

India has been an effective democracy since Independence. In his work Interrogating Caste (2000), Dipankar Gupta rightly points out, 'It is commonplace in the analysis of caste politics to give in to the presumption of numbers. Thus, it is often argued that political outcomes can be determined to a fair degree by the caste composition of electoral constituencies. This falls quite in line with the overall assumption that Hindus are generally bound by their caste loyalties, so why should politics be any different? There are periods when the domination of politics by caste seems like a near truism, but then again there are times when caste does not seem to play that influential a role.'

Thus the locus of power and influence has shifted from the traditionally higher (but numerically lesser) castes to the numerically large, politically mobilized middle-rung and backward castes. In most regions of India, the middle and lower-level castes now enjoy empirical strength. The Nairs and Izhavas in Kerala, Vaniyars in Tamil Nadu, Vokaliggas and Lingayats in Karnataka, Reddys and Khammas in Andhra Pradesh, Patidars and Kshatriyas in Gujarat, Jats in Haryana and Rajasthan, Yadavas and Kurmis in Bihar and Uttar Pradesh, and the Chamars in the whole of North India especially Uttar Pradesh, are examples of this shift in political power.

In his path breaking study, Caste and Politics in India (1969), Rajani Kothari has made a brilliant analysis of the relationship between caste and politics. Describing politics in India as an enterprise, he dubs the politicians as entrepreneurs. Like any intelligent and skilful entrepreneur, they know their resources and how to utilize them effectively. They know that the vast multitude of Indian masses live with their respective caste groups, have primordial caste loyalties, and a strong caste consciousness, and hence can be easily mobilized along caste lines. This intimate interaction between caste and politics has changed the face of both. Kothari describes it as 'politicization of caste'. However, for the traditionally deprived and underprivileged castes, this is a case of democratic assertion for their due rights. Thus it gives rise to a serious debate about whether caste appeal amounts to casteism. Rajni Kothari has specified three typical stages in the relationship between caste and politics in a region.

1. Stage-I: This involves politicization of a powerful elite caste, usually one which responded earliest to the opportunity for Western education. In Maharashtra and Tamil Nadu, this were the Brahmins; in Bihar, they

were the Kayasthas. To the political successes of the entrenched caste, the members of other high castes in the area respond with resentment, with feelings of relative deprivation and possibly antagonism. These castes then challenge the entrenched caste as, what Kothari calls, an 'ascendant caste'. In three examples given in Kothari's work, the ascendant caste is one of the respectable cultivators who had been slower than the entrenched caste in accepting Western education. In Rajasthan, the Rajputs were the entrenched and the Jat cultivators the ascendant caste; in Tamil Nadu, the Brahmins were the entrenched and Shudra non- Brahmins were ascendant; and in Maharashtra the Brahmins were the entrenched and the Marathas were the ascendant.

2. Stage-2: Factionalism and fragmentation take place within the competing castes and multi-caste and multifunctional alignments develop. Lower castes are often brought in to support high caste leaders and to strengthen a faction.

3. Stage-3: Caste identity tends to languish with the progress in education, urbanization, and the development of an orientation towards individual achievement and modern status symbols. Individuals participate in networks which include persons of several loyalties that have been overlaid by a more sophisticated system of social and political participation with cross-cutting allegiances. Institutions are distinctly different. The present political realities suggest that the Indian society is not fixed in either Stage-2 or Stage-3. It is something beyond Stage-2 with the traditionally deprived moving towards domination of society at several levels.

For other scholars of caste, the role of caste associations is also an important factor. A caste organization is a voluntary organization consisting of members of a single caste. It plays an important role as a political instrument. Caste associations link members of a caste within a region and influence the political process, especially electoral politics, significantly. Along with caste associations, the working of democracy at the grassroots level, that is, village level democracy, also shows the significant role of caste.

At the national level, the varna mobilization, that is, the mobilization of all the jatis of a particular varna became a new phenomenon. For instance, Kanyakubja Sabha, a caste organization of Kanyakubja Brahmins, has been an old phenomenon, but the organization of the Brahmins in the form of an All India Brahmin Mahasabha is of much later origin. The same is the case of the Kshatriya Mahasabha. Moreover, the pan-Indian mobilization of a jati like by the All India Kurmi Mahasabha is also a later phenomenon. Such attempts seem to be a part of the political mobilization of castes on an all-India basis, to be used as effective pressure group at the national level. The political alignments of different castes, including the traditionally opposed caste groups, has also emerged as a significant part of the contemporary political scenario.

Caste and Non-Hindus

Though caste is a predominantly Hindu phenomenon, non-Hindu communities have also possess certain specific features of the caste system of the Hindus in India. Many sociologists look at caste as a unique feature of the Hindu society but a number of sociologists and social anthropologists are of the view that caste like groups also exist in non-Hindu societies. Not only this, they see caste-like features in Pakistan, Sri Lanka, Bangladesh, Bhutan, and some of the South-East Asian societies which, at one time or the other, came into contact with centres of Hindu civilization. As a result of cultural contact and the resultant process of Hinduization, they have also come to acquire caste-like features, if not the ideology of caste as sanctioned in Hindu scriptures.

Studies on the impact of the caste system on the non-Hindus reveal the extent to which their life patterns have been influenced by the social organization of the Hindus. When we take a look at the Muslim, Sikh, and Christian societies, we find that the egalitarian ideologies of Islam, Sikhism, and Christianity made social adaptation with the social stratification of the Hindu society. J.H. Hutton (1936) made a perceptible comment saying, 'When Islam and Christianity came to India, caste was in the air and even these egalitarian ideologies could not escape the infection of caste.' This is also true that of all the non-Hindu societies. The impact of caste on the Muslims is visible most strongly.

Caste among the Muslims

The question whether the concept of caste can be applied to the system of social stratification of a community professing a faith other than Hinduism has often been posed. It is true that the egalitarian social order of Islam stands in sharp contrast with the ideology of caste, yet, the Indian Islam and the Hindu caste system have been able to achieve a substantial compatibility. Moreover, a majority of Indian Muslim population comes from the lower caste Hindus, who come into the fold of Islam to escape from social persecution and the oppressive socio-economic disabilities perpetrated by the caste system. However, the search for equality proves a mirage for them. There are improvements in their social conditions, yet the goals of social equality remain elusive. Significantly, in most of the cases, the people embracing Islam gave up their religion but not the caste, which they brought forward to their new socio-religious milieu. Thus, it would be apt to say that while Islam may not be having castes or caste-like groupings, the Indian Muslims do have them. Hence, the interface between ideology and social structure in the context of caste is full of academic issues requiring discussion. Within the larger framework of the Hindu caste system, there are regional variations of caste-like grouping among the Muslims.

Ghaus Ansari (1960), in his pioneering study on caste and social stratification among the North Indian Muslims, places Muslim castes into three categories:

1. Ashraf
2. Ajlaf
3. Arzul

Ashraf includes the Muslim nobility that claims to be the descendants of early Muslim immigrants, either Saiyyad, Shaikh, Mughal, or Pathan, and may also include descendants of higher Hindu castes such as Muslim Rajputs. Even in this category, the Saiyyads occupy the highest rank in the status hierarchy. In the category of Ajlaf (meaning a commoner), clean occupational castes are included such as julaha (weaver), darzi (tailor), qassab (meat seller), hajjam (barber), kunjra (greengrocer or vegetable vendor), mirasi (bards, singers, and musicians), manihar (bangle maker/seller), dhunia (cotton carder), gaddi (grazier, milkman), and so on. In the third category of Arzul (literally the meanest), the unclean or ritually polluting castes such as bhangi/lalbegi or mehter (sweepers and scavengers) are included.

By and large, all these castes or caste-like groupings occupy specific places in the caste hierarchy with their own norms and patterns of behaviour. These are largely endogamous groups and all the relatively lower castes aspire for upward mobility by emulating the lifestyle of the higher ones. This process, in the Indian context, may be described as 'Ashrafization'. It presents a strange synthesis of Islamization, Hinduization, and modernization.

Caste among the Sikhs

The Sikhs or the followers of Sikhism emerged in 16th century. They are popularly considered a reformed sect of Hinduism that was formed as a protest movement against the prevailing orthodoxy of Hinduism, especially in the spheres of ritualism, idolatry, and casteism. Deeply influenced by Islam, it adopted an egalitarian ideology. Thus, in principle, Sikhism like Islam does not recognize the caste system, yet like Islam, the Sikh society too has castes.

The Sikhs are mainly distributed into two groups – upper and lower caste. I.P Singh, in his study of Sikhs, finds the upper and lower castes clearly distinguished and not a single case of inter-marriage. He provides the evidence which shows that unlike the Hindus, in matters such as exchange of food and water and social intercourse, the Sikhs of the upper caste groups can be clearly distinguished from those of the lower caste. The ritual dimension of caste is, therefore, considerably on the hierarchical dimension of the system. The Sikhs are distributed among four endogamous groups which are hereditary occupational groups and are placed in a hierarchical order. These four endogamous groups are:

1. Jats, who are predominantly agriculturists, occupy the highest position in status hierarchy.

2. Trading castes come next.

3. Ram Garhias, who are artisans and clean occupation castes occupy the next lower rung.

4. Mazhabi are the converts from the Hindu untouchable castes and are at the lowest level.

Sikhs practise endogamy but place hardly any restrictions on commensality except in the case of the Mazhabis. The Mazhabis, in most of the cases, are Sikh Scheduled Castes and like other Dalit sections of the Indian society, have developed Dalit consciousness. For instance, the violence in June 2003 in village Talhan, Jalandhar, which attracted national attention was the eruption of the simmering discontent among the Dalits of Punjab. When violence broke out in Talhan, politicians and the media woke up to what sociologists had been warning about for long. Talhan's Dalits, constituting 70 per cent of the village population, wanted a stake in the management of the local gurudwara, controlled by the Jats. It resulted in a Dalit–Jat Sikh clash which showed how religious institutions had defeated Sikhism's central tenet of a casteless society.

Caste in Punjab can perhaps be understood in the framework of agrarianism rather than through the more popular notion of Brahminism. The Punjab Alienation of Land Act, 1901, clubbed the Dalits, including both the Sikhs and Hindus, with non-agriculturist castes, legally denying them access to land ownership. While the Act was scrapped after Independence, its impact is still visible in the general landlessness of the Dalits. The situation has been explosive in a state where the Jats have all the power and where the scheduled castes account for over 30 per cent of the population – the highest proportion in the country. Thus we find that casteism exists even in Sikhism.

Caste among the Christians

The Christians are the second largest community of non-Hindus after the Muslims. An overwhelming majority of the Christian population in India comes from the lower Hindu castes, especially from the untouchable castes. Studies from Kerala and Tamil Nadu, states with substantial Christian population, show the element of caste in the local Christian society. While the converts from higher castes have been largely integrated into the main group of Syrian Christians, social distinctions between Palayas, who are converts from untouchable groups, and Syrian Christians have been maintained. It has also been observed that Bengali Christians continue to use the surnames showing their pre-conversion castes, about which they are very particular in social intercourse and marriage. It has also been observed that in several churches in South India, the lower caste converts are segregated and given back benches. Thus, even the egalitarian Christian ideology could not break the barriers of caste and caste consciousness.

Dalit Identity and Consciousness

Dalits in India have been socially and economically oppressed, culturally subjugated, and politically subordinated and marginalized for centuries. They have begun to articulate their identity, asserting not only equality for themselves but also a struggle to bring about revolutionary changes and a social order based on equality and liberty. Dalit identity conveys their aspirations and quest for a new social order. 'This is essentially political agenda. For that they launch struggles on various issues and participate in electoral politics. Their path is arduous and long drawn' (Ghanshyam Shah, 2001).

The use of the term 'Dalit' does not have a long history. Rooted in a Sanskrit word, it literally means oppressed or crushed. Though in a general sense it refers to all the oppressed and disadvantaged sections of the Indian society, that is, scheduled castes, tribal communities, and backward castes, it is now being used to describe the former untouchables – the scheduled castes. We largely follow this popular usage even in sociological literature.

The usage of the term 'Dalit' goes back to two Marathi leaders, Mahatma Jyotirao Pule and B.R. Ambedkar. They used it to describe the condition of the ex-untouchables – poor, broken, and oppressed victims of the Hindu caste-ridden society. 'The term Dalit, first used in journalistic writings as far back as 1931 to connote the untouchables, did not gain currency until the early 1970s with the Dalit Panther Movement in Maharashtra. As it is now used, it implies a condition of being underprivileged and deprived of basic rights and refers to people who are suppressed on account of their lowly birth' (S.M. Michael, 1999).

A whole body of literature, describing the oppression of the Dalits by the upper castes, became popular, especially in Maharashtra, in the 1970s and 1980s. But the position taken by some of the more militant elements that only Dalits can write truthfully about Dalits split the movement, one group gratuitously excluding from its ranks even those non-backward writers who had wholly identified themselves with Dalit causes.

Dalits are asserting their cultural identity with their folk arts, rejecting the Sanskrit cultural idiom. Thus the word 'Dalit' is a common name, an identity that was discovered by the depressed classes themselves and therefore it has been cherished by them. 'Dalit is not a pejorative designation but rather a positive symbol of identity for the depressed classes which solves the questions of origin, roots and history of these people' (Samuel Jayakumar, 1999). Corresponding to the consciousness of the poor and powerless, Dalit consciousness is an ideological construct. Dalit consciousness is really the question of Dalit identity – the question of Dalit's roots. Dalit consciousness is principally anti-Aryan and anti-Brahminical.

But unlike the West and South India, where steep oppressive caste structures were critiqued through the Bhakti movement, the United Provinces (Uttar Pradesh) experienced no anti-caste cultural or social reform movement which questioned the unequal Hindu social order. This led to a 'delayed development of identity consciousness among the vast masses of Dalits' (Sudha Pai, 2002). In the South, caste mobilization took the form of 'ethnicization' –the posting of an alternative Dravidian identity.

According to a number of Dalit intellectuals, the world-view of Dalits is based on material philosophy which is essentially different from the world-view of Brahminism. 'They were materialists and rejected the idea of karma, punarjanrma (rebirth) and moksha (salvation). They attacked the caste system, considering its ideology a "Brahminical fraud" for deluding and robbing the common people' (Sardesai, 1986). Kancha Ilaiah in Dalitism vs.

Brahminism: The Epistemological Conflict in History, argues, 'The modern Dalit–Bahujan movements, while building up an anti-caste ideology, drew upon the dialectical materialistic discourse that started in a proto-materialist form with Indus based lokayats or charvakas and continued to operate all through the history' (Ghanshyam Shah, ibid). Unlike Brahmins, Dalits do not have material interests in maintaining a caste-based hierarchy. The practice of hierarchy among them is a cultural imposition rather than their own preference.

Dalits may be belonging to one group or category in terms of a common consciousness but the collective Dalit community is not homogenous because of wide variations in terms of language, occupation, customs, and traditions. Yet the task of Dalit solidarity has been at the top of Dalit agenda. From Jyotirao Phule, Periyar Ramaswami Naikar, and Narayan Guru to Bhim Rao Ambedkar, efforts have been made towards social awareness among Dalits about their rights, self-respect, and individuality. Many organizations have made efforts to organize the Dalits, irrespective of their caste affiliations. Among such organizations are All India SC/ST Federation, Dalit Students Association, United Dalit Students Forum, besides several others. The Bahujan Samaj Party is also an example of this mobilization. 'Unlike the Brahmins (and other upper castes) who organized themselves all over India under a common umbrella of RSS irrespective of their sub-castes and language, the sun is just rising on the horizon of Dalit organization and their identity formation. The Brahmins and upper castes were motivated to organize themselves because of the threat to their superior social status from the upward mobility of the non-Brahmins (read Dalits). The Dalits are motivated with the pious thought of eradicating their human suffering' (Avinash Khandare, 1999).

The Dalits are emerging slowly from their own internal contradictions. Dalit identity is still at a nascent stage of development.

Future of Caste System

Though, as discussed, it is true that the traditional caste system has been transformed significantly, but is it fading out? The following features put a question mark over its future:

- Decline of the caste-based system of production and occupational specialization of castes as represented by the jajmani system has led to the dissolution of the caste system. An occupation-free caste structure has emerged in which all castes are now free to choose and follow any occupation. Several skills, like pottery, stitching clothes, hair dressing and so on, are now available in training institutions which previously could be learnt only within the family.

- Democratic assertion of Dalits and Backward Classes through caste-based mobilization has changed the power structure in the society. The dominance and monopoly of upper castes has sharply declined and new dominant castes have emerged in all parts of India.

- Caste is significantly less important in jobs and education, but strongly important in matrimonial alliances and politics. Endogamy (marrying within one's caste) is perhaps the only important feature among the integral features of caste system which is still almost intact. Numerous studies and surveys reveal that no more than 5 per cent of India's population has married outside their castes and most of such cases are from urban India. Many scholars believe that as long as caste endogamy remains the norm, the caste system will not die.

- To counteract the increasing power of the traditionally underprivileged castes, mobilization of upper castes is also seen, thus giving rise to increased caste consciousness.

- Ideas of democracy, equality, and individual self-respect are now redefining social/caste relationships.

- M.N. Srinivas, an eminent sociologist, adding to these trends, makes an eye-opening statement when he says, 'Paradox is that caste as a system is dying but individual castes are thriving, competing with each other for access to material benefits.

Acknowledging the all-pervasive and omnipotent role of caste, he makes a statement in his work Caste: Its Twentieth Century Avatar which may shock many 'Hinduism may or may not remain but caste will.'

With economic growth, market economy has become the privileged avenue for political investment in Indian modernity and development, but can it defeat the caste system? The traditional role of caste is being eroded but new forms of influence are opening up, giving a new lease of life to the caste system.

Critically Thinking Questions

- To what extent is the distribution of power, prestige, and wealth discriminatory in the caste system?

- In what ways does the practice of untouchability put an entire section of population in a life without resources and hope?

- Do you think the caste system is dying?

****

Bibliography

Ansari, Ghaus. 1960. *Muslim Caste in Uttar Pradesh*. Ethnographic and Folk Culture Society, Lucknow.

Amin, Samir. 1997. *Capitalism in the Age of Globalization*. Zed Books, London.

Appadurai, Arjun. 2001. *Globalization*. Duke University Press, London.

Barth, Fredrick. 1969. *Ethnic Groups and Boundaries*. Little Brown, Boston.

Beattie, John. 1969. *Other Cultures*. Routledge, London.

Beitelle, Andre. 1996. *Caste, Class and Power*. Oxford University Press, Delhi.

Bell, Daniel. 1962. *The End of Ideology*. Harvard University Press, London.

Bernard, Jessie. 1972. *The Future of Marriage*. Bantam Books, New York.

Bohnan, Paul. 1963. *Social Anthropology*. Halt, Pinehart and Winston, New York.

Bougle, C.C.A. 1908. *Essays on the Caste System*. Cambridge University Press.

Brake, Elizabeth. 2016. *After Marriage: Rethinking Marital Relationships*. Oxford University Press, New York.

Burton, Ned. 2020. *For Better for Worse: Essay on Sex, Love Marriage and More*. Acheron Press, London.

Chandra, Bipan. 1984. *Communalism in Modern India*. Vikas Publishing House, Delhi.

Collier, J.F. 1981. *Gender and Kinship*. Stanford University Press, Stanford.

Coulanges, Fustel de. 1980. *The Ancient City: A Study of the Religion, Laws and Institutions*. John Hopkins University Press, Baltimore.

De Beauvoir, Simone. 1949. *The Second Sex*. Everyman's Library, New York City.

Desai, A.R. 1994. *Rural Sociology in India*. Popular Prakashan, Bombay.

Dietrich, Gabriele. 1995. *Towards Understanding Indian Society*. Christava Sahitya Samithi Tiruvalla, India.

Dube, S.C. 1974. *Contemporary India and its Modernization*. Vikas Publishing House, Delhi.

Dumont, Louis. 1970. *Homo Hierarchicus*. The University of Chicago Press, Chicago.

Durkheim, Emile. 1997. *The Division of Labour in Society*. Free Press, New York.

Durkheim, Emile. 1915. *The Elementary Forms of Religious Life*. G. Allen & Unwin, London.

Ember, Carol and Melvin R. Ember. 2019. *Cultural Anthropology*. Pearson Education, Noida.

Engels, Fredrick. 1884. *The Origin of the Family, Private Property and the State*. Hottingen, Zurich.

Evans-Pritechard, E.E. 1956. *Nuer Religion*. Clarendon Press, Oxford.

Femia, Joseph. 2002. *Machiavelli Revisited*. University of Wales Press, Cardiff.

Firestone, Shulasmith. 1970. *The Dialectics of Sex*. Bantom Books, New York.

Fox, Robin. 1967. *Kinship and Marriage*. Cambridge University Press, Cambridge.

Frazer, James. 1890. *The Golden Bough*. Macrnillan, London.

French, Marilyn. 1977. *The Women's Room. Penguin Books*, Harmondswarth.

Friedman, J. 1976. 'Tribes, States and Transformations'. In M. Bloch (ed.) *Marxist Analysis and Social Anthroplogy*. Malaby, London.

Fried, Morton. 1959. *Readings in Anthropology*. Crowell, New York.

Fuller, C.J. 2003. *Caste Today*. Oxford University Press, Delhi.

Geertz, Clifford. 1960. *The Religion of Java*. University of Chicago Press Chicago.

Ghurye, G.S. 1932. *Caste and Race in India*. Kegan Paul, Trubner.

Goldberg, David Theo. 1994. *Multiculturalism: A Critical Reader*. Blackwood, Cambridge, MA.

Goldenweiser, A.A. 1910. 'Totemism: An Analytical Religion'. *Journal of American Folklore* 23.

Gough, Kathleen. 1954. *The Traditional Kinship System of the Nayars of Malabar*. Harvard University Press, Cambridge, MA.

Greer, Germaine. 1970. *The Female Eunuch*. MacGibbon & Kee, London.

Guest, Kenneth. 2018. *Cultural Anthropology: A Toolkit for a Global Age*. W.W. Norton, New York.

Gupta, Depankar. 2000. *Interrogating Caste*. Penguin India, Gurgaon.

Harris, Marvin. 1999. *Theories of Culture in Post-Modern Times*. Altamira Press, Walnut Creek.

Hart, H.L.A. 1963. *Law, Liberty and Morality*. Stanford University Press, Stanford.

Hoebel, E.A. 1949. *Anthropology: The Study of Man*. McGraw Hill.

Hutton, J.H. 1963. *Caste in India*. Oxford University Press, Bombay.

Ilaiah, Kancha. 2009. *Post Hindu India: A Discourse in Dalit Bahujan Socio-spiritual and Scientific Revolution*. Sage, New Delhi.

Jain, Jasbir. 1998. *Beyond Post-Colonialism*. Rawat Publications, Jaipur.

Jain, R.K. 1993. *Nation, Diaspora, Trans-nation*. Routledge, Delhi.

Johnson, Allan G. 1995. *The Blackwell Dictionary of Sociology*. Blackwell, Oxford.

Kolenda, Pauline. 1984. *Caste in Contemporary India*. Waveland Press, Long Grove.

Kothari, Rajni. 2010. *Caste in Indian Politics*. Orient Blackswan, Hyderabad.

Lehmann, David. 1979. *Development Theory: Four Critical Studies*. Frank Cass Publishers, London.

Levy, Robert. 1973. *Tahitians: Mind and Experience in the Society Islands*, Chicago University Press, Chicago.

Lyon, David. 2002. *Surveillance Society*. Open University Press, Philadelphia.

Mahajan, Gurpreet. 2002. *The Multicultural Path*. Sage, New Delhi.

Mair, Lucy. 1965. *An Introduction to Social Anthropology*. Oxford University Press, New Delhi.

Malinowski, Bronislaw. 1922. *Argonauts of the Western Pacific*. Routledge Kegan Paul Ltd, London.

Mandelbaum, David. 1972. *Society in India*. University of California Press, Oakland.

Marret, R.R. 1912. *Anthropology*. Henry Halt, London.

Marriot, Mickim. 1990. *India through Hindu Categories*, Sage, New Delhi.

Marx, Karl. 2016. *Capital: A Critique of Political Economy*, Fingerprint Publishing, Delhi.

Michael, S.M. 1999. *Untouchable: Dalits in Modern India*. Boulder, Colorado.

Millet, Kate. 1969. *Sexual Politics*. Columbia University Press, New York.

Moore, Barrington. 1967. *Social Origins of Dictatorship and Democracy*. Beacon Press, University of California.

Morgan, L.H. 1871. *Systems of Consanguinity and Affinity of the Human Family*, The Smithisonian Institution, Washington, DC.

Murdock, G.P. 1949. *Social Structure*. Macmillan, New York.

Nandan, Serena and Richard Warms. 2018. *Culture Courts*. Cangage Learning, Belmont.

Parsons, Talcott. 1951. *The Social System*. Routledge, London.

Polanyi, Karl. 1944. *The Great Transformation*. Farrar & Rinehart, New York.

Popeau, Jean. 1998. *Core Sociological Dichotomies*. Sage, Berkley.

Redfield, Robert. 1941. *The Folk Culture of Yucatan*. University of Chicago Press, Chicago.

Redfield, Robert. 1956. *Peasant Society and Culture*. University of Chicago Press, Chicago.

Rosefield, M.J. 2017. 'Marriage, Choice and Couplehood in the Age of Internet'. *Sociological Science* 4.

Royal Anthropological Institute of Great Britain and Ireland (1892). *Notes and Querries on Anthropology*. London.

Rudolf, Susane. 1967. *The Modernity of Tradition*. Orient Longman, New Delhi.

Sahlins, Marshall. 1974. *Stone Age Economics*, Routledge, London.

Seymour-Smith, Charlotte. 1993. *Macmillan Dictionary of Anthropology*, Macmillan, London.

Shah, Ghanshyam. 2001. *Dalit Identity and Politics*, Sage, New Delhi.

Singer, Milton. 1971. *Beyond Tradition and Modernity in Madras*. Cambridge University Press, Cambridge.

Singh, Harjinder. 1977. *Caste among Non-Hindus in India*. National Publishing House, New Delhi.

Singh, Yogendra. 1973. *Modernization of Indian Tradition*. Thomson Press, New Delhi.

Sokolvosky, Sergay. 1996. 'Identity Politics and Indigeneity Construction'. *Max Planck Institute for Social Anthropology Working Papers*. Munich.

Spiro, Melford E. 1954. *Kibbutz: Venture in Utopia*. Harvard University Press, Cambridge MA.

Srinivas, M.N. 2000. *Caste: Its Twentieth Century Avatar*. Penguin India, New Delhi.

Srinivas, M.N. 1992. *On Living in a Revolution*. Oxford University Press, New Delhi.

Srinivas, M.N. 1965. *Religion and Society among the Coorgs*. Asia Publishing House, Bombay.

Srinivas, M.N. 1972. *Social Change in Modern India*. Orient Longman, Hyderabad.

Stacey, Judith. 1990. *Brave New Families*. Basic Books, New York.

Toynbee, Arnold. 1939. *A Study of History*. Oxford University Press. New York.

Tylor, E.B. 1871. *Primitive Culture*. J. Murray, London.

Van den Berghe, Pierre L. 1981. *Human Family Systems: An Evolutionary View*. Elsevier, New York.

Varshney, Ashutosh. 2002. *Ethnic Violence and Civic Life: Hindus and Muslims in India*. Yale University Press, New Haven.

Weber, Max. 2018. *The Protestant Ethic and the Spirit of Capitalism*, Franklin Classics.

Westermarck, Edward. 1891. *The History of Human Marriage*. Macmillan, London.

Western, Kath. 1991. *Families We Choose*. Columbia University Press, New York City.

Winthrop, Robert. 1991. *Dictionary of Concepts in Cultural Anthropology*. Greenwood Press, New York.

Wiser, William. 1936. *The Hindu Jajmani System*, Lucknow Publishing House, Lucknow.

Wolf, Eric. 2004. *Peasants*. Prentice Hall, Eaglewood Cliffs.

Wolf, Eric. 1969. *Present Wars of the Twentieth Century*. University of Oklahoma Press, Oklahoma.